BREAKING THE DEADLC

Manchester University Press

Breaking the deadlock

Britain at the polls, 2019

Edited by Nicholas Allen
and John Bartle

MANCHESTER UNIVERSITY PRESS

Published by Manchester University Press
Oxford Road, Manchester M13 9PL

www.manchesteruniversitypress.co.uk

British Library Cataloguing-in-Publication Data
A catalogue record for this book is available from the British
Library

ISBN 978 1 5261 6278 6 hardback
ISBN 978 1 5261 5236 7 paperback

First published 2021

Typeset
by Sunrise Setting Ltd, Brixham
Printed in Great Britain
by TJ Books Ltd, Padstow

Contents

Figures

Tables

Contributors

Nicholas Allen is Professor of Politics at Royal Holloway, University of London

John Bartle is Professor of Government at the University of Essex

Sarah Birch is Professor of Political Science at King's College London

Harold D. Clarke is Ashbel Smith Professor at the University of Texas at Dallas

Jane Green is Professor of Political Science and British Politics at the University of Oxford

Robert Johns is Professor of Politics at the University of Essex

Thomas Quinn is Senior Lecturer in Government at the University of Essex

Patrick Seyd is Emeritus Professor of Politics at the University of Sheffield

Maria Sobolewska is Professor of Political Science at the University of Manchester

Paul Whiteley is Professor of Government at the University of Essex

Preface

Most British general elections can be easily understood as stand-alone plays. Parliament is dissolved, the party leaders hit the campaign trail, party activists canvass, the voters cast their ballots, a winner is declared. It helps that elections follow a familiar plot, even as the leading actors come and go. Sometimes the endings are drearily repetitive, such as occurred with the Conservatives' four successive victories in 1979, 1983, 1987 and 1992, or with Labour's three successive wins in 1997, 2001 and 2005. But while every outcome is shaped by the previous contest, and will inevitably shape what happens in the next, most elections make perfect sense as self-contained storylines.

The 2019 general election can certainly be understood as a stand-alone play. But it is perhaps better understood – and may well be viewed as such by historians – as the final instalment in a 'Brexit trilogy'. Just four and a half years separated the 2015, 2017 and 2019 general elections. It was David Cameron's surprise re-election at the head of a single-party Conservative government in May 2015 that paved the way for an in–out referendum in June 2016 on Britain's membership of the European Union (EU). The shock result – a 51.9 per cent vote in favour of Brexit – created monumental political, policy and constitutional challenges that left politicians struggling to respond. The 2017 general election's indecisive outcome, driven by an unexpected spike in support for Labour, multiplied those challenges. Theresa May had sought a snap election to increase her majority, but ended up leading a minority government in a hung parliament. This outcome left May's authority in tatters and provided no clear direction as to the kind of relationship Britain should have with its erstwhile EU partners. Deadlock ensued. Having failed three times to convince MPs to approve her withdrawal agreement, May quit and was succeeded as prime minister by Boris Johnson in July 2019. It was against this backdrop that Johnson laid plans for another snap election to 'get Brexit done'.

The election in December 2019 was as decisive as the 2017 election was not. It comprehensively broke the deadlock, returning the Conservatives to office with a thumping 81-seat majority (excluding the speaker) and a clear mandate for Johnson's vision of Brexit. It was also the party's fourth successive win since 2010 and guaranteed at least a fourteen-year period of Tory-led government. For Labour, the 2019 election was a disaster. The party's four-year dalliance with Jeremy Corbyn, its left-wing leader, ended in its lowest tally of seats since 1935. Labour last won an election with Tony Blair at the helm in 2005. At least a generation will have passed before Labour next has the chance to form a government.

Breaking the Deadlock: Britain at the Polls, 2019 tells the story of the remarkable 2019 general election and its dramatic outcome. It is the eleventh volume in the *Britain at the Polls* series, which has been published after every election since February 1974, with the exception of the 1987 and 2015 elections. As with previous volumes, the book aims to provide general readers, students of British politics and professional political scientists with analyses of key political, economic and social developments, and an assessment of their impact on the election outcome. It also aims to provide readers with informed reflections on the election's long-term significance. Other books, including *The British General Election of 2019* – the latest in the long line of 'Nuffield studies' – and the 2019 volumes in the *Britain Votes* and *Political Communications* series, will provide readers with more detailed accounts of the campaign and how it unfolded. As ever, *The Times Guide to the House of Commons* provides readers with an authoritative guide to the actual results, while the British Election Study (BES) team will provide sophisticated analyses of individual-level survey data.

As with previous volumes of *Britain at the Polls*, the essays included in *Breaking the Deadlock* reflect the editors' judgements about the most distinctive features of the 2019 election and the long-term developments that are central to understanding the contest. This selective approach necessarily entails some gaps in the coverage. Unlike the 2017 volume, for example, there are no detailed chapters on the Liberal Democrats, on developments in Scotland or on the gender balance of the House of Commons. These topics remain important, but they were not as central to the story of the 2019 general election as they were to the 2017 contest.

As ever, *Breaking the Deadlock* includes chapters on the main protagonists in the 2019 election. Nicholas Allen in Chapter 1 focuses on Theresa May's minority government and the ongoing fallout from the 2016 Brexit referendum. He provides a broad survey of the deadlock that gripped Britain's political system after the 2017 election, with a particular focus on failed attempts to secure parliamentary approval for the government's withdrawal agreement with the EU. Thomas Quinn in Chapter 2 focuses more closely on developments within the Conservative Party. He explains why Boris Johnson was elected leader in July 2019 and how the party's

Eurosceptic wing finally triumphed in both the Tories' long-running civil war over Europe and its attempts to secure a 'harder' form of Brexit. In Chapter 3, Paul Whiteley, Patrick Seyd and Harold Clarke explore policy and organisational developments within the Labour Party. They explain how Labour's left-wing leader, Jeremy Corbyn, became an electoral liability as a result of his handling of Brexit and internal tensions.

Other chapters focus on long-term developments central to any account of the 2019 general election. John Bartle in Chapter 4 examines the resilience of the two-party system at Westminster. He describes the importance of institutional factors in sustaining the Conservative–Labour duopoly in British government and explains how the two major parties have been able to incorporate new issues, such as Brexit, within the existing framework of party competition. In Chapter 5, Maria Sobolewska examines long-term changes in the electorate and how education and ethnic diversity have driven the emergence of new identity cleavages. She explains how the Brexit referendum finally brought 'identity politics' to the fore and how Britain's 'culture wars' have shaped post-2016 politics.

The final three chapters explain the outcome of 2019 election and consider its wider significance. Robert Johns in Chapter 6 explains why the Conservatives won. Brexit was, of course, central to the result, but so too were other factors that usually explain election outcomes. Ultimately, the Conservatives were closer to voters ideologically and were seen as more competent than Labour. In Chapter 7, Jane Green examines the 2019 general election's possible status as a 'critical election' and what the wider realignment it revealed means for the future. Finally, in Chapter 8, Sarah Birch steps back to locate the 2019 general election in a wider comparative context. She shows how many of the economic, social and political changes that led to Brexit were by no means exceptional, but that Britain's constitutional arrangements continue to make its electoral politics so distinctive.

Like *None Past the Post*, the 2017 volume, *Breaking the Deadlock* was planned at short notice. Whereas students of US elections know exactly when the next presidential or congressional election will take place, students of British elections face a degree of uncertainty. The Fixed-term Parliaments Act 2011, a legacy of the 2010–2015 coalition government, was meant to fix the electoral cycle and remove the prime minister's traditional power to call an election whenever it suited his or her purposes. Although the Act ensured that the coalition lasted five years, it did not prevent Theresa May or Boris Johnson getting the early elections they wanted. The snap election in June 2017 was triggered through the provisions of the Fixed-term Parliaments Act, with two thirds of all MPs voting in favour of any early poll. The snap election in December 2019 was triggered by circumventing the Act with new legislation. The Fixed-term Parliaments Act's days now look numbered. The 2019 Conservative manifesto pledged to get rid of it. It seems that the British constitution – like the country as a whole – is moving forward into its past.

In addition to the lack of forewarning, this book's production was greatly hampered by one other unforeseen factor: the coronavirus pandemic of 2020. The pandemic's impact on British politics was immediate and significant. It abruptly ended Boris Johnson's honeymoon period as an election-winning prime minister, prompted huge levels of government spending and overshadowed even Brexit. The full political, economic and social ramifications of the pandemic will not be known for some time, but they are likely to be substantial and long-lasting. The fallout from the pandemic, together with the ongoing effects of Brexit, will almost certainly form the backdrop to the next general election.

The pandemic also had personal consequences for the authors in this volume. Trying to write intelligent essays during the academic teaching year is difficult enough. Trying to write them during lockdown, when caring responsibilities and other commitments eat into your time, is even more so. As editors, we are especially grateful to our contributors for their perseverance and enthusiasm in such difficult times.

Nicholas Allen and John Bartle

1

Deadlock: minority government and Brexit

Nicholas Allen

The period between the June 2017 and December 2019 general elections was one of the most turbulent in recent British political history. Hundreds of thousands of citizens took part in protests, dozens of MPs broke with their parties and one prime minister, Theresa May, was forced from office. On the central issue of the day – the terms of Britain's exit from the EU – there was complete deadlock. The combination of a hung parliament and some MPs' deeply held convictions frustrated Conservative ministers' repeated attempts to secure parliamentary approval for a withdrawal agreement with the EU. Theresa May had sought a snap election in 2017 in part to increase her slender parliamentary majority and avoid this scenario. Her gamble backfired spectacularly. A surge in support for Labour cost the Tories seats and forced May to form a minority government propped up by Northern Ireland's Democratic Unionist Party (DUP). Unable to maintain discipline among her ministers and MPs, she failed to take Britain out of the EU and honour her pledge to deliver on the result of the 2016 referendum. Her failure cost her the premiership and catapulted Boris Johnson into Number 10 Downing Street.

This chapter provides an account of the Conservatives in government between 2017 and 2019 and the deadlock that mired Britain's political system. It begins with the formation of May's minority government before turning to the challenge of delivering Brexit. It describes both the government's attempts to negotiate a withdrawal agreement and how internal Tory divisions contributed to the subsequent domestic impasse. It then considers how stalemate at Westminster impacted upon and distorted 'normal' politics. Finally, the chapter examines how Boris Johnson forced an early general election and framed it in terms of 'the people vs. parliament'.

The formation of a minority government

The 2017 general election was Britain's first since the introduction of universal suffrage in which a governing party lost its parliamentary majority but remained in office. The Conservatives, led by Theresa May, secured 42.4 per cent of the popular vote, a 5.5-point increase on their 2015 vote share, but their lacklustre campaign, combined with wider economic and political disillusionment, helped Labour, led by Jeremy Corbyn, to increase its vote share by nearly 10 points. Labour's surge, coupled with the voting system's sensitivity to local dynamics, resulted in the Tories losing seats. They emerged from the election as the largest party, with 317 MPs, but nine seats short of a majority.[1]

Single-party majority rule is the norm in British politics. The first-past-the-post voting system, in which MPs are elected by simple pluralities in their constituencies, tends to manufacture legislative majorities for those parties that win plurality vote shares. This tendency usually results in decisive elections. It also concentrates power in the government of the day, underpinning the 'Westminster model' and the related idea that governments enjoy a 'mandate' – that is, the right and obligation, as well as the parliamentary numbers, to implement their manifesto promises.[2] While the voting system's critics bemoan its disproportionality, its supporters emphasise its promotion of effective government and, above all, accountability. When there is single-party government, voters know who to blame.

Other than 2017, only two elections since 1945 have resulted in hung parliaments and no party winning a majority in the House of Commons. One was the February 1974 election, which led to Harold Wilson forming a minority Labour government before calling another election seven months later.[3] The other was the 2010 election that ushered in a five-year period of coalition government under David Cameron's Conservatives and Nick Clegg's Liberal Democrats.[4] A further two governments initially elected with majorities ended up as minority administrations as a result of deaths, by-election defeats and defections. Labour lost its overall majority in 1976 within hours of James Callaghan succeeding Wilson as prime minister. John Major's Conservative government existed as a minority from late 1996 until its crushing defeat in the 1997 general election. Both governments enjoyed a tenuous hold on power. Both struggled to pursue their agenda.

Whenever an election results in a hung parliament, the incumbent prime minister and government are expected to stay put until it becomes clear that they cannot command the confidence of MPs but an alternative administration might be able to.[5] With 317 MPs, the Conservatives were almost guaranteed to remain in power. Because the seven Sinn Féin MPs would not take their seats (they refused to recognise Parliament's sovereignty over Northern Ireland), and because the speaker and three deputy speakers would abstain from votes, the support of 320 MPs would be enough to guarantee the confidence of the House of Commons. Labour, by contrast, had won 262 seats. Even if it had formed an unlikely 'progressive alliance' with the other centre-left parties – the Liberal Democrats (twelve MPs), the Scottish Nationalists (thirty-five MPs), Plaid Cymru (four MPs) and the Greens (one MP) – the Conservatives would have outnumbered the resulting coalition by three. In any event, the Liberal Democrats had ruled out joining any kind of coalition.

Crucially, there was one other centre-right party whose support could guarantee for the Tories the confidence of the Commons: Northern Ireland's DUP. This party had won ten seats in the election. Although the party was more socially conservative than the Tories, it shared the larger party's commitment to unionism. It was also pro-Brexit. The Conservatives moved quickly to secure the DUP's support. The goal was to establish a 'confidence and supply' agreement, where the DUP would support ministers in key parliamentary votes without entering into government. A full-blown coalition would have been resisted by Tory MPs. It would also have undermined the 1998 Good Friday Agreement and the government's obligation to exercise its powers in Northern Ireland 'with rigorous impartiality'.

After two weeks of negotiations, the DUP agreed to support the government in any confidence motions. Its MPs would also back ministers in any legislative-programme and budget votes, as well as legislation relating to finance, national security or Brexit. In return, the government abandoned some of its manifesto commitments and promised to spend an additional £1.5 billion on infrastructure projects in Northern Ireland. This largesse confounded comments made by May and others during the campaign that there was no 'magic money tree' to fund increases in public spending.

May herself was left gravely weakened.[6] Going to the country had been her initiative. The next general election should have taken place in 2020 under the Fixed-term Parliaments Act 2011. May had sought the early election – which required the backing of two thirds of all MPs – less than three weeks after formally notifying the EU of Britain's intention to leave the bloc. She had previously argued against an early poll but suddenly backtracked, ostensibly on the grounds that the other political parties, as well as the House of Lords, were threatening her plans for Brexit and 'the mandate' created by the referendum.[7] Few people had accepted her words at face value. The Tories had enjoyed a commanding poll lead over Labour, and almost everyone thought May's primary motive was to increase her parliamentary majority.

Early expectations of a landslide win now exacerbated her party's anger. Many Tories blamed the prime minister for both her decision to seek an election and her shortcomings as a campaigner. The ill-judged Conservative campaign had focused on May's personality and ability to provide 'strong and stable leadership', but the prime minister was 'robotic' and lacked spontaneity in interviews. She flunked out of participating in a televised leaders' debate and, worse, was forced into an embarrassing U-turn on an unpopular manifesto pledge to tackle the growing cost of care for the elderly. Conservatives generally campaign on lower taxes, yet the pledge to raise the wealth threshold for free domiciliary social care would have cost millions of voters, especially many traditional Tory voters, thousands of pounds. The whole episode cast doubt on May's political acumen.

On the weekend after the election, a vengeful George Osborne, the former chancellor of the exchequer whom May had sacked the year before, told a television interviewer: 'She is a dead woman walking.'[8] The prime minister appeared even more vulnerable the following week as a result of her response to the Grenfell Tower fire that erupted in a block of flats in West London. Some seventy-two residents were killed, and more were injured. May visited the scene and met with members of the emergency services but did not meet with any of the survivors. It was a public-relations disaster.

For a while it looked like May might be ousted. Senior ministers jockeyed for position, made soundings and hatched plans to replace her. There was speculation that Boris Johnson, the ambitious foreign secretary, leading pro-Brexit campaigner and one-time favourite to replace David Cameron, might make a move. In the event, the plots fizzled out when it became clear that May had no intention of stepping down any time soon. It was a similar story three months later when an excruciating party-conference speech led to renewed speculation about May's future. Her address was first interrupted by a comedian who handed her a mock P45 form indicating that she was about to be dismissed. It was then disrupted by her debilitating cough and finally by a dissolving stage backdrop. The ordeal reminded everyone of both her vulnerability and resilience.

Had the election resulted in the expected landslide, May's authority would have rocketed. She would have gained a 'mandate' for her visions of Brexit and Conservatism.[9] She would have been able to reshuffle her cabinet to her liking and, with a large parliamentary majority, gain much needed leeway to negotiate a withdrawal agreement with the EU. Instead, May was left with no majority or mandate for any particular course of action. She also had to contend with a sour mood on the Tory benches. Everyone knew that governing as a minority would be difficult.

Brexit: the mammoth in the room

All governments are constrained by past policy decisions. The outcome of the June 2016 Brexit referendum meant that Theresa May's government was more constrained than most. David Cameron, May's predecessor as

Conservative leader and prime minister, had pressed for a 'simple' in–out referendum on Britain's membership of the EU in order to resolve deep divisions within his party. He had campaigned strenuously to 'remain'. When 51.9 per cent of voters opted to 'leave', Cameron resigned immediately.[10] The task of leading the government's response fell to his successor.

The referendum result carried enormous moral force even if, legally speaking, the vote had been purely advisory. The Conservatives' 2015 manifesto had committed the party to holding an in–out referendum and respecting the outcome. In June 2015, MPs from every party, except the Scottish Nationalists, had voted overwhelmingly in favour of allowing the people to decide Britain's future in the EU. Everyone campaigning ahead of the subsequent referendum had acted as if it would be binding. A government leaflet, circulated to all households, had stated that this was 'a once in a generation decision' and promised to implement 'what you decide'.[11]

Most MPs were unhappy with the result – around three quarters had declared their support for remaining in the EU – but the general consensus was that it should be respected.[12] Theresa May, who had been a lukewarm Remainer, certainly took this view. Jeremy Corbyn, Labour's leader, also embraced the people's decision. When, after the UK Supreme Court ruled in early 2017 that Parliament needed to authorise the government before it could notify the EU of Britain's intention to leave under the terms of Article 50 of the Lisbon Treaty, MPs voted by an overwhelming margin to do so. The apparent consensus continued into the 2017 general election: both the Conservative and Labour manifestos committed to delivering some form of Brexit.

At this point, many voters might have thought that Brexit was essentially done. They had voted in the referendum in June 2016. Nine months later, the government had finally triggered Article 50 and notified the EU that Britain would be leaving the bloc. A new parliament had been elected and was dominated by two parties committed to honouring the result. The country could move on.

Anyone holding such views was grossly mistaken. Brexit was not done. In policy terms, it was still unclear what Brexit actually meant. The referendum had asked voters if they wanted to remain in or leave the EU, not what kind of future relationship with the EU they wanted if Britain left. Politicians had to interpret Brexit as best they could. The matter boiled down to a simple question: should Britain remain more or less closely aligned with the EU single market and customs union? The two alternatives were known as 'soft' and 'hard' Brexit respectively. Under a soft Brexit, the UK would remain closely aligned, enjoy freer access to EU markets and the associated economic benefits, and there would be no need to impose a 'hard border' and physical checks between Northern Ireland and the Republic of Ireland – the only land border between the UK and EU. The last of these considerations was of particular importance in Northern Irish politics since an open border had helped to underpin the peace process. Close alignment would mean the UK abiding by the EU's rules and regulations, but without any seat at the decision-making table. The UK would also choose not to control immigration from EU countries and lose the freedom to strike new trade deals with non-EU countries. Conversely, a hard Brexit would enable the UK to regain control of its borders and trade policy but would compromise its access to EU markets and require new arrangements for the Irish border.

Proponents of a harder Brexit were able to invoke the official Leave campaign slogan, 'take back control', to justify their case. In contrast, proponents of a soft Brexit found it difficult to articulate and sell a vision in which Britain was no longer a member of the EU but still bound by its rules. Most were further hamstrung by the fact that they had campaigned against any kind of Brexit. Nevertheless, the matter was far from settled. The referendum had not been authoritative on this point.

In political terms, the country was still struggling to move on from the referendum. The campaign had been hugely divisive, cutting across party and especially Conservative lines. Both Leavers and Remainers had made exaggerated claims and appealed to voters' base emotions. One Labour MP, Jo Cox, had been murdered by a far-right sympathiser. The narrowness of the Leave victory, combined with the general conduct of the campaign, made it difficult for some Remainers to accept the result. Indeed, the referendum had created two issue-publics, groups defined by their commitment to one particular position: one was fanatically pro-Brexit, the other fanatically opposed. Their representatives continued to organise marches and haunt Westminster, waving flags and heckling politicians and journalists.

Lastly, in a purely technical sense, Brexit had barely started. The lengthy process for leaving the EU was set out in Article 50 of the Lisbon Treaty. Brexit would be a two-stage affair. The UK would first need to negotiate a withdrawal agreement that set the terms of its 'divorce' from the EU. This agreement would cover issues such as the rights of EU citizens resident in Britain and British citizens resident in the EU, the settlement of Britain's outstanding financial obligations and the status of the UK's land border with the Republic of Ireland. It would also be accompanied by a political framework setting out the UK's likely future relationship with the EU. Article 50 stipulated that withdrawal negotiations had to be concluded within two years unless the other member states agreed to extend the period. Only then, once it had left the EU, could the UK finalise a new relationship with the bloc, including a trade deal.

As well as being a lengthy two-stage process, the Brexit negotiations were also bound to be complex. The withdrawal agreement and framework had to be acceptable to both the EU – in practice a majority in the European Parliament and a qualified majority of the European Council – and the British parliament. The negotiations, in other words, would be what political scientists call a 'two-level game'.[13] Two-level games are complex because the preferences of actors at one level affect the behaviour of actors at the other. The British government would have to spend a great deal of time navigating between the two levels to secure compromise.

These features of the Brexit process were a recipe for popular disappointment. The two years allotted for the withdrawal negotiations constituted a tight timescale for those trying to untangle four decades' worth of EU integration. Most voters saw things differently and expected a speedy resolution. Two years seemed particularly unnecessary for many Leave supporters. Some wondered why Britain was still a member of the EU in June 2017 if it had voted to leave the bloc a year earlier. Moreover, the whole two-year process would be subject to enormous scrutiny. Every disagreement, every twist and turn and every compromise would be scrutinised by journalists and others on social media. Voters would see just how chaotic and convoluted international negotiations could be.

The Brexit negotiations

Theresa May's letter to Donald Tusk, the President of the European Council, on 29 March 2017 had started the two-year process for negotiating a withdrawal agreement.[14] Three months had been lost to the general-election campaign. It was now time to commence formal talks. Britain was scheduled to leave the EU on 29 March 2019, with or without a deal.

The economic consensus was that a 'no-deal Brexit' and leaving without an agreement would damage the country's long-term economic growth. Government studies agreed.[15] A no-deal Brexit risked creating delays at ports and erecting barriers to travel and study. It threatened food, medicine and energy supply chains, as well as the financial-services sector's ability to operate in the EU. Few politicians thought that Britain should actively leave without an agreement and pursue a 'clean Brexit'. But many proponents of Brexit wanted to prepare for the possibility, if only as a means to secure more generous terms from Brussels. After all, Britain's trading partners in Europe would also suffer if there was no deal.

The government's negotiating objectives were framed by a speech given by the prime minister at Lancaster House in London in January 2017. May had advocated a relatively hard Brexit, insisting that Britain would leave the EU's single market and customs union and the jurisdiction of the European Court of Justice. At the same time, and not entirely consistently, she had committed to maintaining the Common Travel Area between the UK and Republic of Ireland and keeping the Northern Irish border open. Looking to put pressure on the EU, May had also hinted at her willingness to walk away from negotiations if need be: 'while I am sure a positive agreement can be reached – I am equally clear that no deal for Britain is better than a bad deal for Britain'.[16] Those in her party convinced that the threat of a no-deal Brexit would elicit concessions from the EU were emboldened.

The British negotiating team was led by David Davis, the swaggering pro-Brexit secretary of state for exiting the EU, and Olly Robbins, a career civil servant who served as May's chief Europe adviser. The EU's chief negotiator was Michel Barnier, a former French foreign minister. Barnier made clear from the outset that the UK could not leave the single market and customs union and continue to enjoy the benefits of access and 'frictionless trade'. Doing so would undermine the bloc's integrity.

Davis, like many Tory advocates of Brexit, was bullish about the prospects for a deal. He was equally bullish when it came to how negotiations should be structured. Ministers wanted concurrent negotiations on both the withdrawal agreement and future relationship. In part, they hoped to expedite the process. They also hoped that concurrent negotiations would enable them to use the divorce issues, including the rights of EU citizens, the UK's outstanding financial obligations and the Northern Irish border, to leverage a better future trade deal. For their part, the EU and Barnier were adamant that the negotiations should be sequenced as laid out in Article 50. Preliminary discussions on the future relationship – ultimately whether there was a softer or harder Brexit – should begin only after progress had been made on the divorce issues.

Davis had promised 'the row of the summer' if the EU insisted on sequencing.[17] There was no row. He was obliged to accept the EU's position in the first round of negotiations in June 2017. The ticking clock and pressure for progress back home meant the British government had little choice but to acquiesce. Davis's bravado merely highlighted the relative weakness of the British vis-à-vis the much larger economic bloc. Images of him appearing without notes at a later meeting – in stark contrast to the folders of material surrounding Barnier – reinforced the sense that the British team was ill prepared.

The most contentious issue to domestic audiences at the start of the negotiations was the size of the divorce bill, the amount of money owed to the EU as a result of existing funding commitments. At one point, it was suggested that the UK might need to pay as much £92bn.[18] In July 2017, the foreign secretary, Boris Johnson, told the House of Commons that the sums then being bandied about were 'extortionate'. The EU, he suggested, could 'go whistle'.[19]

It soon became clear, however, that the real stumbling block would be the Northern Irish border. Whereas the divorce bill could always be haggled over, there was no comparable scope for wiggle room here. Both the government and the EU recognised the border's importance to the Northern Irish peace process. Both were committed to avoiding the re-imposition of a hard border between the North and the Republic of Ireland. To this end, the withdrawal agreement needed to contain provisions, or a 'backstop', that would guarantee an open border in case the two sides failed to reach agreement on a future relationship. The EU initially proposed that Northern Ireland could remain inside the customs union and single market. The problem this posed for May's government was that it threatened the UK's sovereignty that Brexit was meant to return. There would need to be controls between Northern Ireland and the rest of the UK or else British producers could access EU markets without respecting its standards and thereby gain an unfair advantage.

The border question also highlighted more clearly than anything else the two-level nature of the negotiations. In the wake of domestic opposition, including from Northern Ireland's Democratic Unionists, who now threatened to withdraw their support from the government at Westminster, May needed an alternative. The solution was set out in a Joint Report agreed by EU and British negotiators in December 2017. It promised that 'no new regulatory barriers' would be allowed between Northern Ireland and the rest of the UK as part of any backstop, and that Northern Irish business would continue to enjoy 'unfettered access' to the whole of the UK internal market.[20] This concession satisfied the DUP and its leader, Arlene Foster. The document also promised that the UK would remain in 'full alignment' with any EU rules necessary for supporting cross-border trade between the North and South. This concession satisfied the EU.

The Joint Report constituted sufficient progress in the eyes of the EU to accede to preliminary discussions about the future relationship. The government could claim a small victory. But the Joint Report also fuelled concerns among pro-Brexit Conservatives at the direction of travel. In a speech in Florence in September 2017, the prime minister had accepted the need to pay the divorce bill, as well the need for a transition or 'implementation period' that would give time for the EU and UK to negotiate a trade deal after March 2019. During this period, Britain would abide by EU regulations and be a 'rule taker'. May even wanted British judges 'to be able to take into account the judgments of the European Court of Justice'. These concessions had been interpreted as a softening of what Brexit entailed. The backstop outlined in the Joint Report now left open the possibility of Britain being aligned with EU regulations indefinitely. Pro-Brexit Tories were alarmed.

The great challenge for Theresa May was that her government was an uneasy alliance of ambitious ministers with different visions about what form Britain's future relationship with the EU should take. Some, notably the chancellor of the exchequer, Phillip Hammond, favoured closer alignment in order to facilitate trade, especially in financial services. He had pushed hard in cabinet for a transition period after Brexit to help British businesses.[21] Others, notably Boris Johnson, were keen for Britain to leave the EU single market and customs union as soon as possible and pursue a low-tax, lightly regulated economy.[22]

The first of two great domestic tests came in July 2018 when May attempted to establish her government's general vision for the future relationship. Ministers were summoned to Chequers, the prime minister's weekend retreat, where they were given a hard sell on her plans. Mobile phones were confiscated to prevent leaks, and ministers were given cards advertising local taxi firms in case they considered resigning. Eventually the cabinet agreed a common line. Britain would seek a close relationship with the EU underpinned by a 'common rulebook' to facilitate trade in goods, a 'joint institutional framework' to adjudicate on UK–EU agreements and a 'mobility framework' that would allow UK and EU citizens to travel to one another's territories to study and work. There would, however, be an end to the 'free movement of people' and annual payments to the EU budget, and the UK would be free to pursue an independent trade policy. On the thorny question of the Irish border, the government proposed a 'facilitated' customs arrangement: the UK would apply its tariffs for goods intended for the domestic market and EU tariffs for goods intended for the EU market. This arrangement, it was hoped, would make the controversial backstop redundant.

At first, it looked like May had secured cabinet agreement and won an impressive victory. The victory was fleeting. David Davis resigned two days later, claiming the Chequers plan failed to honour the 2016 referendum and return 'control of our laws in any real sense'.[23] He was swiftly joined by Steve Baker, a junior minister, and, more significantly, Boris Johnson, the foreign secretary. Johnson, like Davis, claimed the policy was a repudiation of the referendum result. Britain, he wrote, was heading for a 'semi-Brexit' and 'the status of colony'.[24] May suffered a further setback in September when EU leaders rejected her proposals at a European summit in Salzburg. Of particular concern to them was the UK's wish to maintain alignment with EU rules for trade in goods. This amounted to 'cherry-picking' – that is, seeking to abide by some but not all of the single market's four underlying freedoms: the free movement of goods, services, capital and labour. Barnier had been clear from the outset that the integrity of the single market was non-negotiable. The British government had either failed to listen or appreciate the significance of the point.

The second great domestic test for May's government came in November 2018, when ministers finally signed off on the withdrawal agreement and non-binding political declaration on the future relationship.[25] Britain would pay the EU around £39bn as part of its divorce bill, and both UK and EU citizens would retain their residency and social-security rights in one another's jurisdictions. On the crucial issue of the Northern Irish border, it was agreed that if the EU and UK failed to agree a long-term deal, then the whole of the UK would remain indefinitely in a single customs territory, subject to EU standards, but Northern Ireland would be even more closely aligned with single-market rules and regulations. On the issue of the transition period, the UK would abide by all EU rules until 31 December 2020 but without having a say on them. Lastly, in terms of the future relationship, the non-binding political declaration pledged both parties to 'develop an ambitious, wide-ranging and balanced economic partnership' and create 'ambitious customs arrangements that … build and improve on the single customs territory provided for in the Withdrawal Agreement'.

The backlash among Tories who wanted a harder Brexit was immediate. They were especially alarmed by the proposed backstop and feared that the single customs territory necessary to make it work could become the default setting in any future relationship. Dominic Raab, David Davis's successor as Brexit secretary, promptly resigned from the cabinet, as did Esther McVey, the work and pensions secretary.[26] Two junior ministers also quit, along with several parliamentary private secretaries, MPs who act as ministers' eyes and ears in the Commons. From the Tory backbenches, Boris Johnson denounced it as 'vassal-state stuff', while Jacob Rees-Mogg, the chair of the European Research Group (ERG), a hard-Eurosceptic faction of Tory MPs, called it a 'rotten deal'.[27] Ominously, the DUP leadership declared it would not support the deal.

Meanwhile, there was a backlash among pro-EU Tories. Jo Johnson, the transport minister and younger brother of Boris, resigned from the government in opposition to the deal. He added his voice to growing calls inside and outside Parliament for a second referendum on the terms of the withdrawal agreement and potentially whether or not voters still wanted Brexit. A former cabinet minister, Justine Greening, echoed his sentiments, telling a rally: 'Even if some people in my party can't see this is a bad deal, everyone else around this entire planet can.'[28] A few weeks later, the universities minister, Sam Gymiah, quit the government on similar grounds. The possibility of cancelling Brexit through another referendum was now firmly on the agenda.

The EU, however, was content with the agreement and declaration. On 25 November 2018, the European Council formally endorsed the documents. May's government now needed to secure MPs' approval.

Parliamentary paralysis

With the inter-governmental negotiations apparently concluded, attention shifted to the House of Commons. Under the European Union (Withdrawal) Act 2018, MPs were required to approve the legally binding withdrawal agreement and non-binding political declaration in what had become known as the 'meaningful vote'. On 15 November, Theresa May made a statement to MPs on the agreement. In a three-hour ordeal, she faced criticism from all sides. It was nearly one hour before anyone spoke in support. On 22 November, she made another statement on the political declaration. The criticism was again relentless.

The fundamental problem for the government was that it lacked a clear parliamentary majority to approve the agreement. Its minority status and dependence on the DUP made it vulnerable to backbench rebellions on potentially any issue. Ministers had even started abstaining in non-binding votes in order to avoid defeats. Brexit was not just any issue, however. A sizeable number of Tory MPs, organised around the ERG, were committed to the hardest of Brexits, and a smaller group was equally committed to the softest of Brexits or ideally its cancellation through a second referendum. For every Tory MP that peeled off from either wing, ministers needed to find an opposition MP to support them. Culture and ideology made this easier said than done. Westminster politics is fundamentally adversarial. Labour was nominally committed to accepting the result of the referendum, but its 2017 manifesto had set out a softer vision of Brexit than that envisaged by May's government. Such differences were enough to justify Labour opposing the withdrawal agreement. The other Westminster parties were anti-Brexit. Government whips reckoned a handful of Labour MPs might be tempted to break with their own party and vote for the withdrawal agreement, either because they were personally in favour of Brexit or because they believed the referendum resulted should be honoured and feared losing their seats if it were not. Even so, the numbers would be tight.

The government began a campaign of trying to cajole and persuade its MPs to back the deal. As Theresa May told BBC Radio 4, MPs in practice had three options: 'one is to leave the European Union with a deal … the other two are that we leave without a deal or that we have no Brexit at all'.[29] For Tory MPs wanting a softer Brexit, May hoped to play on fears of crashing out. For those wanting a harder Brexit, May hoped to play on fears that any failure to back her deal could open the way for a second referendum. The problem with this strategy was that it lacked credibility. Both wings believed there were majorities in the House to block the alternative they feared most. So long as that remained the case, there was no incentive for them to approve the agreement.

In early December, MPs began a five-day debate ahead of the planned meaningful vote. The government got off to a dreadful start when MPs defeated it in three votes before the debate proper had even commenced and, for the first time, voted the government in contempt of Parliament for failing to disclose its full legal advice about the withdrawal agreement. The subsequent publication of the advice wrecked ministers' hopes of encouraging Eurosceptic Tories to support the agreement. It confirmed that the Northern Irish backstop could last 'indefinitely' and only be revoked with the EU's consent.

As the debate progressed, it was blindingly obvious that large numbers of Tories were going to rebel and the House of Commons was not going to approve the agreement and declaration. To avoid the ignominy, the prime minister postponed the meaningful vote. Many MPs were outraged. A sufficient number of Tory MPs under internal party rules now demanded a vote of no confidence in May's leadership. The vote was held on the following day. May won it by 200 votes to 117. She was safe from internal challenge for another year, but it was a damning indictment of her waning authority and growing detachment from her parliamentary party.

At this point, the two-level nature of the Brexit process reasserted itself. On the same day that Theresa May signalled the postponement of the meaningful vote, the EU's Court of Justice ruled that the British government could cancel Brexit unilaterally in a case brought by a cross-party group of Scottish politicians and activists. The Court's ruling gave hope to anti-Brexit campaigners in Britain.

Ministers hoped that delaying the meaningful vote until after the Christmas recess would cool MPs' tempers and focus the minds of MPs fearful of a no-deal Brexit. At the same time, ministers sought to focus the minds of pro-Brexit Tory MPs by playing on their fears that Brexit might not happen at all. Speaking early in the New Year, Theresa May again warned of ending up 'with no Brexit at all'.[30] Ministers also sought further concessions from the EU. Little of substance was forthcoming. Donald Tusk and Jean-Claude Juncker, the president of the European Commission, would only provide a letter of reassurance, to the effect that every effort would be made to agree a future relationship and obviate the need for the backstop.

Neither the delay nor the EU's reassurances made a substantive difference. On 15 January 2019, MPs rejected the deal by 432 votes to 202 (Table 1.1). It was the largest government defeat in modern parliamentary history. Over one third of Tory MPs rebelled. Worryingly for government whips, the rebels were drawn from both the pro- and anti-Brexit wings of the party. All ten DUP MPs rejected the deal. Jeremy Corbyn, the Labour leader, immediately moved a motion of no confidence in the government, but when this was debated the following day, all Tory MPs fell into line and the DUP honoured

Table 1.1 The results of the three 'meaningful votes'

	First vote 15 January 2019	Second vote 12 March 2019	Third vote 29 March 2019
Total pro-government	202	242	286
Conservatives	196	235	277
Labour	3	4	4
Others	3	3	5
Total anti-government	432	391	344
Conservatives	118	75	34
Labour	248	238	234
Others	66	78	76
Government majority	−230	−149	−58

Source: House of Commons.

the terms of their confidence-and-supply agreement. The government won by nineteen votes.

The following week, MPs were asked to vote on what they wanted the government to do next. In a series of non-binding votes, opposition MPs, supported by some Tory rebels, rejected a no-deal Brexit, while Tory MPs, supported by some Labour rebels, passed an amendment tabled by Sir Graham Brady, chairman of the influential Conservative backbench 1922 Committee, calling on the government to renegotiate the backstop and find alternative arrangements for the Irish border. Grateful for the breathing space, the prime minister went back to the EU.

In the meantime, three MPs on the Tories' anti-Brexit wing, Heidi Allen, Anna Soubry and Sarah Wollaston, quit the party in protest at its takeover by the 'hard-line anti-EU awkward squad' in the guise of the ERG.[31] They joined the Independent Group, a new parliamentary faction established days earlier by several former Labour MPs unhappy with their own party's position on Brexit. The further reduction in the size of the Tory ranks only added to the government's need to encourage potential Labour rebels to back its deal. To this end, Theresa May now promised to respect and enhance existing EU environmental and employment protections. She also promised to waive the fee for EU citizens applying for 'settled status' and the right to remain in the UK.

Over in Brussels, the government's attorney general, Geoffrey Cox, sought to persuade the EU to accept a legally binding time limit to the Northern Irish backstop. Both the ERG and DUP indicated that such a change could be enough to secure their approval. Ministers hoped that, with such a concession in hand, they could then ask MPs to reconsider their initial judgement and approve the withdrawal agreement in a second meaningful vote.

They also hoped that with Britain's scheduled departure from the EU on 29 March 2019 looming ever closer, MPs would feel greater pressure to approve a deal.

Those were the hopes. The EU refused to renegotiate the substance of the agreement and would only provide further assurances that the backstop was intended to be temporary. Ahead of the second meaningful vote on 12 March, Cox told the Commons that the legal position remain 'unchanged'. Inevitably, the government suffered another catastrophic defeat. There was a silver lining to the cloud, insofar as the margin of defeat fell from 230 votes to 149, and the number of Tory rebels fell from 118 to 75, but nearly one quarter of the Conservative parliamentary party had still rejected the deal.

Speaking to MPs immediately after the vote, Theresa May 'profoundly' regretted their decision and insisted 'the deal we have negotiated is the best, and indeed the only, deal available'.[32] Sounding like an angry teacher, she admonished MPs and reminded them that the time was fast approaching when they would need to decide if they wanted to respect the result of the 2016 referendum – by leaving the EU with or without a deal – cancel it outright or hold a second referendum. The House could vote to request an extension to the Article 50 process, but this would merely delay an inevitable choice.

From this point on, the government lost its ability to set the agenda. A majority of MPs, including seventeen Tory rebels, rejected a no-deal Brexit in a non-binding vote on the day after the second meaningful vote. On the day after that, ministers secured parliamentary approval to seek an extension to the Brexit process. It was a hugely symbolic moment. Promises and commitments to leave on 29 March 2019 had come to naught. The following week, on 21 March, the EU agreed to extend the Article 50 process until 22 May – any later and the UK would need to participate in June's European Parliament elections – provided the Commons approved the withdrawal agreement by 29 March, the original Brexit date. Otherwise, there would be a shorter extension until 12 April, by which point the British government would need to indicate 'a way forward' to EU leaders.

Ministers hoped that an extension might now scare pro-Brexit rebels into backing the agreement or risk sacrificing Brexit altogether. Pressure for a second referendum was intensifying outside and within Parliament. Two days after the EU granted an extension, around one million people took to the streets demanding a 'people's vote'. Meanwhile, over five million people had by now signed a petition to revoke Article 50.[33] It seemed increasingly possible that a majority of MPs could end up voting to refer the matter back to voters. As if to reinforce this point, anti-Brexit rebels, led by the former minister and Tory grandee Sir Oliver Letwin, cooperated with Labour MPs to take control of the Commons' timetable in order to hold a series of

'indicative votes' on MPs' preferred Brexit options. Such cross-party cooperation was extraordinary. Eight options were selected, all were rejected, but
holding a referendum on the withdrawal agreement and remaining in the
EU customs union came closest to winning approval. Both were vehemently
opposed by the ERG.

The speaker of the House of Commons, John Bercow, also asserted
himself. The speaker's role is conventionally neutral, but Bercow judged that
the combination of minority government and Brexit justified him in using
his limited powers to empower the House. When ministers sought to table a
third meaningful vote, Bercow ruled, consistent with parliamentary custom,
that they could not ask MPs to vote on the same matter twice. The EU's
reassurances around the backstop had been sufficient to make the second
meaningful vote different from the first, but nothing had changed since.
Ministers huffed and puffed. The solicitor general, Robert Buckland, called
it a 'constitutional crisis'. Bercow insisted he was merely upholding the
rights of MPs.

To circumvent the ruling, ministers asked MPs to vote only on the
withdrawal agreement. This vote took place on 29 March, the last possible
day if the government was to avoid an extension beyond 22 May. To
incentivise those in her party who wanted her gone, the prime minister
promised to step down if MPs backed the deal. It was a courageous offer
and recognition of her untenable situation. A number of former rebels,
including Boris Johnson, now agreed to support the withdrawal agreement,
but thirty-four Tories, including a handful of anti-Brexit MPs and a larger
core of hard Eurosceptics, known as the 'Spartans' for their refusal to back
down, refused. The DUP also voted against. The government was defeated
by 344 votes to 286.

The initiative now passed to MPs. Once again taking control of its timetable, a cross-party group of backbenchers proposed a second round of
indicative votes to determine if there was a majority for any way out of the
impasse. Again, no option commanded majority support, although holding
a referendum to approve the agreement and remaining in the customs union
after Brexit both came close. There was a sense that MPs had flunked the
chance to take the initiative. One Conservative MP, Nick Boles, who had
advocated remaining in the EU single market, immediately quit the party
over his colleagues' refusal to compromise.[34]

The one thing that a majority of MPs could agree on was the need to
request yet another extension to the Article 50 process. A cross-party group
led by Sir Oliver Letwin and Yvette Cooper, a Labour MP, introduced and
passed legislation that obliged MPs to debate whether or not they should
require the government to request an extension to 30 June. When that
debate happened on 9 April, some 420 MPs voted in favour of the request.

The government acted accordingly, and the EU granted a six-month extension until 31 October. The UK would now be participating in May's European Parliament elections.

With virtually nothing else left to try, and still desperate to fulfil her pledge to honour the result of the 2016 referendum, Theresa May initiated formal discussions with the opposition parties. Labour's position was crucial since it was also committed to honouring the referendum result albeit retaining the benefits of single-market and customs-union membership. May's desperate embrace of bipartisanism went down like lead balloon among Tory MPs. Those on the pro-Brexit wing feared it could lead to a soft Brexit. Almost everyone on the Conservative benches was unhappy about the prospect of Jeremy Corbyn, Labour's far-left leader, influencing government policy. Two more ministers quit. The talks ended up going nowhere.

Tory MPs now openly asked when Theresa May would step down.[35] With absolutely nothing else left to try, the prime minister promised MPs a vote on a second referendum if they approved the withdrawal agreement. It was the final straw for many in her party. Yet another minister resigned and pressure on her became irresistible. On 24 May, as the Tories prepared for a dreadful set of European Parliament election results, a tearful Theresa May announced she would resign towards the end of July once her party had elected a new leader.

The domestic impact of the Brexit process

Brexit had completely paralysed Britain's parliamentary system of government. A majority of MPs opposed the government's withdrawal agreement, a different majority opposed leaving the EU without a deal and a third majority opposed cancelling Brexit. On the related matter of process, there was no majority for referring the matter to voters in a second referendum, and there was no majority, for the time being, for a fresh general election. There was also no majority in favour of creating a 'national government', which some politicians and commentators had proposed.[36] The combination of minority government, internal Tory divisions, Theresa May's toxic leadership and the terms of the withdrawal agreement, all reinforced by the straitjacket of the party system, had led inexorably to stalemate. There would be no way forward until something changed.

Beyond the parliamentary paralysis, the impact of Brexit was far-reaching. In broad terms, it entirely frustrated Theresa May's own personal agenda. Back in 2016, when she had contested and won the Tory leadership, the prime minster had promised a new direction for British Conservatism.[37] She had spoken of more government intervention and of introducing 'a proper industrial strategy'. She had also talked of helping those who were 'just about managing', not just the 'privileged few', of fighting against 'burning' economic, racial and gender injustices, and of promoting social mobility: 'We will do everything we can to help anybody, whatever your background, to go as far as your talents will take you.'[38] This agenda was almost entirely thwarted, however, as the prime minister invested and lost all her political capital in the pursuit of Brexit. Her singular premiership was a twin failure in this respect. May sought to salvage some kind of legacy in the dying days of her government, establishing a new Office for Tackling Injustices, for instance, but her domestic vision was ultimately unfulfilled.

Brexit also ate up the government's bandwidth. Most Whitehall departments were overloaded.[39] Thousands of additional civil servants were recruited to help plan for and administer Britain's withdrawal from the EU, and many were redeployed as the government ramped up planning for a no-deal Brexit, known as Operation Yellowhammer. Mistakes were inevitable. In one case, the transport secretary, Chris Grayling, was mocked for awarding a £13.8 million contract to Seaborne Freight, a start-up ferry company that had no ferries and whose website's 'terms and conditions' had been written for a food-delivery firm.[40] The wider disruption wrecked departments' abilities to develop and pursue other policies. Important pieces of domestic policy, including a planned NHS Reform Plan, a Domestic Abuse Bill and action to address the challenges of social care, were significantly delayed.[41]

At Westminster, a significant portion of the legislative timetable was taken up by Brexit-related matters. The 2017–2019 parliamentary session was the longest on record, and Brexit consumed approximately one sixth of the time spent on the floor of the House of Commons.[42] Ministers had identified a dozen bills that needed to be passed ahead of Brexit, covering trade, fisheries, agriculture, taxation, nuclear safeguarding and countless other issues. Yet, only five of them had made it on to the statute book by 29 March 2019, the day when Britain was meant to have left the EU. Among them was the European Union (Withdrawal) Act 2018, a vital piece of legislation that gave domestic effect to Brexit by transposing existing EU law into UK law. More controversially, the Act contained a number of so-called 'Henry VIII clauses', which allowed ministers to change other acts of Parliament through secondary legislation, subject to less scrutiny. The government claimed the measures were needed for the sake of efficiency. Its critics warned of a power grab.

Beyond Westminster, Brexit dominated the agenda in most voters' minds. Table 1.2 shows changes in responses to Ipsos MORI's 'most important issue' question, averaged over the 2010, 2015 and 2017 parliaments.[43] Between the 2010 and 2015 elections, the economy was the top issue,

Table 1.2 The most important issues facing Britain today, 2010–2019

	2010–2015	*2015–2017*	*2017–2019*
Europe	6	28	55
NHS	24	40	44
Education	15	17	20
Crime	17	11	19
Immigration	30	43	19
Economy	49	25	18
Housing	9	17	18
Poverty	12	15	17
Environment	5	7	12
Defence and foreign affairs	11	16	11
Ageing population and social care	7	9	10
Unemployment	29	15	10

Source: Ipsos MORI. Average responses to: 'What would you say is the most important issue facing Britain today? What do you see as other important issues facing Britain today?' The numbers are the average scores for each issue across the three parliaments.

followed by immigration, unemployment and the NHS. Europe was not an issue on most voters' radars. Between the 2015 and 2017 elections, immigration was the top issue, ahead of the NHS. Europe was now far more prominent, an obvious consequence of the 2016 referendum. Between the 2017 and 2019 elections, Europe was *the* top issue.

None of this is to say that other issues were absent from the agenda. Stories of winter health crises reminded voters of the NHS's vulnerability. The 2017 Grenfell Tower fire highlighted the dreadful quality of housing for many on low incomes. The 2018 'Windrush scandal', where a number of people, particularly members of Britain's African-Caribbean community, were wrongly deported, brought criticism of the government's 'hostile environment' policy for reducing immigration. Rising levels of knife crime, Russian attempts to poison an exiled spy in Salisbury and anti-climate-change protests also contributed to the changing issue agenda. Nevertheless, the constant drip-drip and occasional torrent of Brexit-related media coverage was inescapable. It was a source of bewilderment and worry for many people.

The relative unimportance of the economy after 2017 was striking. In part, the issue's low salience reflected the relatively stable economic conditions. As Table 1.3 shows, growth during this period was low but consistent. Inflation, interest rates and unemployment also remained low. The general outlook was sufficiently good for Philip Hammond, Theresa May's chancellor of the exchequer, to increase public spending and promise voters

Table 1.3 Objective economic indicators, 2015–2019

		GDP quarterly growth (%)	Inflation (%)	Unemployment (%)	Interest rates (%)
2015	Q3	0.4	−0.1	5.5	0.5
	Q4	0.7	−0.1	5.2	0.5
2016	Q1	0.2	0.3	5.2	0.5
	Q2	0.5	0.2	5.1	0.5
	Q3	0.5	0.6	5.0	0.25
	Q4	0.6	1.1	4.9	0.25
2017	Q1	0.6	2.0	4.7	0.25
	Q2	0.3	2.6	4.5	0.25
	Q3	0.3	2.7	4.4	0.25
	Q4	0.4	2.9	4.4	0.5
2018	Q1	0.1	2.7	4.3	0.5
	Q2	0.5	2.4	4.1	0.5
	Q3	0.6	2.5	4.2	0.75
	Q4	0.2	2.2	4.1	0.75
2019	Q1	0.6	1.8	3.9	0.75
	Q2	−0.1	2.1	4.0	0.75
	Q3	0.5	1.8	3.9	0.75
	Q4	0	1.4	3.8	0.75

Sources: Office for National Statistics (for Gross Domestic Product (GDP), inflation and unemployment) and Bank of England (interest rates). Gross Domestic Product (GDP) growth is shown as the percentage increase in GDP at market prices compared with the previous quarter. The inflation measure is the Consumer Price Index annual percentage change. Unemployment is shown as the International Labour Organization rate, including all adults (16+) to retirement age. Interest rates are the end-of-quarter offical Bank Rate.

in his 2018 budget that the era of 'austerity', a legacy of the 2007–2008 financial crisis, was 'finally coming to an end'.[44] The economy's low salience also reflects the way it was often framed by Brexit and speculation about Britain's future relationship with the EU. Hammond and others, notably Mark Carney, the independent-minded head of the Bank of England, frequently warned against the economic effects of a no-deal Brexit. Hammond also talked up the 'war chest' he had accumulated to cushion against a no deal.[45] Most voters, when they read or heard about the economy, usually read or heard about Brexit and the economy.

Many of the political consequences of Brexit have already been alluded to. Nearly two-dozen ministers resigned from the government, and several Tory and Labour MPs broke from their parties and formed a centrist party, the Independent Group, later Change UK.[46] Both Conservative and Labour MPs routinely voted against their party. When it came to Brexit, Jeremy

Corbyn's problems were the mirror image of Theresa May's. Labour's largest and most wobbly wing comprised committed pro-Europeans. Over one third of Labour MPs declared their support for another referendum in defiance of the party's official line.[47]

Among voters, the Brexit process merely reinforced the divisions created by the 2016 referendum. Passions often ran high, especially on social media, and many politicians were subjected to abuse and intimidation. The minority of voters who cared most deeply about Brexit were the least likely to compromise. For those who favoured Brexit, anything less than a 'clean break' would violate their vote to 'take back control'. For those opposed to Brexit, full-blown EU membership was preferable to a soft Brexit. Although some surveys suggested membership of the single market and customs union might constitute an acceptable compromise, this option never attracted passionate support.[48] There were marches and protests in favour of leaving the EU immediately and in favour of cancelling Brexit. No one marched for compromise.

Since the referendum, the polling organisation YouGov had routinely asked respondents whether they thought Britain was right or wrong to leave the EU. As Figure 1.1 shows, there was no sudden dramatic change in public opinion. To be sure, many voters were influenced by the delays and political wrangling, and the proportion saying 'wrong to leave' increased slightly over time, especially after the withdrawal agreement's publication in November 2018. Yet, the delays and wrangling also reaffirmed many voters' beliefs that Britain was right to leave. For them, it was evidence of why Brexit was necessary.

Voters may have disagreed on the virtues of Brexit but most agreed that ministers were bungling it. Figure 1.2 shows changes in response to another YouGov question, which asked how well or badly voters thought the government was doing at negotiating Britain's exit from the EU. Other than in the immediate wake of Theresa May's letter to the EU in March 2017 formally triggering the Brexit process, the net judgement was negative. It became progressively more negative. By the time of the third meaningful vote in March 2019, net evaluations were at around *minus* 80. Voters who wanted Brexit blamed the government for failing to deliver it. Voters opposed to Brexit blamed the government for pressing ahead with it.

If most voters disdained the government's performance, they were even more disdainful of the Labour Party's performance as the official opposition. Figure 1.3 shows respondents' answers to another regular YouGov question: which of the political parties would handle the problem of Britain's exit from the EU best? Throughout the Brexit process, Labour's handling was judged more negatively than the Tories. Labour found itself torn

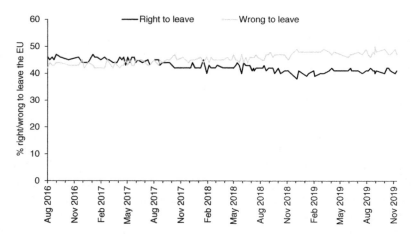

Figure 1.1 Was Britain right or wrong to vote to leave the EU?
Source: YouGov, 'EU tracker questions (GB)', available at: https://d25d2506sfb94s.
cloudfront.net/cumulus_uploads/document/042fsto5vj/YG%20Trackers%20-%20
EU%20Tracker%20Questions_W.pdf, last accessed 26 June 2021. Responses to: 'In
hindsight, do you think Britain was right or wrong to vote to leave the European
Union?'

between its programmatic commitment to European integration and some
of its traditional working-class voters' support for Brexit. Jeremy Corbyn's
attempts to fashion a middle way was confusing if not confused. He was
also blamed for the parliamentary deadlock. The public understandably
concluded 'a plague on both your houses'.

Voters' disdain for the Tories' and Labour's handling of Brexit was
manifested in a dramatic upsurge in support for the Brexit Party and the
Liberal Democrats (Figure 1.4). The Brexit Party, co-founded by Nigel
Farage, the former leader of the United Kingdom Independence Party
(UKIP), was little more than a single-issue pressure group. It wanted a
swift and 'clean Brexit' and argued the UK should leave the EU without a
deal if necessary. It soon found a following among frustrated former Leave
voters. The Liberal Democrats, once Britain's third party, found a possible
way to recover from the toxic reputation it had acquired from being the
junior partner in the 2010–2015 coalition government. As an unambiguously pro-European party, it reached out to former Remain voters, especially those frustrated by Labour's opaque policy. By the summer of 2019,
the Brexit Party had eaten into much of the Tories' support, and the Liberal
Democrats into Labour's.

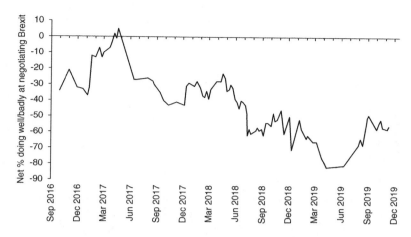

Figure 1.2 Evaluations of the government's handling of Brexit
Source: YouGov, 'EU tracker questions (GB)', available at: https://d25d2506sfb94s.
cloudfront.net/cumulus_uploads/document/56vc0xf7fa/YG%20Trackers%20-%20
EU%20Tracker%20Questions_W.pdf, last accessed 26 June 2021. Calculated from
responses to: 'How well or badly do you think the government are doing at negotiating
Britain's exit from the European Union?'

Voters had an opportunity to register their disdain in the May 2019
European Parliament elections, which were necessitated by the second Brexit
extension, to 31 October 2019. Many did so. Ominously for the Tories and
Labour, the 36.9 per cent turnout was the second highest it had ever been
for European elections in the UK, suggesting their failures had mobilised
voters. The results were catastrophic for both parties. The Brexit Party won
a commanding plurality of votes and topped the polls in every region outside London and Scotland, as shown in Table 1.4. The Liberal Democrats
were second, some way ahead of Labour in third place, and came top in
London. The Conservatives were a distant fifth, taking only 9 per cent of the
popular vote. Labour tended to do worse in Scotland and the southern
regions of England. The Tories did badly everywhere.

European Parliament elections employ a form of proportional representation. This ensured at least four Conservative MEPs were elected. Had the
contest followed the single-member plurality rules of a general election, the
Tories might have failed to win a single seat. It remained anybody's guess if
the results heralded a realignment of the British party system. The confusion
was exacerbated by the relatively low turnout in some regions – 33 per cent
in the North East and North West – making it harder to predict how voters
might behave in a general election.

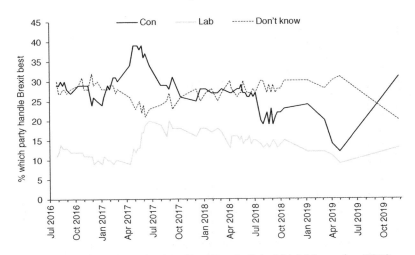

Figure 1.3 Best party for handling Brexit, July 2016–November 2019
Source: YouGov, 'Best party on issues (GB)', available at: https://d25d2506sfb94s.
cloudfront.net/cumulus_uploads/document/h1webgz4u8/YG%20Trackers%20-%20
Best%20Party%20On%20Issues.pdf, last accessed 26 June 2021.
Responses to: 'Here is a list of problems facing the country. Could you say for each of
them which political party you think would handle the problem best? Britain's exit
from the EU.'

Beyond its policy and party-political consequences, Brexit affected aspects of the wider UK polity. The pressures facing the civil service have already been noted. One of the consequences was the testing of norms of civil-service neutrality and the fraying of trust between officials and politicians. Civil servants are meant to implement the government's policies without public question, but some started voicing their concerns, especially over preparations for a no-deal Brexit.[49] Speaking in the summer of 2019, Lord Kerslake, the former head of the civil service, warned: 'We are reaching the point where the civil service must consider putting its stewardship of the country ahead of service to the government of the day.'[50] Such warnings reinforced some politicians' suspicions that the civil service was seeking to sabotage Brexit.[51] Civil servants, in turn, became fair game. Olly Robbins, Theresa May's chief Europe adviser, was publicly criticised. In one apparently related incident, Sir Kim Darroch, Britain's ambassador to the US, resigned after emails critical of President Donald Trump were leaked. Many believed that he had been sacrificed to improve the prospects of striking post-Brexit trade deals with the US.

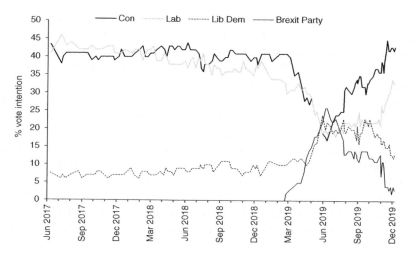

Figure 1.4 Voting intentions, 2017–2019

Source: YouGov, 'Voting intention tracker (GB)', available at: https://d25d2506sfb94s.
cloudfront.net/cumulus_uploads/document/jb4i486dc5/YG%20trackers%20-%20
Voting%20Intention%20since%20GE%202017_W.pdf, last accessed 26 June 2021.
Responses to: 'If there were a general election held tomorrow, which party would you
vote for?'

Table 1.4 Party vote shares in the 2019 European Parliament elections (%)

Region	Brexit Party	Lib Dem	Lab	Green	Con	SNP	Plaid	Others
North East	39	17	19	8	7	0	0	10
North West	31	17	22	13	8	0	0	10
Yorkshire and Humber	37	16	16	13	7	0	0	12
East Midlands	38	17	14	11	11	0	0	9
West Midlands	38	16	17	11	10	0	0	8
East	38	23	9	13	10	0	0	8
London	18	27	24	12	8	0	0	11
South East	36	26	7	14	10	0	0	7
South West	37	23	7	18	9	0	0	7
Wales	33	14	15	6	7	0	20	6
Scotland	15	14	9	8	12	38	0	4
Great Britain	32	20	14	12	9	4	1	8
MEPs elected (number)	29	16	10	7	4	3	1	0

Source: Stefano Fella, Elise Uberoi and Richard Cracknel, *European Parliament Elections 2019: Results and Analysis*, House of Commons Library, Briefing Paper 8600, 26 June 2019, available at: https://researchbriefings.files.parliament.uk/documents/CBP-8600/CBP-8600.pdf, last accessed 26 June 2021.

Brexit also strained the UK's devolution settlement.[52] The introduction of devolved rule for Scotland, Wales and Northern Ireland had been one of the Blair government's most enduring legacies. Brexit was now a source of multiple tensions between the central and devolved governments, or at least between the UK and Scottish and Welsh governments, since Northern Ireland had been under direct rule from London after the collapse of its power-sharing government in January 2017. Sixty-two per cent of Scottish voters had backed Remain in the 2016 referendum. The Scottish National Party, which governed in Edinburgh, favoured the softest of Brexits, if there had to be Brexit, but it also wanted another opportunity to vote on leaving the UK and thereby remain in the EU. One of the arguments made against independence in the 2014 Scottish referendum had been that Scotland's membership of the EU depended on remaining part of the UK. That argument no longer applied. Labour and the Liberal Democrats, which governed together in Cardiff, were also opposed to Brexit, although 52.5 per cent Welsh voters had voted Leave in 2016.

Debates about the repatriation of powers from the EU compounded the tension. The broad policy framework set by the EU in areas like agriculture and the environment had provided scope for divergence among the home nations. The devolved governments wanted some of the powers being returned from Brussels in order to protect their autonomy. The central government in London wanted these powers to ensure the UK could function as a single market and make future trade agreements for the whole country. Scottish and Welsh politicians vented their frustrations. By convention, the Westminster Parliament was expected to secure the 'legislative consent' of the devolved parliaments when legislating in areas that had been devolved. Initially, the Scottish and Welsh governments refused to consent to the European Union (Withdrawal) Bill. The Welsh Assembly eventually provided its consent, but the Scottish Parliament did not. After the UK government pressed ahead with the law, Nicola Sturgeon, Scotland's first minister, tweeted that ministers had 'ripped up the 20-year-old devolution convention'.[53] Scottish Nationalist MPs at Westminster staged a walkout in protest.

The judges too found themselves entangled in the political morass created by Brexit. Reflecting the trend towards the 'judicialisation' of British politics and the courts being drawn into political matters, campaigners on both sides pursued legal means to advance their cause.[54] Anti-Brexit campaigners were visibly more successful in utilising the courts. In early 2017, for instance, the UK Supreme Court had ruled that the government needed parliamentary approval before it could trigger the Article 50 process. It had accepted the campaigner Gina Miller's claim that any attempt by the government to leave the EU using executive or royal prerogative powers – powers exercised by the monarch on the advice of ministers – would be illegal, since Britain's membership had been established in law. From that point on, the judges, who had been asserting the constitutional importance of the doctrine of 'parliamentary sovereignty' and Parliament's ultimate legal authority, were subject to intense suspicion from pro-Brexit campaigners.

Last but by no means least, Brexit even challenged some of the ideas that underpinned Britain's political system. Consistent with the doctrine of parliamentary sovereignty, British democracy traditionally entailed a clear 'division of labour' between politicians and voters: it was politicians' job to act as 'trustees' and govern in what they thought was the country's best interests. Brexit was driving Britain, at least discursively, to resemble a different model of democracy, one premised on the idea of popular sovereignty in which politicians operated as delegates, acting faithfully on the wishes of 'the people'.[55] The discourse had been apparent in the *Daily Mail*'s coverage of the Miller case, when it described three judges as 'the enemies of the people' for ruling that Parliament needed to authorise the prime minister to trigger Article 50. It was also apparent in some of Theresa May's attempts to strong-arm MPs into supporting her withdrawal agreement by appealing directly to voters:

> as we have seen over the last few weeks, there are some in Westminster who would wish to delay or even stop Brexit and who will use every device available to them to do so ... We all have a duty to implement the result of the referendum.[56]

The dangers of this discourse were threefold. The first was that it risked crossing the boundary into outright populism and undermining the norms of liberal democracy. The 2016 referendum had been won by a narrow margin of 51.9 per cent. What of the rights and opinions of the 48.1 per cent? The second danger was that such talk was based on a fallacy. There was no clear 'will of the people' in favour of Brexit, or any particular form of Brexit.[57] The original referendum had only asked voters to choose whether or not Britain should remain in or leave the EU. Third, the discourse cut both ways. Opponents of May's withdrawal agreement could point to opinion polls or estimates of how their constituents voted in the referendum and invoke the will of the people. The notion that politicians were the delegates of those they represented merely reinforced the deadlock.

The ball comes loose

On 24 July 2019, one of the factors that had contributed to the deadlock changed. For reasons that Thomas Quinn explains in Chapter 2, Boris Johnson became the new Conservative leader and prime minister. Back in

2013, when he was the mayor of London, a BBC interviewer had tackled Johnson about his ambition to be prime minister. Invoking the game of rugby and the Corinthian spirit, Johnson had replied: 'If the ball came loose from the back of the scrum, which it won't of course, it would be a great, great thing to have a crack at.'[58] In terms of Brexit, Johnson's entry into 10 Downing Street was akin to that ball coming loose.

Johnson's election as Tory leader was a sign of his party's desperation. He had a chequered past – he had been sacked as the party's shadow arts minister in 2004 for lying about an extra-marital affair – and there were wider doubts about his trustworthiness and suitability for high office. Michael Gove had sabotaged his leadership bid in 2016 by declaring that Johnson could not 'provide the leadership or build the team for the task ahead'.[59] The new prime minister was certainly divisive. His colourful language offended those on the left, while many of those opposed to Brexit despised him for his role in the 2016 campaign. For the same reasons, Johnson was adored by many on the right, although some Eurosceptics wondered whether his support for Brexit had been heartfelt or driven by personal ambition.

Johnson immediately conducted a wide-ranging cabinet reshuffle, shifting the balance in government towards a hard Brexit.[60] The ministerial clear-out restored discipline but was risky: it sent to the backbenches several high-ranking former cabinet ministers, who now swelled the ranks of anti-Brexit Tory rebels. Johnson also appointed Dominic Cummings, the former director of Vote Leave, as his chief adviser. Cummings was an iconoclast when it came to Britain's governing institutions. David Cameron had once described him as a 'career psychopath'.[61] Cummings asserted himself immediately, sacking one of the special advisers who worked for Sajid Javid, the new chancellor of the exchequer. Javid complained but could do nothing.

Johnson's approach to Brexit mirrored his robust approach to government. He offered one clear pledge: Britain would leave the EU on 31 October, when the second extension period came to an end, 'do or die, come what may'.[62] All ministers were obliged to commit themselves to this goal. The new prime minister preferred to leave the EU with a deal, of course, but vowed to renegotiate the withdrawal agreement and especially the Northern Irish backstop. Nothing would alter his timetable.

Johnson's do-or-die pledge was aimed at his base, at Leave voters tempted by Nigel Farage's Brexit Party and at the EU. He believed that a credible threat of no deal would force new concessions from Brussels. To underline the point, no-deal preparations were ramped up. Johnson also declined to offer proposals on how to replace the Northern Irish backstop, putting the ball firmly in the EU's court. Some diplomats concluded that the government was now reconciled to a no-deal Brexit.[63]

Despite his more robust approach to Brexit, Johnson faced the same fundamental challenges that had confronted Theresa May. A majority of MPs remained opposed to a no-deal Brexit, and there was the risk, albeit small, that they might bring down his government or force a second referendum. But Johnson had two options open to him that May had not. One was to go back to the EU, since it was now clear that MPs would not vote for the existing withdrawal agreement. The other was to change the parliamentary arithmetic by seeking and winning a general election. If he could do the latter, he would have a mandate for his vision of Brexit and a Commons majority to deliver it. The risk, of course, was that he might suffer the same fate as May's 2017 electoral gamble. There was also the practical difficulty of persuading two thirds of all MPs to vote for an election under the terms of the Fixed-term Parliaments Act. Since an election would eat into the time remaining before the new deadline, it increased the prospects of a no-deal Brexit. Since most MPs were opposed to a no-deal Brexit, they would not yet vote for an election.

The conventional wisdom was that Johnson and Cummings were laying the ground for a 'people vs. parliament' election.[64] If MPs ratified a new withdrawal agreement, Johnson could fight an election as the man who had delivered Brexit. If there was a no-deal Brexit, Johnson could still say he had delivered Brexit and pin the blame for any economic disruption on the EU. If there was a further extension, Johnson could attack the other parties for frustrating his attempts to deliver Brexit. To reinforce Johnson's popular if not populist appeal, he promised cash injections for the NHS.

For the time being, the prime minister insisted he would not seek an early election.[65] Downing Street also worked to put pressure on its opponents in the House of Commons. In late August 2019, during the summer recess, ministers announced plans for a five-week prorogation of parliament. The power to prorogue is one of the remaining royal prerogatives. Theresa May had been criticised for running down the clock and using the looming Brexit deadline to cajole MPs into supporting her deal. The prorogation took this strategy to another level.

Prorogations refer to the periods between parliamentary sessions when MPs do not sit. Most are unremarkable and brief: between 1930 and 2017, the mean length was just eight days, with most lasting around five days or fewer.[66] The 2017–2019 parliamentary session was already the longest on record, and a new session would enable the new government to set out its legislative agenda. However, every day parliament was prorogued was a day in which MPs could not debate Brexit or take action to prevent a no-deal Brexit. Anticipating the government's move back in July, Dominic Grieve, a Conservative MP and former attorney general, had tabled amendments to the Northern Ireland (Executive Formation etc.) Bill requiring ministers to produce fortnightly reports and allow MPs time to debate them. This requirement, it was hoped, would make a lengthy prorogation illegal.

The announcement of a five-week prorogation infuriated opposition and some Tory MPs. They reacted as soon as the House of Commons returned from its summer recess on 3 September. Sir Oliver Letwin, now an habitual rebel, secured an emergency debate to introduce legislation that would prevent a no-deal Brexit by asking for a further extension to the Brexit process. Introducing a bill in this way was unprecedented: John Bercow, the speaker, stretched his powers to the limit in allowing it. No fewer than twenty-one Conservative MPs voted in favour, including nine former cabinet ministers. Johnson immediately expelled them from the party. In protest, two cabinet ministers, including the prime minister's brother, Jo Johnson, quit the government and party. On 9 September, the European Union (Withdrawal) (No. 2) Act 2019 became law. Known as the Benn Act, after its chief sponsor, the Labour MP Hilary Benn, it required the prime minister to seek a further delay to Brexit if MPs failed to approve either a withdrawal agreement or leaving the EU without an agreement by 19 October. Johnson insisted that he would 'rather be dead in a ditch' than seek an extension.[67] There were even hints that the government might disregard it.[68]

Whether the prime minister's response was sincere or feigned, it reflected his plans to fight a 'people vs. parliament' election. The government was now a minority administration, even with the DUP's support. An early general election was inevitable. The only question was whether it would be before or after any deal. In response to the Benn Act, ministers had twice asked MPs to consent to an early election, knowing that the opposition parties' refusal would merely reinforce the narrative of a 'broken parliament'.

At this point, the prorogation took effect. It was met by angry scenes at Westminster. With parliament suspended, all eyes now turned to the courts. Over the summer, a cross-party group of MPs and peers had, like Dominic Grieve, anticipated a lengthy prorogation and launched a petition in the Scottish courts seeking an injunction against one. The petition was rejected but then successfully appealed. Meanwhile, Gina Miller, the anti-Brexit campaigner, started a separate action in the English courts. Both cases swiftly converged on the UK Supreme Court in London. To the government's chagrin, the court's president, Baroness Hale, ruled that ministers' advice to the queen had been unlawful on the grounds that the prorogation was excessive in length, undermined parliamentary sovereignty and prevented MPs from carrying out their duties. The court declared the prorogation null and void. Parliament could resume immediately.[69]

Things now began to move swiftly. At the beginning of October, the government announced another, shorter prorogation. It also finally published its proposals for resolving the impasse around the withdrawal agreement.

Two weeks later, Boris Johnson and Jean-Claude Juncker shook hands on a revised deal. The main changes related to the Northern Irish backstop. The UK would not now remain within a single customs territory if it was unable to negotiate a new trade deal. Only Northern Ireland would remain within the single market for goods. Formally, Northern Ireland would also leave the customs union along with the rest of the UK; in practice, checks on goods would take place between Northern Ireland and the rest of the UK at special 'points of entry'. Moreover, taxes would only be paid on goods moving from Great Britain into Northern Ireland if they were likely to proceed on to the Republic of Ireland. As a sop to the DUP, the Northern Irish Assembly would be able to end the arrangement four years after the end of the transition period.

The new deal was a great fudge, blurring legal formalities and practicalities. It was also a remarkable U-turn from Johnson, who had previously promised the DUP that no Conservative government could or should ever agree to additional regulatory checks and customs controls between Northern Ireland and the rest of the UK.[70] Nevertheless, many voters, especially Conservative supporters, considered it a marked improvement on May's deal.[71] More importantly, the changes were sufficient to garner the ERG's backing. On 22 October, in a rare Saturday sitting, the House of Commons voted to approve the deal laid out in the European Union (Withdrawal Agreement) Bill by 329 votes to 299. However, a majority of MPs, still wary of a possible no-deal Brexit, opposed attempts to expedite the bill's passage through the Commons. The government, in turn, pulled the bill and made it clear that a general election was now needed.

Pulling the bill meant that Johnson had to request an extension to the Brexit process in line with the Benn Act. He did so reluctantly. On 28 October, the EU agreed to extend the deadline a third time, until 31 January 2020. Johnson's critics mocked his earlier 'do or die' promises. The prime minister's cheerleaders could frame the extension as yet another instance of other politicians thwarting Brexit and the will of the people.

Now that no deal had been taken off the table, at least temporarily, the Scottish Nationalists and Liberal Democrats suddenly came out in favour of an early election. Their U-turns created the simple majority necessary to pass new legislation that bypassed the Fixed-term Parliaments Act. The resulting Early Parliamentary General Election Act 2019 set the date for Thursday 12 December. Speaking in Downing Street at the start of the campaign, Johnson's populist message was laid bare. Parliament was paralysed, he told reporters: 'our MPs are just refusing – time and again – to deliver Brexit and honour the mandate of the people'. Targeting former Leave voters and everyone else frustrated by the Westminster deadlock he declared: 'Let's get Brexit done.'[72]

Conclusion

After two years of parliamentary paralysis, there was now an opportunity to escape the deadlock that had mired British politics. The change in prime minister had made the difference. Boris Johnson had been ruthless in dealing with internal opposition, purging his party of anti-Brexit dissidents. He had played hard and fast with constitutional norms and drawn the queen into party politics. He had also shown himself willing to compromise on the integrity of the UK. If leaving the EU required barriers between Northern Ireland and Great Britain, so be it. To paraphrase his earlier words about the Brexit divorce bill, the DUP 'could go whistle'. The Conservatives could now look forward to fighting an election largely on their terms and united around a vision of a hard Brexit. Johnson could claim credit for having renegotiated a viable Brexit deal. He could also campaign by the populist rule book, setting himself up as the leader trying to deliver on the 2016 referendum result but frustrated by the political establishment and opposition parties. Johnson had once said that his policy on cake was 'pro having it and pro eating it'. By design and luck, he would get his electoral cake and eat it.

Notes

1 For a thorough analysis of the result, see John Bartle, 'Why the Conservatives lost their majority – but still won', in Nicholas Allen and John Bartle (eds), *None Past the Post: Britain at the Polls, 2017* (Manchester: Manchester University Press), pp. 160–189.

2 See Richard I. Hofferbert and Ian Budge, 'The party mandate and the Westminster Model: Election programmes and government spending in Britain, 1948–85', *British Journal of Political Science*, 22 (1992), 151–182.

3 See Howard R. Penniman (ed.), *Britain at the Polls: The Parliamentary Elections of 1974* (Washington, DC: American Enterprise Institute for Public Policy Research, 1975).

4 See Nicholas Allen and John Bartle (eds), *Britain at the Polls 2010* (London: Sage, 2011).

5 See Cabinet Office, *The Cabinet Manual: A Guide to Laws, Conventions and Rules on the Operation of Government* (London: Cabinet Office, 2011), available at: https://assets.publishing.service.gov.uk/government/uploads/system/uploads/attachment_data/file/60641/cabinet-manual.pdf, last accessed 26 June 2021.

6 See Rosie Campbell, 'A coalition of chaos: Where next?', in Allen and Bartle (eds), *None Past the Post*, pp. 190–211.

7 See BBC News, 'Theresa May's general election statement in full', 18 April 2017, available at: www.bbc.co.uk/news/uk-politics-39630009, last accessed 26 June 2021.

8 See Sam Coates, '"I have no wish to be PM": Johnson protests his loyalty', *The Times*, 12 June 2017, available at: www.thetimes.co.uk/article/i-have-no-wish-to-be-pm-boris-johnson-protests-his-loyalty-mhfq5r9r7, last accessed 26 June 2021.

9 See Nicholas Allen, '"Brexit means Brexit": Theresa May and post-referendum British politics', *British Politics*, 13 (2018), 105–120.

10 For a thorough account of the referendum, see Harold D. Clarke, Matthew Goodwin and Paul Whiteley, *Brexit: Why Britain Voted to Leave the European Union* (Cambridge: Cambridge University Press, 2017).

11 The leaflet, entitled 'Why the Government believes that voting to remain in the European Union is the best decision for the UK' is available at: assets.publishing.service.gov.uk/government/uploads/system/uploads/attachment_data/file/515068/why-the-government-believes-that-voting-to-remain-in-the-european-union-is-the-best-decision-for-the-uk.pdf, last accessed 26 June 2021.

12 A list of MPs' positions can be found at BBC News, 'EU vote: Where the cabinet and other MPs stand', 22 June 2016, available at: www.bbc.co.uk/news/uk-politics-eu-referendum-35616946, last accessed 26 June 2021.

13 Robert D. Putnam, 'Diplomacy and domestic politics: The logic of two-level games', *International Organization*, 42 (1988), 427–460.

14 Much of the following narrative draws on three excellent books: Tim Shipman, *Fall Out: A Year of Political Mayhem* (London: William Collins, 2017), Lode Desmet and Edward Stourton, *Blind Man's Brexit: How the EU Took Control of Brexit* (London: Simon & Schuster, 2019) and Anthony Seldon with Raymond Newell, *May at 10* (London: Biteback, 2019).

15 BBC News, 'Brexit: No-deal impact assessment published', 26 February 2019, available at: www.bbc.co.uk/news/uk-politics-47379308, last accessed 26 June 2021.

16 Theresa May, 'The government's negotiating objectives for exiting the EU', speech delivered on 17 January 2017, available at: www.gov.uk/government/speeches/the-governments-negotiating-objectives-for-exiting-the-eu-pm-speech, last accessed 26 June 2021.

17 Oliver Wright, 'Timetable for talks will be row of the summer, says Davis', *The Times*, 15 May 2017, available at: www.thetimes.co.uk/article/timetable-for-brexit-talks-will-be-row-of-summer-says-davis-zr0nsmrxr, last accessed 26 June 2021.

18 See James Tapsfield, Martin Robinson and Mario Ledwith, '"We won't pay": David Davis DISMISSES Brussels demand for £92 billion after Germany, France and Poland gang up to DOUBLE the Brexit divorce bill', MailOnline, 2 May 2017, available at: www.dailymail.co.uk/news/article-4467612/Europe-raises-Britain-s-bill-Brexit-92billion.html, last accessed 26 June 2021.

19 Oliver Wright, 'Go whistle, Johnson tells Brussels', *The Times*, 12 July 2017, available at: www.thetimes.co.uk/article/go-whistle-johnson-tells-brussels-25k8 p7vb3, last accessed 26 June 2021.

20 See paragraphs 49 and 50 of 'Joint report from the negotiators of the European Union and the United Kingdom government on progress during phase 1 of

negotiations under Article 50 TEU on the United Kingdom's orderly withdrawal from the European Union', available at: https://assets.publishing.service.gov.uk/government/uploads/system/uploads/attachment_data/file/665869/Joint_report_on_progress_during_phase_1_of_negotiations_under_Article_50_TEU_on_the_United_Kingdom_s_orderly_withdrawal_from_the_European_Union.pdf, last accessed 26 June 2021.

21 Sarah Gordon, 'Hammond seeks "off-the-shelf" transition', *Financial Times*, 28 July 2017, available at: www.ft.com/content/cc1dbf04-71fc-11e7-aca6-c6bd07df1a3c, last accessed 26 June 2021.

22 Boris Johnson, 'My vision for a bold, thriving Britain enabled by Brexit', *Daily Telegraph*, 16 September 2017, available at: www.telegraph.co.uk/politics/0/boris-johnson-vision-for-brexit-bold-thriving-britain/, last accessed 26 June 2021.

23 BBC News, 'Brexit: David Davis' resignation letter and May's reply in full', 9 July 2018, available at: www.bbc.co.uk/news/uk-politics-44761416, last accessed 26 June 2021.

24 BBC News, 'Boris Johnson's resignation letter and May's reply in full', 9 July 2018, available at: www.bbc.co.uk/news/uk-politics-44772804, last accessed 26 June 2021.

25 Both documents are available at: www.gov.uk/government/publications/withdrawal-agreement-and-political-declaration, last accessed 26 June 2021.

26 Katy Balls, 'Dominic Raab's resignation could spell the end for May's Brexit plan', *Guardian*, 15 November 2018, available at: www.theguardian.com/commentisfree/2018/nov/15/dominic-raab-resignation-may-brexit-plan, last accessed 26 June 2021.

27 BBC News, 'Brexit: Cabinet backs draft agreement', 14 November 2018, available at: www.bbc.co.uk/news/uk-politics-46215930, last accessed 26 June 2021.

28 BBC News, 'Brexit: UK and EU "agree text" of draft withdrawal agreement', 14 November 2018, available at: www.bbc.co.uk/news/uk-politics-46188790, last accessed 26 June 2021.

29 Quoted in Reuters, 'PM May says – It's my deal, no deal or no Brexit at all', 6 December 2018, available at: uk.reuters.com/article/uk-britain-eu-may-idUKKBN1O50RT, last accessed 26 June 2021.

30 BBC News, 'Brexit: PM warns of "uncharted territory" if MPs reject deal', 6 January 2019, available at: www.bbc.co.uk/news/uk-politics-46772601, last accessed 26 June 2021.

31 BBC News, 'Independent Group: Three MPs quit Tory party to join', 20 February 2019, available at: www.bbc.co.uk/news/uk-politics-47306022, last accessed 26 June 2021.

32 House of Commons Debates, volume 656, 12 March 2019, col. 295.

33 Lucy Fisher, 'Petition to stop Brexit passes the 5m mark', *The Times*, 25 March 2019, available at: www.thetimes.co.uk/article/petition-to-stop-brexit-passes-the-5m-mark-pwqvk93gp, last accessed 26 June 2021.

34 Sam Coates, 'Boles quits with swipe at Tory party incapable of compromise', *The Times*, 2 April 2019, available at: www.thetimes.co.uk/article/cabinet-to-hold-marathon-session-on-next-step-ztc67svm8, last accessed 26 June 2021.

35 BBC News, 'Theresa May: Senior Tories rule out early challenge to PM', 24 April 2019, available at: www.bbc.co.uk/news/uk-politics-48032990, last accessed 26 June 2021.

36 Ed Davey, 'Only a national government can deliver Britain from its Brexit nightmare', *Observer*, 2 June 2019, available at: www.theguardian.com/commentisfree/2019/jun/02/only-a-national-government-can-deliver-britain-from-its-brexit-nightmare, last accessed 26 June 2021.

37 Allen, '"Brexit means Brexit"', pp. 116–117.

38 See 'Statement from the new prime minister Theresa May', 13 July 2016, available at: www.gov.uk/government/speeches/statement-from-the-new-prime-minister-theresa-may, last accessed 26 June 2021.

39 See the Institute for Government's *Whitehall Monitor 2019*, p. 3, available at: www.instituteforgovernment.org.uk/sites/default/files/publications/Whitehall%20Monitor%202019%20WEB1.pdf, last accessed 26 June 2021.

40 Matt Chorley, 'In this ferry tale, Grayling is Peter Pan looking for his Lost Buoys', *The Times*, 5 January 2019, available at: www.thetimes.co.uk/article/in-this-ferry-tale-grayling-is-peter-pan-looking-for-his-lost-buoys-kjxk0tb2x, last accessed 26 June 2021.

41 Lewis Lloyd, *The Brexit Effect: How Government Has Changed since the EU Referendum* (London: Institute for Government, 2019), p. 14, available at: www.instituteforgovernment.org.uk/sites/default/files/publications/brexit-snapshot-final-web-vd_0.pdf, last accessed 26 June 2021.

42 Lloyd, *The Brexit Effect*, p. 34.

43 Ipsos MORI combines responses to two questions: 'What would you say is the most important issue facing Britain today?' and 'What do you see as other important issues facing Britain today?' See 'Issue index archive', available at: www.ipsos.com/ipsos-mori/en-uk/issues-index-archive, last accessed 26 June 2021.

44 Rachael Sylvester, 'Hammond's budget dodged the big decision', *The Times*, 30 October 2018, available at: www.thetimes.co.uk/article/budget-2018-hammond-s-budget-dodged-the-big-decision-6lbdhpkd3, last accessed 26 June 2021.

45 Szu Ping Chan, 'Spring statement: Hammond promises "deal dividend"', BBC News, 13 March 2019, available at: www.bbc.co.uk/news/business-47554876, last accessed 26 June 2021.

46 Louise Thompson, *The End of the Small Party? Change UK and the Challenges of Parliamentary Politics* (Manchester: Manchester University Press, 2020).

47 Sienna Rodgers, 'The list of all Labour MPs openly backing a "people's vote"', LabourList, 29 November 2019, available at: labourlist.org/2018/11/the-list-of-all-labour-mps-openly-backing-a-peoples-vote/, last accessed 26 June 2021.

48 Will Jennings, 'In search of the "median voter" on Brexit…', YouGov, 29 August 2019, available at: yougov.co.uk/topics/politics/articles-reports/2019/08/29/search-median-voter-brexit, last accessed 26 June 2021.

49 The Civil Servant [anonymous], 'I'm a civil servant. Trust me, we're nowhere near ready for no-deal Brexit', *Guardian*, 5 February 2019, available at: www.

theguardian.com/commentisfree/2019/feb/05/civil-servant-no-deal-brexit-operation-yellowhammer, last accessed 26 June 2021.

50 Polly Toynbee, 'A civil war state of mind now threatens our democracy', *Guardian*, 28 August 2019, available at: www.theguardian.com/commentisfree/2019/aug/28/prorogation-parliament-boris-johnson-brexit, last accessed 26 June 2021.

51 See, for example, Nicholas Watt, 'Lord Lawson: Civil servants want to "frustrate Brexit"', BBC News, 22 January 2019, available at: www.bbc.co.uk/news/uk-42782637, last accessed 26 June 2021.

52 See Vernon Bogdanor, *Beyond Brexit: Towards a British Constitution* (London: I. B.Tauris, 2019), pp. 169–255.

53 Stuart Nicolson, 'Reality check: Has the UK's devolution settlement been ripped up?', BBC News, 14 June 2018, available at: www.bbc.co.uk/news/uk-scotland-scotland-politics-44470777, last accessed 26 June 2021.

54 See Jonathan Sumption, *Trials of the State: Law and the Decline of Politics* (London: Profile Books, 2019).

55 For an overview of these models, see Anthony King, *Running Scared: Why America's Politicians Campaign Too Much and Govern Too Little* (New York: Free Press, 1997), pp. 52–56.

56 Theresa May, 'PM's Brexit speech in Stoke-on-Trent', speech delivered on 14 January 2019, available at: www.gov.uk/government/speeches/pms-brexit-speech-in-stoke-on-trent-14-january-2019, last accessed 26 June 2021.

57 See Albert Weale, *The Will of the People: A Modern Myth* (Cambridge: Polity, 2018).

58 Chris Mason, 'Boris Johnson and the future PM question', BBC News, 26 March 2013, available at: www.bbc.co.uk/news/uk-politics-21936681, last accessed 26 June 2021.

59 Matt Chorley, 'Tears, betrayal and Brexecutions: The week that shook the world', *The Times*, 2 July 2016, available at: www.thetimes.co.uk/article/tears-betrayal-and-brexecutions-the-week-that-shook-the-world-l989md56x?shareToken=5c6 72a5587e2eb6ebea5897f7cdf308f, last accessed 26 June 2021.

60 Nicholas Allen, 'Cabinet reconstruction: The calculations and risks behind Johnson's "second-chance" government', LSE: British Politics and Policy, 9 August 2019, available at: blogs.lse.ac.uk/brexit/2019/08/09/cabinet-reconstruction-the-calculations-and-risks-behind-johnsons-second-chance-government/, last accessed 26 June 2021.

61 Tim Shipman, '"Career psychopath" Dominic Cummings weeps as his dream comes true', *Sunday Times*, 2 February 2020, available at: www.thetimes.co.uk/article/career-psychopath-dominic-cummings-weeps-as-his-dream-comes-true-n7256j0b8, last accessed 26 June 2021.

62 George Parker, 'Johnson sparks election warning with "do or die" pledge on Brexit', *Financial Times*, 25 June 2019, available at: www.ft.com/content/403eafe6-972c-11e9-8cfb-30c211dcd229, last accessed 26 June 2021.

63 Daniel Boffey and Rowena Mason, 'Boris Johnson has no intention of renegotiating Brexit deal, EU told', *Guardian*, 5 August 2019, available at: www.theguardian.com/politics/2019/aug/05/no-deal-brexit-is-boris-johnsons-central-scenario-eu-told, last accessed 26 June 2021.

64 Kate Devlin, 'Boris Johnson lays ground for "people versus politicians" general election', *The Times*, 5 August 2019, available at: www.theguardian.com/politics/2019/aug/05/no-deal-brexit-is-boris-johnsons-central-scenario-eu-told, last accessed 26 June 2021.

65 BBC News, 'Boris Johnson "absolutely" rules out pre-Brexit election', 26 July 2019, available at: www.bbc.co.uk/news/uk-politics-49125078, last accessed 26 June 2021.

66 Matthew Purvis, 'Lengths of prorogation since 1900', House of Lords Library, 3 October 2019, available at: lordslibrary.parliament.uk/research-briefings/lln-2019–0111, last accessed 26 June 2021.

67 Kate Devlin, 'I'd rather die in a ditch than ask for Brexit delay, says Boris Johnson', *The Times*, 6 September 2019, available at: www.thetimes.co.uk/article/id-rather-die-in-a-ditch-than-ask-for-brexit-delay-says-boris-johnson-mprnrrdg0, last accessed 26 June 2021.

68 James Blitz and Sebastian Payne, 'Can Johnson defy the law against no-deal Brexit?', *Financial Times*, 7 October 2019, available at: www.ft.com/content/28180c0e-e91c-11e9-a240-3b065ef5fc55, last accessed 26 June 2021.

69 Steven Swinford, Francis Elliott and Kieran Andrews, 'PM flies back to chaos', *The Times*, 25 September 2019, available at: www.thetimes.co.uk/article/pm-flies-back-to-chaos-over-supreme-court-ruling-nps0c5g97, last accessed 26 June 2021.

70 Steerpike, 'Boris Johnson's speech to DUP conference: "We are on the verge of making a historic mistake"', *Spectator*, 24 November 2018, available at: www.spectator.co.uk/article/boris-johnson-s-speech-to-dup-conference-we-are-on-the-verge-of-making-a-historic-mistake-, last accessed 26 June 2021.

71 YouGov, 'YouGov Results', 21 October 2019, available at: http://d25d2506s-fb94s.cloudfront.net/cumulus_uploads/document/epib6jirg7/YouGov%20-%20Brexit%20deals%20Results.pdf, last accessed 26 June 2021.

72 See Johnson's speech marking the start of the election campaign, delivered on 6 December, available at: www.conservatives.com/news/boris-begins-the-general-election-outside-10-downing-street, last accessed 26 June 2021.

2

The Conservative Party: the victory of the Eurosceptics

Thomas Quinn

Britain's Conservative Party is one of the oldest and most successful political parties in the democratic world. The events of the 2017–2019 parliament could have destroyed it. As seen in Chapter 1, a minority government dependent on a shaky deal with Northern Irish unionists was split over how to implement the result of the 2016 referendum on EU membership. Tory Eurosceptics demanding a clean break with the EU were opposed by a powerful array of ministers and backbenchers who had never wanted to leave and were now determined to minimise the damage they feared that Britain's exit from the bloc would inflict. In between these groups stood Theresa May, a prime minister whose authority had drained away with her party's parliamentary majority after the 2017 general election, who presided over the collapse of collective cabinet responsibility and who negotiated a lopsided withdrawal agreement with the EU that pleased no one.

The Conservatives had been deeply divided over the question of the UK's membership of the EU since the days of Margaret Thatcher's premiership. For much of the 2017 parliament, it looked as though the likeliest scenario for the party was the type of deep and enduring split it had experienced during the debate over the Corn Laws in the 1840s and that had kept it out of power for a generation. In the event, a new Conservative prime minister, Boris Johnson, ended up securing the party's best election result for over thirty years. Extraordinarily, he did so by uniting his party on the European question. The main ideological victors were a radical Eurosceptic faction that could count on the support of just twenty-eight out of 650 MPs. This chapter explains how this miraculous outcome was achieved.

The European question in the Conservative Party

For an entire generation, the principal ideological fissure within the Conservative Party has been the issue of Britain's place within the EU. The process of European integration, whereby EU member states have progressively ceded control over law-making powers and political decisions, touches on values at the heart of conservatism. These include the nation's primacy as a political and social institution; the state's independence, sovereignty and authority, including its monopoly of law-making; scepticism about abstract blueprints for radical change, as advocated by the supporters of European federalism; and suspicion of the EU bureaucracy's big-state economic ambitions.[1] What came to be described as the 'Eurosceptic' position was most memorably set out by the then Conservative prime minister, Margaret Thatcher, in her famous speech to the College of Europe at Bruges in 1988:

> willing and active cooperation between independent sovereign states is the best way to build a successful European Community ... Europe will be stronger precisely because it has France as France, Spain as Spain, Britain as Britain, each with its own customs, traditions and identity. It would be folly to try to fit them into some sort of identikit European personality ... We have not successfully rolled back the frontiers of the state in Britain, only to see them reimposed at a European level, with a European superstate exercising a new dominance from Brussels.[2]

These ideas are now commonplace in the British Conservative Party. This makes it unusual among the major centre-right parties of Western Europe, especially when compared with the consensus-seeking Christian Democrats in Germany, Benelux and, historically, Italy. French Gaullists are spiritually closer to the Tories, but European integration has long been accepted by political elites in France as a facilitator of French power, not a constraint on it. Integration could be seen as a path to a superstate. Alternatively, it could be seen as a way of fostering European cooperation and rescuing nation states from the dead-end of nationalism and authoritarianism that had led directly to the Second World War.[3]

In the UK, by contrast, the lesson drawn by some within the political elite, as well as by many voters, was that the sovereign nation state was the guarantor of national survival and independence. The experience of war had not damaged the nation state's credibility in the UK in the way it had on the continent. What is sometimes denounced as British 'exceptionalism' is a consequence of these different experiences.[4] It is no surprise that this way of thinking should be strongly reflected in a major political party that is founded on the principles of the nation, tradition and scepticism towards grand – or grandiose – plans.

The Conservative Party has always been pulled in two different directions on the question of 'Europe'. From the outset, many Tories were prepared to go along with membership because of the economic benefits of integration in a major trading bloc. Relatively few were 'true-believers' in the European project. One such true-believer, however, was Edward Heath, the former

Conservative prime minister, who took Britain into what was then the Common Market, in 1973.[5] The more common profile of a 'pro-European' Tory was that of a pragmatist who accepted that Britain's membership of the EU was, on balance, good for the country economically and politically but did not necessarily support every move towards integration.

At the same time, there were those Conservatives, most notably Enoch Powell, who, from the start, were suspicious of British involvement with the Common Market because of the threat that membership posed to UK sovereignty. While Powell's was a fairly lonely voice in the 1970s, things would soon change. The key figure was Margaret Thatcher. Despite signing the 1986 Single European Act, which ushered in a new era of integration, she came to regret her decision and became a fierce critic of the federalist agenda.[6] Her growing Euroscepticism led to her famous speech at Bruges, ultimately contributed to her downfall in 1990 and laid bare the increasing divisions in her party.

These divisions poisoned the tenure of Thatcher's successor, John Major, who was prime minister between 1990 and 1997. The main point of contention among Conservative MPs in this period was between those generally favourable to further European integration and those strongly opposed, particularly in relation to monetary union. Re-elected with a much reduced parliamentary majority in the 1992 general election, Major's government was rocked, first, by the debacle of 'Black Wednesday' and Britain's forced departure from the Exchange Rate Mechanism, the precursor to a single European currency, on 16 September 1992, and, second, by a series of parliamentary rebellions by Tory MPs opposed to the 1992 Maastricht Treaty. This treaty created the EU in its modern form and extended its reach into new policy fields.[7] Its most controversial element was its provision for monetary union, and although Major had secured an opt-out of that part of the treaty for the UK, the matter was far from settled. A number of Conservative MPs, known as the 'Maastricht rebels', repeatedly voted against their own government's attempts to ratify the treaty. These rebellions and the government's responses – withdrawing the party whip from some rebels and making key votes issues of confidence in the government so that defeat would lead to the government's resignation and a general election – soured relations on the Conservative benches and in government. Major referred to three of his cabinet colleagues as 'bastards'. The infighting over Europe contributed to the Tories' crushing defeat in the 1997 election.

In opposition between 1997 and 2010, the pro-EU faction was sidelined, and the Conservatives adopted increasingly stronger forms of Euroscepticism.[8] Successive leadership contests saw the most popular candidate among voters, Kenneth Clarke, repeatedly rejected because of his pro-European convictions.[9] William Hague, leader between 1997 and 2001, ruled out joining the single currency for two parliaments. His successors ruled out joining it forever. The Conservatives' opposition to Europe was reinforced by the New Labour government's enthusiasm for it. The Tories trenchantly opposed new EU treaties signed by the Blair and Brown governments that extended integration.[10] Tory Eurosceptics even campaigned to have a referendum on the 2009 Lisbon Treaty that revived the aborted European Constitution. David Cameron, elected leader in December 2005, initially argued in favour of referring it to the people. Once he became prime minister in 2010, any notion of a plebiscite was abandoned, not least because the Conservatives' Liberal Democrat coalition partners would not countenance it. The coalition government passed the European Union Act in 2011, requiring further transfers of sovereignty to be subject to a referendum, but Eurosceptics were largely unconvinced. The Cameron government did not attempt to repatriate powers from the EU back to the UK, despite successive Conservative manifestos pledging to do so.[11]

Cameron's unwillingness or inability to push for the repatriation of powers helped to create a new dividing line in the party. 'Soft' Eurosceptics, who included Cameron himself, remained suspicious of further integration but were prepared to continue pursuing Britain's interests in the EU. 'Hard' Eurosceptics drew the lesson that the failure to commit credibly to repatriating powers meant that the only option was for the UK to leave the EU altogether.[12] They fired a warning shot in 2011 when eighty-one backbench Tory MPs supported a motion calling for a referendum on EU membership, despite the government imposing a three-line whip against the motion. It was, at the time, the largest post-war rebellion on Europe.[13] Within two years, Cameron caved in, promising to offer an 'in–out' referendum in the next Conservative manifesto.

Meanwhile, all Conservatives were increasingly mindful of the danger posed by Nigel Farage's UKIP. This party had campaigned for Britain's withdrawal from the EU and threatened the Tories on their Eurosceptic flank. Its rise gave the hard Eurosceptics in the Conservative Party an electoral justification for their position. That justification only grew stronger after UKIP topped the poll in the 2014 European Parliament elections, pushing the Conservatives into third place.

The Tories' unexpected majority in the 2015 election meant that they now had to implement their referendum pledge.[14] Cameron attempted to renegotiate the terms of Britain's membership of the EU before the referendum in 2016, although the concessions he achieved were modest. The party was bitterly divided during the ensuing campaign. A majority of Conservative MPs – 187 out of 330 – publicly backed 'remain', but they were heavily skewed towards the government's 'payroll vote' of ministers. Fully 140 backed 'leave', including a majority of backbenchers.[15]

The Remainers were largely soft Eurosceptics who had been highly critical of the 2009 Lisbon Treaty that extended EU powers. The predominant belief among this group was that Britain could best achieve its goals by being a member of the EU, but that it had to guard against any further erosion of sovereignty. The Leavers were hard Eurosceptics who believed there was no realistic prospect of reforming the EU, only the promise of fighting an endless war of attrition to resist further integration.

The electorate's decision to leave the EU caused lasting convulsions in the Conservative Party. Cameron resigned as prime minister, triggering an eventful leadership contest. Boris Johnson, the former mayor of London and a leading figure in the Leave campaign, was the favourite to replace him, not least because party members – who had the final say – were overwhelmingly Eurosceptic. But Johnson's campaign imploded after Michael Gove, a fellow Leave campaigner and erstwhile ally, declared him unfit for the post. Theresa May, a reluctant Remainer, was the beneficiary, succeeding Cameron as prime minister in July 2016.[16] She staked out her position on Brexit in a speech at Lancaster House in January 2017, pledging to take Britain out of the EU's single market and customs union and paving the way for a 'harder' Brexit based on a new customs arrangement with the bloc.

During this time, May scaled high peaks of popularity as voters compared her favourably with Labour's left-wing leader, Jeremy Corbyn. It led her to seek an early election in the hope of increasing her slim parliamentary majority. As recounted by Nicholas Allen in Chapter 1, the 2017 election ended in a hung parliament, with the Conservatives the largest party but dependent on a confidence-and-supply deal with Northern Ireland's DUP for a majority.

Brexit divisions within the Conservative Party

Following the 2017 election, Conservative MPs remained deeply divided over Brexit. The party had campaigned on a manifesto that pledged to seek a Brexit based on the ideas set out in Theresa May's Lancaster House speech. This represented a relatively 'hard' form of Brexit. But the author of that speech, May's joint chief-of-staff Nick Timothy, had been forced out following the election fiasco. With the government deprived of its majority, the expectation was that it would seek a softer form of Brexit, with the UK remaining more closely aligned to the single market and customs union.

That was precisely what pro-EU Tory MPs desired and their hard-Eurosceptic colleagues feared. In between these two groups, a large mass of MPs, comprising the payroll vote and backbench loyalists, could potentially be swung either way. What made the situation so delicately poised was that either of the pro- and anti-EU factions could torpedo any Brexit deal struck by the government if they were joined by the opposition parties in rejecting it. In the UK's adversarial party system, there was a strong likelihood of that happening.

Theresa May was not an ideological Eurosceptic. But she had insisted during her ascent to the leadership in 2016 that 'Brexit means Brexit', taken as a signal that she saw the referendum as a clear mandate to leave the EU.[17] May seemed to interpret the referendum result as a backlash against large-scale immigration, which had been an important and contentious issue in British politics for over a decade. This interpretation chimed with her own view that immigration levels needed to be reduced, a position that she became closely associated with during her six years as home secretary in Cameron's government, from 2010–2016. While at the Home Office, May had sought to tighten immigration rules for people from outside the EU and was associated with the 'hostile environment' strategy, but she could do nothing about EU immigration because of the single market's principle of freedom of movement. Brexit provided the opportunity to control EU immigration. At the same time, with the disappearance of the pro-Brexit Timothy from her team, she became increasingly persuaded of the importance of retaining close economic ties to the EU post-Brexit.

The parliamentary party that May led after the 2017 election retained a majority of Remainers, but had a large Leave component (Table 2.1). Because it was a snap election, most sitting Conservative MPs were reselected as candidates. Since a majority of them had publicly declared for Remain in the EU referendum – as had the overwhelming majority of opposition MPs – the 2017–2019 parliament was dominated by Remainers. Most Conservative MPs switched to backing the government's Brexit policy, but some Remainers within the government sought softer forms of Brexit, while a handful on the backbenches hoped, ultimately, to stop it altogether. May's chancellor of the exchequer, Philip Hammond, and her home secretary, Amber Rudd, were both ex-Remainers who opposed a no-deal Brexit, and Hammond was accused of obstructing it in government.[18] Other prominent ex-Remainers in the cabinet included David Gauke, the work and pensions secretary, Greg Clark, the business secretary, and David Lidington, the justice secretary. Overall, about three quarters of cabinet ministers and junior ministers under May were ex-Remainers.

Up to thirty pro-EU Conservative MPs on the backbenches were determined to preserve close links between the UK and the EU. The most prominent among them were Dominic Grieve, a former attorney-general, and Sir Oliver Letwin, an ex-minister from the modernising wing of the party. These two led later efforts to rule out a no-deal Brexit, sponsoring legislative bills and amendments in alliance with opposition Remainers. Another leading

Table 2.1 EU referendum positions of Conservative MPs and ministers

	Leave		Remain		Undisclosed	
All MPs (June 2017)	140	44%	172	54%	5	2%
May government (June 2017)						
Cabinet ministers	7	26%	20	74%	-	-
Junior ministers	15	23%	49	74%	2	3%
Johnson government (July 2019)						
Cabinet ministers	14	44%	18	56%	-	-
Junior ministers	40	42%	54	56%	2	2%

Source: Phillip Lynch, 'The Conservative Party', *Parliament and Brexit* (The UK in a Changing Europe: 2020), pp. 11–12, available at: https://ukandeu.ac.uk/wp-content/uploads/2020/03/Parliament-and-Brexit-report.pdf, last accessed 26 June 2021. Cabinet ministers include all ministers entitled to attend cabinet.

Conservative critic was Kenneth Clarke, chancellor under John Major. The former prime minister himself was also a vocal opponent of Brexit from outside Parliament. In the House of Lords, Michael Heseltine – Major's deputy prime minister – added his own criticisms of the government.

Some of the most sustained and public opposition to the government came from three previously little-known backbenchers, Anna Soubry, Heidi Allen and Sarah Wollaston. All three would eventually defect from the Conservative Party to join the new Independent Group in 2019. Allen and Wollaston, in turn, later joined the Liberal Democrats, along with Phillip Lee and Sam Gyimah, who were also elected as Conservatives in 2017.

Confronting the largely ex-Remain party elite was a strong Leave cohort. May's cabinet included the two leading figures from the victorious Vote Leave referendum campaign, Boris Johnson, the foreign secretary, and Michael Gove, the environment secretary. Other prominent former Leavers in the cabinet included David Davis, the Brexit secretary, in charge of negotiations with the EU, as well as Liam Fox, Priti Patel, Chris Grayling and Andrea Leadsom.

The bulk of Eurosceptic opinion among Conservative MPs, however, continued to sit on the backbenches. Some were ex-cabinet ministers, such as Iain Duncan Smith, but most had low public profiles. The most notable pro-Brexit group in the party was the ERG. Despite its name, the ERG was not primarily a research body but an organised faction. Formed in 1993 by some of the Maastricht rebels, the ERG initially opposed the federalist direction of European integration. Later, many ERG members shifted towards supporting Britain leaving the EU altogether. Under the Conservative–Liberal

Democrat coalition government of 2010–2015, parliamentary rebellions by the ERG were instrumental in pushing David Cameron into pledging a referendum on EU membership. The group acquired greater public prominence under Jacob Rees-Mogg, its chairman between 2018 and 2019, amid its determined opposition to May's Brexit policy.

The ERG is sometimes described as a 'party within a party', electing its own chairs, adopting policy positions, briefing MPs, coordinating MPs through WhatsApp groups and running its own whipping operation in the House of Commons.[19] However, it cannot offer patronage to incentivise supporters in the way party leaders do, and it cannot 'punish' its members (or, more accurately, subscribers) if they do not take its advice on policy. Consequently, there are varying levels of cohesion within, and attachment to, the ERG among Tory MPs. In the 2017–2019 parliament, about eighty to ninety MPs were sometimes described as being part of the ERG (no membership or subscription lists are publicly provided).[20] Within that, a hard core consisting of about twenty-five MPs, most without realistic hopes of high office, was surrounded by an outer ring of another thirty ideologically aligned supporters, and beyond that perhaps another thirty occasional supporters. The challenge for the ERG was always to seek to maximise its mobilisation of parliamentary support beyond its hard core.

The degree of broader ideological uniformity among Conservative Eurosceptics should not be overstated. All were keen to see sovereignty and law-making powers repatriated from the EU to the UK, but beyond that there were sharp differences over long-term visions for Britain. Many, like the prominent Tory MEP Daniel Hannan, were free-marketers who wanted to break away from the EU's customs union so that Britain could strike its own trade deals around the world. A minority, such as May's one-time adviser Nick Timothy, saw the need for a more economically interventionist state.[21] Boris Johnson wanted the best of both worlds, advocating both a 'global Britain' and more interventionist policies to 'level up' the UK and reduce regional inequalities. Meanwhile, a sizeable minority were open to large-scale immigration, including Hannan and Johnson, whereas others, such as Priti Patel, wanted to reduce immigration levels. However, all agreed that it should be the UK government that ultimately decided the issue. Many Eurosceptics, such as Rees-Mogg, were socially conservative, but others, like Johnson, were socially liberal.

The ideological heterogeneity among Tory Eurosceptics made them potentially uneasy bedfellows for each other, let alone for the rest of their party or indeed MPs in other parties. Yet if they were to succeed in achieving a form of Brexit that was not, in their view, to be hollowed out by a Remain parliament, they would need to demonstrate a unity of purpose and strategic acumen.

The ERG's struggle against 'Brexit in name only'

Despite the Leave victory in the 2016 referendum, many Eurosceptics, particularly those within the ERG, were anxious about the prospects for Brexit.[22] They feared that a Remain-dominated cabinet and a largely pro-EU civil service would devise a 'Brexit in name only', or 'BRINO', a soft Brexit that tied the UK into key EU institutions such as the single market and the customs union after Britain had nominally left the bloc. Ahead of the 2017 general election, senior figures in the ERG worried that a landslide victory for May would give her the parliamentary strength and political authority to impose BRINO. The eventual hung parliament, which dismayed most Tories, was immediately recognised by the ERG leadership as its big opportunity to secure a hard Brexit.[23] May's minority government would need almost all Conservative and DUP MPs to support any deal she negotiated with the EU.

The ERG developed a parliamentary strategy for achieving a harder Brexit. In the light of the government's pledge to hold a 'meaningful vote' in Parliament on any final Brexit deal, and mindful of the party composition of the House of Commons, ERG leaders made three calculations.

First, they determined that Labour and the other opposition parties, such as the Liberal Democrats and the Scottish and Welsh nationalists, would be unlikely to support any Brexit deal negotiated by the government. The smaller parties were ideologically committed to remaining in the EU, while Labour was internally divided on whether to campaign for a second referendum, and opposing a 'Tory Brexit' was the only policy on which it could unite (Chapter 3). Second, ERG leaders believed that the parliamentary arithmetic was tight enough to ensure that its own inner core of MPs, together with its DUP allies, could outnumber any pro-Brexit Labour rebels prepared to support the government.[24] Third, the ERG judged that the opposition parties could neither force an early election nor replace the government before an election. The Fixed-term Parliaments Act stipulated that an early election could take place only if two thirds of all MPs voted for one. Defeating the government in a confidence vote would require the support of pro-EU Tory rebels, who would effectively be ending their own careers in order to make Jeremy Corbyn prime minister. It seemed inconceivable that any would consider doing that.

These three assumptions led to three conclusions. First, the ERG and the DUP could veto any soft-Brexit deal negotiated by the government because it could rely on the votes of the opposition parties to form a blocking coalition. Second, another referendum was unlikely in the post-2017 parliament. No Conservative government would ever be able to implement it because of the scale and depth of opposition within the party. A non-Conservative government, which might want to implement it, could not be formed before the next election. Finally, a hard Brexit was achievable provided that the government actively pursued it and fully mobilised Conservative and DUP support in the Commons, perhaps buttressed by a handful of pro-Brexit Labour rebels.

The ERG's suspicions about the government's intentions were quickly confirmed (Chapter 1). The Chequers plan of July 2018 envisaged Britain becoming a rule-taker and accepting regulations made in Brussels without any say. It led to the resignations of the foreign secretary, Boris Johnson, and the Brexit secretary, David Davis. One of Davis's junior ministers, Steve Baker, also resigned. Baker was a former – and future – chairman of the ERG, and would play a crucial organising role in the following eighteen months.[25] The final withdrawal agreement signed off by Theresa May and the EU in November 2018 was, in the ERG's view, even worse. It kept the UK tied to areas of EU law and under the European Court of Justice's supervision. Most controversially, the backstop mechanism for avoiding a hard border between Northern Ireland and the Republic of Ireland would leave the province subject to some single-market rules and keep the UK tied to the EU's customs union. If the UK and the EU failed to agree a free-trade deal, the UK could remain indefinitely in the backstop. To the ERG, the withdrawal agreement was the embodiment of BRINO. It might even be followed by a referendum to rejoin the EU after a few years.[26] Several ministers shared this view, including the new Brexit secretary, Dominic Raab, who resigned from the government.

The ERG's immediate response was to launch an assault on May's leadership. It had long ago reached the conclusion that the only way to change the party's Brexit policy was to change its leader. In November 2018, opponents of May had narrowly failed to trigger an internal-party confidence vote in her leadership. Party rules stipulated that for a ballot to be triggered, 15 per cent of Conservative MPs – forty-eight in total – would need to send letters requesting one to the Chairman of the 1922 Committee, the parliamentary group of Tory backbenchers, but the rebels had fallen short. After the prime minister pulled the planned meaningful vote on the withdrawal agreement in December, they tried again and reached the threshold. A secret ballot of Tory MPs was arranged for the following day. Theresa May won the ballot by 200 votes to 117, making her seemingly safe from another challenge for twelve months. That could have given her the confidence to fight a war of attrition to secure support for her deal with the EU, shielded from another ERG assault. But it was also now clear that her opponents had enough support to frustrate her withdrawal agreement if they were joined by the opposition parties.[27]

If Labour and the smaller parties voted against May's deal, as the ERG's leaders assumed they would, the ERG could scupper it altogether by maximising anti-deal votes among Conservative and DUP MPs. Most of the ERG's hard core of about twenty MPs could be trusted. So too could the DUP's ten MPs, who were vehemently opposed to the Northern Irish backstop, as it would potentially undermine the cohesion of the union. Eurosceptic MPs in the ERG's outer rings might also be prepared to vote against the government. However, their numbers would be expected to fall as government whips made the usual array of threats and promises. Primarily, however, the whips argued that Brexit could be lost altogether if the agreement were not passed. But since the prime minister herself had publicly warned that any failure to pass the withdrawal agreement could also lead to the hardest of no-deal Brexits, the credibility of the whip's argument was somewhat undermined.

In the three meaningful votes in January and March 2019, opposition MPs voted almost unanimously against the withdrawal agreement (Table 1.1). The number of Labour MPs supporting the government never exceeded five, while no more than four independents did so. In contrast, 118 Conservative MPs voted against the government in the first vote, resulting in the biggest parliamentary defeat in history. That number was squeezed down to seventy-five Tories in the second vote and thirty-four in the third as the government's whipping operation went into full swing.

Those switching from opposing to supporting the withdrawal agreement between the second and third meaningful votes included Boris Johnson, Dominic Raab and even the ERG chair, Jacob Rees-Mogg. All cited the fear of losing Brexit altogether if the agreement were not passed, with Remainers being emboldened to secure a second referendum to break the deadlock. Some supporters of Brexit indicated that it might be possible to unpick the deal later, as Michael Gove, the environment secretary, had suggested after the Chequers plan.[28] Others were sceptical whether the UK would be prepared to violate an international treaty in this way. Meanwhile, other rebels were persuaded to switch after it was made clear that May would step down as prime minister once parliament had approved the withdrawal agreement.[29]

Ultimately, the government's hopes, regularly briefed to the media, of reducing the ERG to about ten holdouts and relying on pro-Brexit Labour MPs to approve the agreement came to nothing. Some within the core of the ERG, including Baker, came close to voting for the deal before deciding to reject it.[30] In a 'very emotional' speech to other ERG MPs in a packed Westminster committee room before the third meaningful vote, Baker said:

> What is our liberty for if not to govern ourselves? Like all of you I have wrestled with my conscience about what to do. I could tear this place down and

bulldoze it into the river. These fools and knaves and cowards are voting on things they don't even understand. We've been put in this place by people whose addiction to power without responsibility has led them to put the choice of No Brexit or this deal. I may yet resign the whip than be part of this.[31]

Of the thirty-four Conservatives who opposed the deal in the third meaningful vote, six were pro-EU rebels hoping for a second referendum but the other twenty-eight were ERG hard-Brexiters. The latter were nicknamed Spartans by their supporters since – like the defenders of Thermopylae in 480 BC – they seemed to be prepared to sacrifice everything for their cause. In alliance with the DUP, whose MPs voted against the withdrawal agreement in all three votes, they helped to kill off May's deal. Baker acknowledged that his approach was 'a huge gamble'.[32] The ERG had come under considerable pressure, including from some Brexiters, to back May's deal. Not only might a miscalculation have meant they lost Brexit altogether, but some in the ERG feared that they might have the whip withdrawn by May.[33] If they remained, they had to consider how far they were willing to go to prevent a soft Brexit in the event that the government persisted with it. If at some point the government looked to have enough votes to approve the withdrawal agreement or there was a cross-party deal that softened Brexit even further, the only way to halt the process would be for the Tory rebels to signal their willingness to vote against their own government in a no-confidence vote. Doing so would be the nuclear option, although Baker, who prioritised the principle of Brexit above party loyalty, hinted that he could potentially do so.[34]

The Spartans had not killed the deal by themselves. Labour's leader, Jeremy Corbyn, played a crucial role in its defeat.[35] Under a different leader, Labour may well have pivoted towards supporting a second referendum, as a majority of its MPs and an overwhelming majority of its members wanted. But that might have prompted some of those Labour MPs who opposed a second referendum to support May's withdrawal agreement. In those circumstances, May might well have been able to secure its passage. In contrast, Corbyn's policy of opposing the agreement in order to force an election and a renegotiation of the deal under a Labour government served to unite Labour's factions, enabling the ERG to play the decisive role in vetoing the deal.

The government was forced to seek an extension to the Brexit process, and the EU agreed to delay Britain's departure until 31 October. The prime minister subsequently made a final attempt to rescue her withdrawal agreement by seeking a deal with Labour. It failed. When May indicated she was open to holding a second referendum, her support within the Conservative Party, already severely undermined, collapsed entirely. Former Tory supporters flocked to Nigel Farage's new vehicle, the Brexit Party, which campaigned for a no-deal Brexit if necessary. On the day after the disastrous European Parliament elections, described in Chapter 1, May confirmed she would step down as leader in June.

The Conservative leadership election of 2019

Having seemingly stopped Theresa May's Brexit deal, Eurosceptics now had the opportunity to replace the outgoing leader with one who was more to their ideological liking. The leadership contest would focus almost exclusively on Brexit. Mindful of the party's fifth place in the recent European Parliament elections, many in the party feared that if the next leader did not secure Brexit, the Conservatives could splinter and be finished as a major political force.[36] In order to avoid this catastrophe, the party had to unite around an agreed policy and restore the internal discipline required to implement it. May's approach of seeking deals with the opposition had failed. Something else had to be tried.

Boris Johnson quickly emerged as the strong favourite. His resignation from the cabinet over the Chequers plan gave him credibility on Brexit and helped secure him the endorsement of key ERG figures, including Baker and Rees-Mogg, even if others in the group were concerned by his voting for the withdrawal agreement at the third asking.[37] Johnson confirmed that he was now prepared to take the UK out of the EU without a deal by 'Brexit Day' on 31 October if necessary, although his preference was to renegotiate the agreement, something the EU had insisted it would not do.[38] Fellow Leavers Dominic Raab, the ex-Brexit secretary, as well as Johnson's former ally-turned-nemesis Michael Gove, the environment secretary, also joined the contest. The main threats to Johnson from the ex-Remain wing of the party were expected to be the foreign secretary, Jeremy Hunt, and the home secretary, Sajid Javid.

No fewer than thirteen MPs announced their intentions to stand. The 1922 Committee, which oversees Conservative leadership elections, modified the rules in order to winnow out weaker candidates and speed up the contest. Normally, candidates would require nominations from two other Conservative MPs, and those securing them would enter a series of parliamentary ballots designed to whittle them down, one by one. The final two candidates would then go through to a one member, one vote (OMOV) postal ballot of the party's 160,000 individual members. This time, however, each candidate would require eight nominations, which succeeded in reducing the field to just ten candidates. The 1922 Committee also set thresholds of support for the first two rounds of parliamentary ballots. In the first round, each candidate would need to secure at least 5 per cent of the 313 Conservative MPs plus their own vote, meaning seventeen votes in total. In the second round, they would require 10 per cent plus their own vote, meaning thirty-three votes in total. After that, there would be no further thresholds and candidates would be eliminated one at a time, although they could also withdraw of their own volition.

The fact that only two candidates go through to the all-member ballot in Conservative leadership contests can lead to tactical voting during the parliamentary ballots.[39] A candidate who looks certain to top the final parliamentary vote, as Johnson did in 2019, can direct some supporters to vote for other candidates in order to eliminate those deemed to be threats in the membership ballot. For Johnson, the ideal scenario was to face a former Remainer in the final run-off, since the overwhelming majority of party members – approximately 80 per cent – had voted Leave in the referendum. One of the biggest potential threats to Johnson came from Raab, whose resignation from the cabinet over May's withdrawal agreement had also strengthened his credibility on Brexit. In a poll of party members conducted at the start of the contest, 77 per cent of respondents viewed Johnson as likely to make either a very or fairly good leader, with 19 per cent saying he would make a very or fairly poor leader (Table 2.2). Raab was his closest rival. Facing Raab would leave Johnson competing for the majority bloc of

Table 2.2 Conservative Party members' views of candidates' leadership abilities

	Very/fairly good leader	Very/fairly poor leader	Don't know	Net score
Boris Johnson	77	19	4	+58
Dominic Raab	68	21	11	+47
Sajid Javid	61	30	10	+31
Andrea Leadsom	55	34	11	+21
Jeremy Hunt	56	37	8	+19
Esther McVey	45	38	17	+7
Michael Gove	50	45	6	+5
Rory Stewart	31	50	19	−19
Matt Hancock	25	44	32	−19
Mark Harper	14	35	50	−21

Source: YouGov, 'YouGov Survey Results' [poll of 892 Conservative Party members], 18 June 2019, available at https://d25d2506sfb94s.cloudfront.net/cumulus_uploads/document/mxtlaay6zu/YouGov%20-%20Conservative%20members%20poll%20190614.pdf, last accessed 26 June 2021. Responses to: 'Thinking of who becomes party leader after Theresa May steps down, do you think each of the following would or would not make a good party leader?'

Leavers. After the chaos of his previous aborted leadership campaign in 2016, Johnson wanted to leave nothing to chance.

The first round of voting among Tory MPs saw three candidates fail to meet the seventeen-vote threshold (Table 2.3). Johnson finished far ahead of the field, collecting 114 votes, with Hunt second on forty-three and Gove third on thirty-seven. Raab finished fourth on twenty-seven, with Javid, Matt Hancock, the health secretary, and Rory Stewart, the maverick international development secretary, also qualifying for the next round. By the time it took place, five days later, Hancock had withdrawn. Most people predicted his support would go to Hunt and that Stewart would miss the thirty-three-vote cut. Instead, Raab was eliminated, while Stewart surged

Table 2.3 Results of the Conservative leadership election of 2019

	Parliamentary ballots					Members' ballot
	13 June	*18 June*	*19 June*	*20 June*	*20 June*	*22 July*
Boris Johnson	114	126	143	157	160	92,153 (66.4%)
Jeremy Hunt	43	46	54	59	77	46,656 (33.6%)
Michael Gove	37	41	51	61	75	
Dominic Raab	27	*30*				
Sajid Javid	23	33	38	*34*		
Matt Hancock	20	withdrew				
Rory Stewart	19	37	*27*			
Andrea Leadsom	*11*					
Mark Harper	*10*					
Esther McVey	*9*					
Abstained/ spoilt	0	0	0	2	1	
Total	313	313	313	313	313	138,809

Source: Neil Johnston, *Leadership Elections: Conservative Party*, House of Commons Library, Briefing Paper 01366, 8 August 2019, pp. 10–11, available at: https://commonslibrary.parliament.uk/research-briefings/sn01366/, last accessed 26 June 2021. Eliminated candidates denoted in italics.

from nineteen votes to thirty-seven. It was a perplexing result given that the three candidates eliminated in round one were Brexiters, whose votes were expected to transfer to other Leavers. Some suspected that pro-Johnson MPs had backed Stewart in order to engineer Raab's removal.[40]

In the third round, Stewart fell back, losing ten votes and finding himself knocked out with twenty-seven. In the fourth found, Johnson hit the psychologically important tally of 157, which represented an overall majority of Conservative MPs. Hunt and Gove were far behind but almost level-pegging on fifty-nine and sixty-one votes respectively. Javid fell back to thirty-four and was eliminated, choosing to endorse Johnson. In the fifth and final round, held on the same day as the fourth, Hunt pipped Gove to the post for second place by just two votes. Despite Javid's endorsement, Johnson increased his tally by just three. More accusations followed that Johnson's supporters had engaged in tactical voting.[41] Although Hunt enjoyed a relatively good image among party members (Table 2.2), Johnson's team saw Gove as the greater threat. They suspected he would fight a dirty campaign in the membership ballot and inflict damage on Johnson, whereas a run-off against Hunt (who had campaigned for Remain) would be more sedate.

The final choice now shifted to the Conservative Party's 160,000 individual members in the OMOV ballot. Johnson remained the clear favourite. The members' ideological leanings and views of the candidates' characters were decisive. In 2019, party members were preoccupied with Brexit: a YouGov poll found that 68 per cent wanted to hear more about the candidates' Brexit plans than their domestic policies, while only 29 per cent preferred the opposite. Although four fifths of members were Leavers, they were prepared to accept an ex-Remainer as leader provided that he was now committed to Brexit and, crucially, was prepared to leave the EU without a deal. Their preferred candidate was one who had voted Leave in the referendum, supported Brexit now and was willing to leave the EU without a deal. Such a leader would be acceptable to 83 per cent of members. But an ex-Remainer who now supported Brexit and leaving without a deal would also be acceptable to 68 per cent. Any leader who would not be willing to leave without a deal was deemed unacceptable by around two thirds of members, while 83 per cent of members said it was unacceptable to have a leader who now wanted to stay in the EU.[42]

For party members, Brexit was an existential issue. Whether their MPs liked it or not, they had been given the historic mission of delivering Brexit. Fully 62 per cent of members believed the Conservatives would win at least the next election, perhaps multiple ones, if it achieved Brexit with a deal, while 58 per cent thought it could do the same with a no-deal Brexit. In contrast, 56 per cent believed the party would lose the next or multiple elections if there were a second referendum, and a further 31 per cent thought this would mean the Tories never leading another government. If Brexit did not occur and Britain remained in the EU, fully 51 per cent of members thought their party would never lead a government, and a further 41 per cent believed it would lose the next or multiple elections. Most party members were prepared to make significant sacrifices to secure Brexit, including Scotland (63 per cent) or Northern Ireland (59 per cent) leaving the UK, significant economic damage to the country (61 per cent) and their own party being destroyed (54 per cent). Just about the only thing that most members (51 per cent) were not prepared to countenance to achieve Brexit was the Labour leader, Jeremy Corbyn, becoming prime minister. In their minds, Corbyn was an even greater threat to the country than ongoing EU membership.[43]

Given this context, the nature of Johnson's advantage over Hunt was made clear in a second YouGov poll of Conservative members (Figure 2.1). His attraction was not his perceived ability to succeed where Theresa May had failed. Although twice as many respondents thought Johnson could renegotiate the withdrawal agreement with the EU as thought Hunt could, a plurality thought he could not. Similarly, only 36 per cent believed Johnson could get MPs to support any deal in the Commons (23 per cent thought Hunt could). Instead, Johnson's major attraction was his perceived willingness to take Britain out of the EU without a deal. No less than 90 per cent of party members believed he was prepared to do so, whereas 60 per cent judged that Hunt was not. Indeed, given what they viewed as the EU's intransigence in the negotiations, 54 per cent of members thought that no deal was the most likely outcome if Johnson became prime minister, and a further 26 per cent believed Britain would leave with a deal by 31 October. In contrast, 72 per cent of members believed that if Hunt became prime minister, Britain would still be in the EU by the scheduled leaving day. To party members, Johnson was the man who was willing and able to follow through with a no-deal Brexit. Not surprisingly, the poll gave Johnson a 74–26 lead over Hunt among party members.[44]

It was now fairly clear that only Johnson would be acceptable as leader to the majority of members. Too many believed that Hunt would continue with May's policy of futile negotiations and endless delays. A widely used academic approach to the study of leadership elections posits a three-level framework for explaining the outcomes. Since the most basic requirement for a party is internal unity, without which it cannot win elections or govern effectively, the most broadly acceptable candidate tends to win in divided parties.[45] Ideologically, that was Johnson. There were questions over his character – specifically, his honesty and conduct in his private life – but these were largely discounted by party members who wanted Brexit done. Over

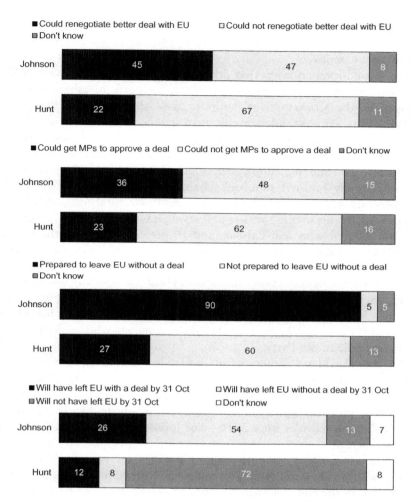

Figure 2.1 Conservative Party members' views of Johnson and Hunt on Brexit
Source: YouGov, 'YouGov/*The Times* survey results' [poll of 1,119 Conservative Party members], 5 July 2019, available at: https://d25d2506sfb94s.cloudfront.net/cumulus_uploads/document/mazvho8f5m/TimesResults_190705_ConMembers_w1.pdf, last accessed 26 June 2021. Responses to: 'Thinking about if [Johnson/Hunt] became the next Prime Minister: 'Do you think he would or would not be able to renegotiate a better deal with the EU?', 'Do you think he would or would not be able to get the House of Commons to approve a Brexit deal?', 'Do you think he would or would not actually be prepared to take Britain out of the EU without a deal?' and 'And taking everything into account, if [Johnson/Hunt] became Prime Minister what do you think would end up happening?'.

three quarters believed that Johnson's private life, including a litany of extra-marital affairs, made no difference to whether or not he would make a good prime minister.

The second-level criterion that drives leadership selection is electability. That had become a more pressing concern for party members since the collapse in the Conservatives' support after the European Parliament elections. On this count, Johnson enjoyed a significant advantage over Hunt. Johnson could reach out to non-Conservative voters: he had twice won the mayoralty of London, despite the city being heavily skewed towards Labour. He was also a formidable campaigner, as he had shown in the EU referendum. But what really boosted Johnson's chances was that most Conservative members now saw the Brexit Party as their major electoral rival, with 67 per cent of respondents in one YouGov poll saying it was a 'big threat' compared with 34 per cent who said Labour (and 10 per cent who said the Liberal Democrats).[46] Johnson was seen as someone who could win back ex-Tory supporters from the Brexit Party, unite Leave voters behind the Conservatives and win the next election. In contrast, Hunt was a steady but uninspiring figure, the archetypal 'safe pair of hands'. Given the suspicion among Tory members that he would not countenance no-deal, whatever his protestations to the contrary, Hunt was not seen as someone who could win back voters from the Brexit Party.

On the third-level criterion of leadership selection, governmental competence and suitability to be prime minister, the two candidates were largely tied. Hunt was the serving foreign secretary, having replaced Johnson in that post. Hunt had spent longer in government – he had had held a number of cabinet-level roles since 2010 – but Johnson had spent eight years as London mayor.

A month-long campaign consisting of hustings, interviews and televised debates was largely uneventful. The result had long been thought a forgone conclusion. In the end, Johnson won 66–34 on a turnout of 87.1 per cent, more than enough for him to claim a mandate to pursue a new Brexit deal or to leave the EU without a deal if necessary. The following day, he became the first British prime minister to come to office mid-term through an all-member ballot.

A Vote Leave government?

If Boris Johnson's victory in the leadership contest was expected, what came next was not. On the day he took office as prime minister, Johnson undertook one of the most extensive cabinet reshuffles in modern political history. Eleven senior ministers were sacked and a further six resigned, as Johnson created an entirely new government committed to delivering Brexit.[47] The cabinet contained significantly more Leavers than previously, although they were still a minority (Table 2.1).

Key Remainers were prominent among those removed, including Jeremy Hunt, Johnson's final opponent in the leadership contest, and Theresa May's deputy, David Lidington. The chancellor of the exchequer, Philip Hammond, the business secretary, Greg Clark, and the justice secretary, David Gauke, all resigned before they could be sacked. Hard Brexiters were promoted, including Raab as foreign secretary and Priti Patel as home secretary. Patel was one of the 28 Spartans who had voted against the withdrawal agreement in the third meaningful vote, as was another returnee to the cabinet, Theresa Villiers. The main survivors were the former home secretary, Javid, who became chancellor, and Steve Barclay, who stayed on as Brexit secretary. The ERG chair, Rees-Mogg, also joined the government, as leader of the House of Commons, although, ominously, Steve Baker declined a junior ministerial position. Baker replaced Rees-Mogg as the ERG's chairman.

Johnson also brought in Dominic Cummings as his chief adviser, a key strategist in the pro-Brexit campaign group during the referendum, Vote Leave. With the ascent of the Brexiters in cabinet, it had the feel of a Vote Leave government.

The reshuffle sent a strong signal that Johnson was determined to take a tougher line with the EU. He repeated his call to reopen the withdrawal agreement and to remove the Northern Irish backstop. It was notable that Johnson limited his criticism of the agreement to this one element, indicating that he was prepared to accept the other compromises it contained if this part were excised. Crucially, there was a chance that MPs would pass the withdrawal agreement if the backstop could be ditched. Back in January 2019, a majority of MPs in the House of Commons had voted for the 'Brady amendment', a backbench initiative to unite the various Tory factions and DUP, which had called for alternative arrangements for the Irish border. It was still the only substantive Brexit policy, other than avoiding no-deal, that had won a parliamentary majority.[48]

The events of the summer months, set out by Nicholas Allen in Chapter 1, also sent a signal that Johnson was determined to take a tougher line with his own MPs. When, after the summer recess, a group of backbench MPs sought to introduce legislation requiring the government to seek an extension to the Brexit process unless a deal could be passed by parliament in advance of 31 October – the so-called Benn Act – ministers warned that any Conservative who supported a motion to debate the bill would have the whip withdrawn. Despite that, twenty pro-EU Tory MPs supported the motion and one more abstained. The rebels included recent cabinet ministers, notably Hammond, Clarke, Stewart and Gauke, who joined regular backbench rebels, such as Grieve and Letwin. The government followed through with its threat and removed the whip from them, which would prevent them from standing as Conservative candidates in any general election. Further attrition of pro-EU Tory numbers was to follow. The prime minister's brother, Jo Johnson, resigned from the cabinet and announced he would not stand at the next election, while Amber Rudd also resigned from the cabinet and surrendered the Conservative whip.

The removal of the whip from the pro-EU rebels confirmed Johnson's ruthlessness in reorienting his party to a harder Brexit. Both it and the earlier reshuffle helped to instil a unity of purpose in the parliamentary Conservative Party, which it had lacked under May. Potential rebels would now have to think hard, for fear of expulsion, about whether they would vote against the government. For those who had been expelled, only a new attitude of loyalty would give them any chance of being readmitted and allowed to stand as Conservative candidates. In the event, ten rebels had the whip returned, of whom only four stood again as Tory candidates. Far from undermining the government, the harsh treatment of the rebels helped to restore discipline to the Conservative Party.

This new-found unity was important. It showed that the Conservatives under Johnson could be mobilised behind one position, on a harder Brexit. As Johnson reopened talks with the EU, it became apparent that there was more scope to renegotiate the withdrawal agreement than most observers had previously believed. After successful talks with the Irish prime minister, Leo Varadkar, over provisions for the Irish border, Johnson struck a new deal with the EU. The backstop was removed, although it was replaced by extra customs checks between Great Britain and Northern Ireland, with the province's devolved assembly able to vote on ending these arrangements after four years.

The ERG initially equivocated.[49] Its main worry was over the provisions for Northern Ireland, which could potentially undermine the union between Great Britain and the province. The DUP's outright rejection of the new deal only emphasised this concern. Yet, Johnson's ascent to the premiership had altered the ERG's calculations. First, he was a Leaver, like them, and he had delivered on his promise to renegotiate the withdrawal agreement. Rejecting it now would condemn it to defeat and severely damage his premiership. From there, it might be the case that Brexit could only get softer. Second, two Spartans, Patel and Villiers, were now in the cabinet, and it seemed unlikely that either would resign over the new deal. Other Spartans might also break away, leaving only a small rejectionist group that could be defeated. Third, Johnson had been ruthless in removing the whip from pro-EU rebels, and he could conceivably do the same with rejectionist Spartans. Ultimately, the ERG came on board. Conservative unity was vital to achieve Brexit, and that meant all sides would need to swallow some compromises. The government's opponents now had a choice to make. Some Labour MPs representing Leave-voting constituencies signalled they could support the new agreement, unenthusiastic about facing their electors before Brexit had been achieved.

The new Brexit deal was offered to parliament as part of legislation to implement the withdrawal agreement. The bill secured a clear majority at its second reading and was backed by all remaining Conservative MPs, as well as nineteen ex-Tory independents and nineteen Labour MPs. However, the government was defeated in its attempts to timetable the legislation's passage through the Commons. Johnson interpreted this defeat as a sincerity test: those who wanted the Brexit deal would agree to a quick timetable but those who wanted to undermine it with wrecking amendments on customs unions or a second referendum did not really support it at all. He chose to pull the legislation and called for a general election to break the deadlock. Johnson would have to wait for the election to give him his own majority to force it through. But he had succeeded in uniting his party around a new Brexit deal, something that had appeared all but impossible a few months earlier.

Conclusion

The Conservative Party had become *the* party of Brexit by the end of the 2017–2019 parliament. While most Tory MPs elected in 2017 had backed Remain in the 2016 referendum, none was speaking out against Brexit by the time of 2019 general election. The party had been effectively purged of its remaining pro-Europeans. The ERG had played a critical role in this outcome. It had exploited the conditions created by a hung parliament and the adversarial nature of Labour's opposition to defeat May's withdrawal agreement. The Conservatives' rout in the European Parliament elections then persuaded a critical mass of Tory MPs to unite behind a harder position or face a haemorrhage of votes to the Brexit Party. For the ERG, Johnson's revised withdrawal agreement was a bittersweet moment. It came closer to the Spartans' preferences than to those of any other faction in the Conservative Party or of any other party in the House of Commons. But it also potentially weakened the union between Great Britain and Northern Ireland. Nevertheless, the outcome was a remarkable achievement for a twenty-eight-strong group in a parliament of 650 MPs.

The victory of the Tory Eurosceptics is one of the more remarkable stories in British politics. It was based on a long march through the institutions of the Conservative Party over a period of decades, facilitated at times by external pressure from UKIP and later the Brexit Party. The approach of the Eurosceptics throughout these years had been to focus on the big picture, seeking to turn the party into a Eurosceptic force in the long-term, even at the price of election defeats in the short-term. Leaders came and went, usually on the basis of the European question. Backbenchers became increasingly rebellious – and opposed to Europe. The Eurosceptics' goal shifted from ruling out membership of the single currency to leaving the EU altogether. Eventually, perseverance and luck paid off in the 2016 referendum. Even then, a momentous parliamentary battle had to be fought to confirm the Eurosceptic victory. It was entirely in keeping with all that had gone before it.

Notes

1 Andrew Heywood, *Political Ideologies*, 6th edn (London: Palgrave Macmillan, 2017), pp. 62–94.

2 Margaret Thatcher, *The Downing Street Years* (London: Harper Press, 1993), pp. 744–745.

3 Alan Milward, *The European Rescue of the Nation-State*, 2nd edn (London: Routledge, 1999).

4 Stephen George, *An Awkward Partner: Britain in the European Community*, 3rd edn (Oxford: Oxford University Press).

5 Hugo Young, *This Blessed Plot: Britain and Europe from Churchill to Blair* (New York: Overlook Press, 1999).

6 Thatcher, *Downing Street Years*.

7 Philip Cowley and Philip Norton, 'Rebels and rebellions: Conservative MPs in the 1992 Parliament', *British Journal of Politics and International Relations*, 1 (1999), 84–105.

8 Philip Lynch, 'The Conservatives and Europe, 1997–2001', in Mark Garnett and Philip Lynch (eds), *The Conservatives in Crisis* (Manchester: Manchester University Press, 2003), pp. 146–163.

9 Thomas Quinn, *Electing and Ejecting Party Leaders in Britain* (Basingstoke: Palgrave Macmillan, 2012).

10 Tim Bale, *The Conservative Party from Thatcher to Cameron* (Cambridge: Polity Press, 2010).

11 Philip Lynch and Richard Whitaker, 'Where there is discord, can they bring harmony? Managing intra-party dissent on European integration in the Conservative Party', *British Journal of Politics and International Relations*, 15 (2013), 317–339.

12 On the ideological composition of Cameron's Conservative Party, see Timothy Heppell, 'Cameron and liberal conservatism: Attitudes within the Parliamentary Conservative Party and Conservative ministers', *British Journal of Politics and International Relations*, 15 (2013), 340–361.

13 The motion was voted for by 79 Tory MPs, with two tellers. Nicholas Watt, 'David Cameron rocked by record rebellion as Europe splits Tories again', *Guardian*, 25 October 2011, available at: www.theguardian.com/politics/2011/oct/24/david-cameron-tory-rebellion-europe, last accessed 26 June 2021.

14 Nicholas Allen, 'Gambling with the electorate: The Conservatives in Government', in Nicholas Allen and John Bartle (eds), *None Past the Post: Britain at the Polls, 2017* (Manchester: Manchester University Press, 2018), pp. 1–33.

15 Three MPs' preferences were undisclosed. See Table 2.1 for details.

16 Thomas Quinn, 'The Conservative Party's leadership election of 2016: Choosing a leader in government', *British Politics*, 14 (2019), 63–85.

17 Quinn, 'The Conservative Party's leadership election of 2016'.

18 Camilla Tominey, 'How Philip Hammond used his time as chancellor to block No Deal preparation at every turn', *Daily Telegraph*, 14 August 2019, available at: www.telegraph.co.uk/politics/2019/08/14/philip-hammond-used-time-chancellor-block-no-deal-preparation/, last accessed 26 June 2021.

19 Colin Murray, 'A mobile phone in one hand and Erskine May in the other: The ERG's parliamentary revolution', The UK in a Changing Europe, 21 February 2019, available at: https://ukandeu.ac.uk/a-mobile-phone-in-one-hand-and-erskine-may-in-the-other-the-ergs-parliamentary-revolution/, last accessed 26 June 2021.

20 Sebastian Payne, Cale Tilford and Martin Stabe, 'The Conservative Party's Brexit tribes: An interactive guide', *Financial Times*, 28 March 2019, available at: https://ig.ft.com/brexit-tory-tribes, last accessed 26 June 2021.

21 Nick Timothy, *Remaking One Nation: The Future of Conservatism* (Cambridge: Polity Press, 2020).

22 For an inside account of the ERG's approach to securing a hard Brexit, see David Scullion, 'Spartans who remade Britain', *The Critic*, February 2020, available at: https://thecritic.co.uk/issues/february-2020/spartans-who-remade-britain/, last accessed 26 June 2021.

23 Scullion, 'Spartans who remade Britain'.

24 The ERG's understanding of the DUP's position was facilitated by the fact that the ERG strategist Christopher Montgomery had previously been the DUP's chief of staff.

25 Patrick Maguire, 'Meet Steve Baker, the Brexiteers' shop steward', *New Statesman*, 18 July 2018, available at: www.newstatesman.com/politics/uk/2018/07/meet-steve-baker-brexiteers-shop-steward, last accessed 26 June 2021.

26 Scullion, 'Spartans who remade Britain'.

27 BBC News, 'Theresa May survives confidence vote of Tory MPs', 12 December 2018, available at: www.bbc.co.uk/news/uk-politics-46547246, last accessed 26 June 2021.

28 Henry Zeffman, 'Support Chequers plan for now, Michael Gove tells Eurosceptics', *The Times*, 17 September 2018, available at: www.thetimes.co.uk/article/support-chequers-plan-for-now-michael-gove-tells-eurosceptics-z5qgj50bz?region=global, last accessed 26 June 2021.

29 Heather Stewart, Rowena Mason and Peter Walker, 'Brexit: May vows to resign before next phase of negotiations if deal is passed', *Guardian*, 28 March 2019,

available at: www.theguardian.com/politics/2019/mar/27/theresa-may-to-resign-before-next-phase-of-brexit, last accessed 26 June 2021.

30 Patrick Maguire, 'Steve Baker: "I'm never tasting surrender again"', *New Statesman*, 3 April 2019, available at: www.newstatesman.com/politics/uk/2019/04/steve-baker-i-m-never-tasting-surrender-again, last accessed 26 June 2021.

31 Cited in David Scullion, 'Steve Baker resigns as ERG chair', *The Critic*, 25 February 2020, available at: https://thecritic.co.uk/exclusive-steve-baker-resigns-as-erg-chair/, last accessed 26 June 2021.

32 Scullion, 'Steve Baker resigns as ERG chair'.

33 Scullion, 'Spartans who remade Britain'.

34 Maguire, 'Steve Baker: "I'm never tasting surrender again"'.

35 Daniel Finkelstein, 'Remainer rebels may pave way to hard Brexit', *The Times*, 19 June 2018, available at: www.thetimes.co.uk/article/remainer-rebels-may-pave-way-to-hard-brexit-f06jglrvj, last accessed 26 June 2021.

36 Robert Peston, 'Will Brexit destroy – or save – the Tory party?', *Spectator*, 7 June 2019, available at: www.spectator.co.uk/article/will-brexit-destroy-or-save-the-tory-party-, last accessed 26 June 2021.

37 Edward Malnick, 'Boris Johnson wins over top Eurosceptics with "clean Brexit" pledge', *Daily Telegraph*, 8 June 2019, available at: www.telegraph.co.uk/politics/2019/06/08/boris-johnson-wins-top-eurosceptics-clean-brexit-pledge/, last accessed 26 June 2021.

38 Boris Johnson, 'Full text: Boris Johnson launches his Tory leadership campaign', *Spectator* blog, 12 June 2019, available at: www.spectator.co.uk/article/full-text-boris-johnson-launches-his-tory-leadership-campaign, last accessed 26 June 2021.

39 Quinn, *Electing and Ejecting Party Leaders in Britain*.

40 Jessica Elgot, Heather Stewart and Rajeev Syal, 'Stewart out as Johnson extends lead', *Guardian*, 20 June 2019, available at: www.theguardian.com/politics/2019/jun/19/tory-leadership-race-stewart-out-as-johnson-extends-lead, last accessed 26 June 2021.

41 John Connolly, 'Did Boris's dirty tricks help Hunt over Gove?', *Spectator* blog, 20 June 2019, available at: www.spectator.co.uk/article/did-boris-s-dirty-tricks-help-hunt-over-gove-, last accessed 26 June 2021.

42 YouGov, 'YouGov Survey Results' (poll of Conservative Party members), 18 June 2019, available at: https://d25d2506sfb94s.cloudfront.net/cumulus_uploads/document/mxtlaay6zu/YouGov%20-%20Conservative%20members%20poll%20190614.pdf, last accessed 26 June 2021.

43 Matthew Smith, 'Most Conservative members would see party destroyed to achieve Brexit', YouGov, 18 June 2019, available at: https://yougov.co.uk/topics/politics/articles-reports/2019/06/18/most-conservative-members-would-see-party-destroye, last accessed 26 June 2021.

44 Chris Curtis, 'Boris Johnson holds his 48 point lead in the Conservative leadership election', YouGov, 6 July 2019, available at: https://yougov.co.uk/topics/politics/articles-reports/2019/07/06/boris-johnson-holds-his-48-point-lead-conservative, last accessed 26 June 2021.

45 Leonard Stark, *Choosing a Leader: Party Leadership Contests in Britain from Macmillan to Blair* (Basingstoke: Macmillan, 1996); Quinn, *Electing and Ejecting Party Leaders in Britain*.

46 Smith, 'Most Conservative members would see party destroyed to achieve Brexit'.

47 Francis Elliott and Olivia Coles, 'Boris Johnson's cabinet carnage', *The Times*, 25 July 2019, available at: www.thetimes.co.uk/article/boris-johnson-s-afternoon-of-cabinet-carnage-v663vjmj9, last accessed 26 June 2021.

48 Tom Quinn, 'Boris Johnson and the Irish Backstop', The UK in a Changing Europe, 29 July 2019, available at: https://ukandeu.ac.uk/boris-johnson-and-the-irish-backstop, last accessed 26 June 2021.

49 Rowena Mason and Rajeev Syal, '"It's painful to choose": ERG locked in internal talks over Brexit deal', *Guardian*, 17 October 2019, available at: www.theguardian.com/politics/2019/oct/17/its-painful-to-choose-erg-locked-in-internal-talks-over-brexit-deal, last accessed 26 June 2021.

3

The Labour Party: leadership lacking

Paul Whiteley, Patrick Seyd and Harold D. Clarke

Any analysis of the politics of the Labour Party up to the 2019 general election has to be situated within the context of the remarkable 2017 general election result. All the opinion-poll data before the 2017 contest had predicted a significant loss of Labour votes and seats, an outcome that would have made it virtually impossible for Jeremy Corbyn to continue as party leader. It was widely anticipated that the voters would thus succeed in securing what the majority of the Parliamentary Labour Party (PLP) had hoped for but had failed to achieve in the previous parliament, namely Corbyn's removal. However, as a consequence of both Theresa May's disastrous performance in the Tory campaign and Labour's remarkable election campaign, Labour achieved a net increase of thirty seats and a 10-point increase in its vote share. After this strong showing Corbyn's leadership of the party was no longer in doubt. What was in fact the party's third consecutive electoral defeat and a failure came to be regarded by both the party leadership and membership as an electoral success. These assessments enhanced Corbyn's standing in the party and influenced the conduct of Labour's internal affairs over the next two years. Yet, even as Corbyn's team now sought to remould the party, it failed to connect with many parts of the electorate. The 2019 election ended up being the disaster that the opinion polls had predicted in 2017. Labour made a net loss of sixty seats, and its tally of 202 seats was its worst result since the 1935 general election.

The outcome of the 2019 general election gives rise to a puzzle: if Jeremy Corbyn was so successful in the 2017 election, why was he such a failure in 2019? The public's attitudes to Corbyn made a big difference to voting behaviour in both elections, so the explanation does not lie in the proposition that his role was significant in one election but not the other. To address this puzzle, we need to carefully look at changes in public attitudes to the Labour leader over time. This involves examining trends in his popularity after he became party leader and also drilling down to identify what the voters thought about him in the 2019 election campaign. Part of the answer to the puzzle lies in some of the decisions that Corbyn made as the 2019 election approached. Strategic errors were made during this period that proved very damaging to Labour on polling day. Corbyn dominated Labour politics in the 2017–2019 period. His decisions played a key role in explaining why success in 2017 was turned into failure in 2019.

Corbyn's leadership in context

Jeremy Corbyn was the ultimate outsider in Labour Party politics. He had been a serial rebel for the whole of his long career as a backbench MP. Some in the party viewed him as Tony Benn's natural successor and the authentic voice of a radical tradition in the party that had been sidelined during the Blair/Brown years.[1] Others – particularly in the PLP – viewed him as either a dangerous radical or simply dangerous. Indeed, one has to go back to the leadership of Michael Foot in the early 1980s to see such a divisive choice of new leader. Corbyn won a surprise victory in the 2015 leadership contest largely because he was able to surf a wave that shifted the party leftwards following defeats in 2010 and 2015. In this regard at least, his victory fitted a pattern. There is a long history of internal left–right ideological conflicts after Labour loses power that invariably result in a swing to the left. This has happened several times in the post-war period and it has usually benefited the Conservatives.

The pattern is illustrated in Figure 3.1, which shows the relationship between the percentage of seats in the House of Commons won by the

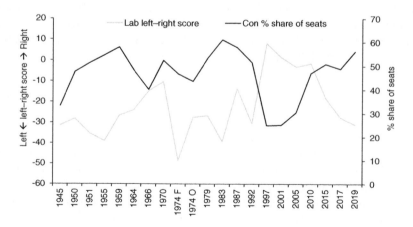

Figure 3.1 Labour's left–right position and Conservative seat share, 1945–2019
Source: Manifesto Project, available at: https://manifesto-project.wzb.eu/, last accessed 26 June 2021.

Conservative Party and the overall left–right policy positions adopted by the Labour Party in post-war general elections, as measured by the Manifesto Research on Political Representation (MARPOR) project team.[2] It has been commonly argued that Labour needs to move towards 'the middle ground' to win elections. The 'median voter theorem' popularised by the economist Anthony Downs shows why this is necessary.[3] The median voter is the person who has as many voters to their left as to their right. If voting is driven by policy and there are just two parties, the support of the median voter is essential to win elections.

Figure 3.1 shows that the party has usually swung to the left after a Labour government was defeated. This occurred after the defeat of the post-war Labour government in 1951, when Aneurin Bevan, the founder of the National Health Service, led a left-wing revolt against the party leadership.[4] It happened again (rather more dramatically) after Harold Wilson's government was defeated by Edward Heath's Conservatives in 1970. It happened yet again after Margaret Thatcher won the 1979 election. Labour's move to the left on that occasion culminated in the 1983 manifesto, which was memorably described by the Labour MP Gerald Kaufman as 'the longest suicide note in history'. The most recent manifestation of this tendency followed the election of Ed Miliband as party leader after the Labour government's defeat in 2010.[5] Labour's move to the left ahead of the 2015 general election paved the way for Jeremy Corbyn's election as Labour leader.

Figure 3.1 also shows that as the party has moved left, the Conservatives have generally benefited in terms of seats won.[6] There was a 3.2-point increase in the Tories' seat share between the 1951 and 1955 elections, a 7.7-point increase between the 1979 and 1983 elections and a 3.8-point increase between the 2010 and 2015 elections.[7] History suggested that the strategy of moving left was likely to help the Tories.

The Corbyn factor

Corbyn appeared to buck the association between leftward moves and increasing Conservative seat share in 2017. On this occasion the party moved left, the Conservative seat share decreased and Theresa May lost her majority. The relative success of the 2017 campaign meant that Corbyn's critics within the PLP were forced to recognise that any move to oust him as leader would fail. It also implied that any attempt to remove him would very likely result in them not being reselected as Labour parliamentary candidates in future elections. Corbyn's support within the PLP remained weak, but he was able to appoint a shadow cabinet, the majority of whom were his supporters. Some of the party's most experienced parliamentarians went to the backbenches or to chair select committees.

Throughout the next two years Corbyn could rely on the extra-parliamentary party for support. The grassroots party had largely been marginalised during the Blair/Brown years, and Corbyn had long campaigned to give them more power and influence. The result was that a majority of the party's individual members – around 500,000 throughout this period – were supportive of his leadership.[8] Corbyn could also rely on a majority on the party's ruling body, the National Executive Committee (NEC).[9] Furthermore, from April 2018 the party headquarters was directed by a Corbyn supporter, Jennie Formby. The previous incumbent, Iain McNicol, was widely supposed to be hostile to the Labour leader. Corbyn and his left-wing allies dominated the party after the 2017 election. Tensions and differences within the left faction over policies and personalities emerged on occasion, but its overriding objective – to defend and maintain the Corbyn project and to ensure that when he eventually retired his successor would be cast in the same political mould – prevailed. A great deal of the party's efforts and resources were expended on this internal project rather than the more fundamental task of regaining the electorate's support and trust.

Intra-party faction fighting was a major contributor to the decline in Labour support after 2017. Nevertheless, it is also important to recognise that for the electorate as a whole Jeremy Corbyn was never a very popular leader, except for a relatively brief period during the 2017 election campaign. Figure 3.2 charts public satisfaction with his role as leader of the opposition from the time he won the leadership in 2015 up to the 2019 election. Corbyn's popularity started to decline as soon as he was elected Labour leader. By the start of the 2017 general-election campaign, just over 60 per cent of respondents in an Ipsos MORI survey said they were dissatisfied with his leadership, while only just over 20 per cent were satisfied. Things improved as a result of the successful 2017 election campaign. By June 2017 50 per cent were dissatisfied and 38 per cent satisfied. Net satisfaction with the Labour leader had widened to a chasm, however, by the 2019 election.

Factional fighting started immediately after Corbyn won the leadership contest in 2015 when many senior figures in the party such as Yvette Cooper, Chuka Umunna and Rachel Reeves refused to serve in his shadow cabinet. Subsequently there were revolts in the parliamentary party over Corbyn's opposition to Britain's involvement in the war in Syria and his attitude to the UK's nuclear deterrent.[10] Labour's official policy was to retain nuclear weapons. Corbyn, however, was a long-standing supporter of the Campaign for Nuclear Disarmament, an organisation committed to unilateral nuclear disarmament. There was much embarrassment when he announced that if

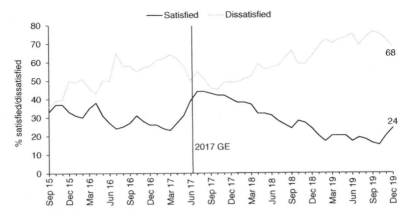

Figure 3.2 Public satisfaction/dissatisfaction with Jeremy Corbyn, 2015–2019
Source: Ipsos MORI, 'Political monitor: Satisfaction ratings 1997–present', available at:
www.ipsos.com/ipsos-mori/en-uk/political-monitor-satisfaction-ratings-1997-present,
last accessed 26 June 2021. Responses to: 'Are you satisfied or dissatisfied with the way
Jeremy Corbyn is doing his job as Leader of the Opposition?'

he were prime minister, he would not use these weapons under any circumstances.[11]

These intra-party divisions were widely publicised, and it quickly became
apparent to the public that a civil war was going on within the party. This
turmoil culminated in a leadership challenge in 2016, following an overwhelming vote of no confidence in his leadership by the PLP (172 votes to
40).[12] The Welsh MP Owen Smith took on the task of challenging Corbyn
for the leadership under the rules set out in the party's constitution. Corbyn
easily fought off the challenge, defeating Owen by 62 to 38 per cent in the
ballot of Labour members.

Corbyn won this challenge to his leadership because he retained the support of the grassroots party membership, which by this point had doubled
in size to more than half a million members. He could take personal credit
for bringing in large numbers of new members, and in return most supported him. One little noticed indicator of this grassroots support came
from the party activists who sit on the general management committees in
constituency parties. They clearly disapproved of the 2016 challenge to his
leadership. A total of 399 constituency parties refused to nominate any candidates in the leadership contest.[13] As far as they were concerned, Labour
MPs should not have precipitated a leadership contest only a year after the
previous one, and they boycotted the whole exercise.

This infighting had a significant impact on Labour's support in the
country. In September 2015, when Corbyn was first elected leader, support

for the party stood at 32 per cent in the polls.[14] By March 2017, just before Theresa May called for an early general election, a mere 26 per cent expressed an intention to vote Labour. It is a well-known fact of life in electoral politics that voters are reluctant to support a party that is seriously internally divided. Labour's infighting also reinforced existing concerns about Corbyn and his policies among voters.

These observations naturally raise the question: why did Corbyn do so well in the election campaign in 2017? One reason is that it was seen as an opportunistic election. Theresa May had repeatedly promised that she would not call an early election after replacing David Cameron as prime minister in 2016. The massive Conservative lead over Labour in the polls proved too tempting for her to resist. Reneging on this promise for opportunistic reasons, however, was a mistake. A second reason why Labour did so well was that the unusually long campaign gave Corbyn a chance to shine at the one thing he was really good at: face-to-face campaigning in mass rallies. For many people who did not normally pay much attention to politics, particularly the young, he was a fresh face with a new radical message.

Corbyn's message and the subsequent Labour manifesto addressed many of the concerns of younger voters, particularly the promise to scrap university tuition fees. Some viewed voting Labour as an opportunity for Britain to remain in the EU. A year earlier, young voters had overwhelmingly supported Remain in the EU referendum, and this defeat mobilised them to get involved in the 2017 election.[15] Labour's official stance was to accept the outcome of the EU referendum but insist on protections for labour, the environment and consumers. This was sufficiently 'pro-European' to provide an opportunity for Remainers to rerun that campaign and, as far as they were concerned, to try to change the outcome. Corbyn also spoke to young persons' concerns about growing insecurity in the labour market, particularly zero-hours contracts that disproportionately affected them.[16]

As a consequence, Corbyn mobilised large numbers of young people to turn out and vote Labour in a series of barnstorming election rallies. His central message focused on providing a radical alternative to the Conservative's record on austerity, something that had been muted in Labour's 2015 campaign, led by Ed Miliband.[17] Indeed, the age division in British politics, which is now very wide, goes a long way to explaining Corbyn's success in 2017. The young viewed Labour's swing to the left differently from the old. As we shall see, however, Corbyn and Labour's appeal had faded by the time of the 2019 election.

Although the Conservatives started off the 2017 campaign well ahead of Labour, there were clear signs that the electorate had their doubts about Theresa May. In the Essex–University of Texas at Dallas (UTD) pre-election survey in 2017 some 54 per cent of respondents thought that the government was not honest and trustworthy, compared with only 30 per cent who thought that it was.[18] Furthermore, 34 per cent approved of the government's overall record and 48 per cent disapproved. Corbyn ploughed potentially fertile ground with his attacks on the prime minister and her party.

The Conservative press relentlessly attacked Corbyn and Labour during the campaign, but this had little effect on young voters. They do not read what is often described as the 'legacy' media, but get their political information largely from the internet, as our later 2019 survey showed.[19] Labour's online campaign in 2017 was particularly effective and left the Conservative campaign standing in this respect.[20] Theresa May's robotic repetition of the slogan 'strong and stable' was rapidly undermined by a U-turn on the manifesto policy for social care of the elderly within a few days of its publication. This was labelled a 'dementia tax'. It was hugely damaging for the Conservative party, particularly among the key constituency of the retired and elderly.

The authors of the Nuffield election study summarised May's 2017 campaign succinctly: 'She had called the election. She had been the focus of the party's campaign, in which role she had been found wanting.'[21] As Figure 3.2 shows, this culminated in a rapid rise in Jeremy Corbyn's public standing and also in Labour voting intentions in the polls. He succeeded in overcoming his earlier unpopularity at exactly the right time. However, his approval ratings rapidly faded after the 2017 election.

The role of Brexit

The dominance of the Brexit issue in the 2019 election campaign was probably greater than in 2017. In our Essex–UTD 2019 election survey, 64 per cent of respondents thought that Brexit was the most important issue facing the country, twice as many as the second most salient issue, the NHS, chosen by 31 per cent. In one respect the importance of the issue accentuates the puzzle about Labour's poor performance in 2019, because there was evidence of 'Bregret' among the electorate. Many voters were starting to think that Britain had made the wrong decision when it voted to leave the EU in the 2016 referendum.

A YouGov poll conducted in June 2017 indicated that 45 per cent of respondents thought that Britain was wrong to leave the EU, and 45 per cent thought it was the right thing to do. By November 2019, just before the next election, 49 per cent of respondents thought that Britain was wrong to leave the EU, compared with 40 per cent who thought it was the right thing to do.[22] This evidence of increasing 'Bregret' naturally raises the question as to why Labour was unable to capitalise on this feeling in 2019. Arguably, the party should have won more Remain supporters as well as these 'Bregreters'.

However, things were different in the 2019 general election compared with 2017. In 2017 many Remain supporters saw their chance to change the referendum result by supporting Labour. By the time of the 2019 election widespread fatigue with the Brexit issue had set in. Many people just wanted it to be over and done with. Labour seemed to propose prolonging the issue. Corbyn changed the party's stance by promising to renegotiate a 'sensible' withdrawal agreement and hold a second referendum with the option to 'remain'. He then declared that he would sit on the fence in that referendum. Corbyn's position was characterised as 'constructive ambiguity', a willingness to implement whatever the public decided, without providing any clear leadership himself. It failed to offer the necessary clarity, direction or coherence required on this fundamental issue. Corbyn claimed that this approach was the same as that taken by Harold Wilson in the 1975 referendum on Common Market membership, but this comparison was misleading. Wilson had remained distant in the early stages of the referendum campaign, leaving it to senior party figures, such as Jim Callaghan and Roy Jenkins, to make the case for remaining within the Common Market. But Wilson joined in during the later stages of the campaign to support British membership.[23] He certainly did not announce that he would sit on the fence over the issue.[24]

Although the party's 2017 election manifesto had affirmed Labour's acceptance of the referendum result, the party promised that it would negotiate to retain the benefits of the single market and the customs union.[25] In all subsequent parliamentary debates and votes the party's official policy accepted the referendum result but demanded guarantees to go with it, particularly in relation to jobs and the environment. However, Labour found it impossible to maintain any semblance of unity on this issue. This, together with Corbyn's traditional scepticism about EU membership, produced the fence-sitting strategy offered to the electorate in 2019.

The fence-sitting strategy undoubtedly represented an attempt to reconcile competing views within the party. On the one hand, pro-EU MPs were critical of Corbyn's half-hearted endorsement of the Remain vote in the 2016 EU referendum. Many of them blamed Corbyn personally for the referendum outcome. They wanted that outcome reversed and demanded that Labour commit to a second referendum. On the other hand, there was a smaller group within the PLP that was consistently sceptical or even hostile to the EU. This group was reinforced by MPs from Leave-voting constituencies who had been Remain campaigners in the referendum but had subsequently changed their minds. The 2017 general election convinced them that their best chance of re-election was to back the decision to exit the EU. During the passage of the European Union Withdrawal Act a total of

128 Labour MPs rebelled on at least one occasion from the official party position of abstention, and in March 2019 a total of 198 voted in favour of a second referendum.

The shadow cabinet member in charge of the party's EU stance was Sir Keir Starmer, the former director of public prosecutions, who had entered the House of Commons at the 2015 general election. Starmer did not support Corbyn in either of the party leadership elections in 2015 or 2016. He was an ardent pro-European who slowly steered the party to a policy of renegotiating the withdrawal agreement and holding a referendum with an option to remain.

What the Brexit debate revealed, other than Corbyn's failure to give the party a clear sense of direction, is a significant cultural divide in the party. The party membership is socially skewed. A majority of members are middle-class professionals. This is something that has been true for a long time.[26] The membership surge, however, accentuated this divide by bringing in a younger, cosmopolitan, pro-European, well-educated, media-literate group of predominantly middle-class idealists.[27] The party no longer had trade-union figures in its leadership echelons of the stature of the former deputy prime minister John Prescott or the former home secretary Alan Johnson, who could appeal to Labour's historic working-class constituency. Yet a significant proportion of the party's parliamentary seats contained large numbers of working-class voters who had voted Leave in the 2016 referendum. Some of the Labour MPs who most consistently rebelled to support the government's withdrawal agreement, such as Caroline Flint (Don Valley), Dennis Skinner (Bolsover) and John Mann (Bassetlaw), represented constituencies with rock-solid Labour majorities and a history of permanent Labour representation. These were some of the constituencies identified after the 2019 general election as being in Labour's 'red wall'. In 2019 much of that wall collapsed.

Party policies in the run-up to 2019

The overall context within which any discussion of policy in this two-year period should be located is the desire of almost everyone in the party to move on from the politics and policies associated with New Labour. Only a small minority were comprehensively critical of Labour government policies between 1997 and 2010. The great majority recognised positive achievements, such as the Sure Start programme, the minimum wage and the reduction in relative poverty.[28] But many also believed that New Labour had done very little to advance the socialist case for public enterprise, public expenditure and progressive taxation. The party's timid response to the coalition government's austerity programme in the 2015 general election added to the desire for something new at all levels of the party. As a result, a general policy consensus prevailed throughout the party during Corbyn's time as leader.

The 2017 election manifesto had set out a distinctive set of post-New Labour commitments that commanded wide support within the party. The 2019 manifesto, *It's Time for a Real Change*, hardly differed from its predecessor. There was a greater emphasis on the party's proposed green industrial revolution, which involved commitments to renewable-energy investment in rail and electric cars, to energy-efficient housing and to creating a million environmentally friendly jobs in the UK. There was also a promise to provide free fibre-optic broadband to every home by 2030, but in other respects the commitments were very similar to those in the 2017 manifesto.

The commitments carried forward to 2019 included the nationalisation of the railways, the Royal Mail and water and energy companies, an end to privatisation in the NHS, free personal care for all older people, a living wage of £10 per hour, free university tuition and free lifelong learning. To help pay for these Labour proposed to raise income tax for those earning above £80,000 per year. The promises and commitments were extensive, but it was less a coherent programme for the next five years in government and more a wish list of left-wing causes. As such, it was very popular among the party membership. Yet while many voters supported specific policy commitments, they were not convinced that it represented a realistic programme for government.[29]

In the two years separating the 2017 and 2019 elections, very few policy disagreements emerged, apart from the party's stance on the EU. One topic that did prompt debate and division, however, was the Brexit-related issue of immigration and the free movement of people into Britain. There was a continuing tension between those who believed in free movement with only a very limited system of immigration controls, and those who believed that stricter immigration controls were necessary. This latter group were particularly concerned that the issue played a very important part in explaining why a majority had voted Leave in the EU referendum.[30]

The intra-party debates on immigration again very much reflected the geographical and cultural differences in the membership that we have already referred to. Younger, cosmopolitan, highly educated party members were more in favour of a relaxed attitude to immigration, while members in the industrial-based constituency parties leaned towards the restrictive immigration views of their working-class voters. The 2019 manifesto contained warm words on the subject, such as: 'A Labour government will establish a humane immigration system' and 'we recognize the social and economic benefits that free movement has brought both in terms of EU citizens here and UK citizens abroad'.[31] But in practice the manifesto did not come down firmly on one side of the argument or the other.

Anti-Semitism

The accusation that anti-Semitism was rife in Labour caused significant problems for the party during this period. It prompted the resignation of three high-profile Labour MPs of Jewish origin: Luciana Berger, Louise Ellman and Ian Austin.[32] Allegations of anti-Semitism were cited by some of those MPs, including Berger, who left Labour in February 2019 to form the short-lived Independent Group (also known as Change UK) in an attempt to challenge the electoral hegemony of the Labour and Conservative parties. There were also very public criticisms of the leadership's response to the problem from a number of prominent individuals, such as Dame Margaret Hodge, a Labour MP, and the Chief Rabbi, Ephraim Mirvis. These criticisms were used by opponents as proof of Labour's dysfunction and inability to govern the country.

Labour's commitment to a two-state solution in the Middle East, support for the Palestinians in their plight and criticism of the state of Israel's policies was clear. However, for a small number of party members their criticisms of the state of Israel extended to Jewish people in general and involved advocacy of Jewish conspiracy theories, Holocaust denial and a linking of Jewish power and influence with the worst features of capitalism. There is no doubt that there was anti-Semitism among some of the party's membership. It was exacerbated from 2015 onwards by the considerable growth in the numbers of party members, and further stimulated by the explosion of internet platforms pushing conspiracy theories.

Corbyn's critics accused him of weak leadership on this issue, particularly his failure to speak out and condemn anti-Semitism and his failure to expel anti-Semites from the party. However, his record does not justify the first of these criticisms. In April 2016, a fortnight before he asked Shami Chakrabarti, a prominent human-rights lawyer, to conduct an inquiry into anti-Semitism in the party, Corbyn had stated that 'Antisemitism is absolutely abhorrent and wrong. Anyone that commits any act of antisemitism, that makes antisemitic remarks, is also excluded from the party.'[33] At its annual conference in October 2017 the party adopted a new rule making it explicit that anti-Semitism, Islamophobia and other forms of racism and prejudice were unacceptable in the party. Speaking in support of this new rule, Corbyn stated that 'Anyone using such antisemitic language, anyone using any form of racist language, is completely at odds with the beliefs of this party.'[34]

With regard to the second criticism – that Corbyn dragged his feet on the expulsion of anti-Semites from the party – the evidence is mixed. It is clear that both the party machinery and the party staff at national and regional level were ill equipped and ill trained to deal with the problem and, as party leader, Corbyn should have taken a more direct and interventionist role in remedying this problem. However, the legal and administrative details in dealing with expulsion from the party were complex and difficult. This was a consequence of the changes that were made following legal challenges to the expulsion of members of Militant from the party in the 1990s.[35] The party had established an independent National Constitutional Committee to adjudicate and expel those deemed to be ineligible for party membership. This committee and the party's disciplinary institutions and procedures in general were overwhelmed and inadequate for the task. As a result, the majority of complaints of anti-Semitism in this period were not adequately addressed.[36]

There are numerous reasons for these failures, including insufficient personnel and a lack of training. However, another factor is that the party headquarters at this time was dysfunctional, with pro- and anti-Corbyn factions fighting each other. A report prepared by Jennie Formby claimed that certain senior officers in Labour's headquarters and in some of the regions used this issue to undermine Corbyn's leadership.[37] Whatever the truth, the party undoubtedly paid a price in terms of credibility for its hyper-factionalism.

Factionalism in the party

Factionalism has been a permanent feature of Labour politics over the years, with various lobbying organisations existing on both the left and the right of the party. At times the intensity of the factional divisions has harmed the party electorally – for example, in the 1950s and 1980s. It did so again between 2017 and 2019, when Labour once again acquired a public image of a bitterly divided party that was unfit to govern. The two most prominent factions in this period were Momentum on the left and Labour First on the right.

Momentum was first established as a group to campaign for Corbyn in the 2015 leadership election and then to support him after he became party leader. In effect, Momentum was a party within the party, with its own officers, paid organisers, funds and membership, and fully organised local branches.[38] Labour First was less well organised, but attempted to counter the influence of Momentum in NEC elections and the selection of parliamentary candidates. Momentum and other left groups, in particular the Campaign for Labour Party Democracy, agreed a slate of people to run as candidates in the annual elections to the NEC. These arrangements were both very well organised and successful.

At the time of Momentum's formation its declared commitment had been to community activism and campaigning, but it increasingly became more concerned with Labour's internal politics and the defence of Corbyn.[39] One of its main objectives was to rid the PLP of Corbyn critics by reintroducing a demand closely associated with the left in the 1980s: the mandatory reselection of all Labour MPs before a general election. This would have required existing MPs to face competition for nomination. However, the apparently inexorable forward march of the left was halted on this issue at Labour's 2018 annual conference by some affiliated trade unions. They preferred a compromise solution in which reselection procedures would only be triggered if a specific number of local party and trade-union branches demanded it.[40]

In previous studies of Labour politics, it would have been impossible to explain the development of the party's policies and practices without a detailed examination of the role of the trade unions. But the compromise agreed at the 2018 party conference on the procedure for the reselection of Labour MPs is one of the very few instances of the unions playing a significant part in the party's deliberations in recent years. This reflects their declining memberships, reduced influence in the economy and diminished role in funding the party as a consequence of the rapid growth in individual membership. They have been relatively marginalised in local party deliberations as well because of the cultural transformation in the party's individual membership. The only exception to this generalisation is the role played by Len McCluskey, the general secretary of the Unite union, who supported Corbyn very publicly throughout this period. His union was both a major financial donor and a provider of key personnel in the leader's office and, eventually, in the party headquarters.

During this period the leadership made great play of the fact that Labour had the largest individual membership of any party in Europe. The increased numbers came with significant benefits, particularly financial resources. Previous budgetary deficits and short-term loans were replaced by surpluses.[41] However, very little thought was given to the role of these members within the wider party, apart from sustaining Corbyn and providing foot soldiers in campaigns. For all the talk of 'a people powered movement' and 'a transformational movement', very little change to traditional practices within the party actually occurred.[42]

Jeremy Corbyn's election as Labour leader in 2015 was a very clear reaction to the politics of New Labour. But the qualities required of political leadership extend far beyond the immediate repudiation of predecessors. Archie Brown, in his book on political leadership, itemises some of the essentials required of political leaders. These include 'integrity, intelligence, articulateness, collegiality, shrewd judgement, a questioning mind, willingness to seek disparate views, ability to absorb information, flexibility, good memory, courage, vision, empathy and boundless energy'.[43] Although no party leader displays all of these qualities, Corbyn lacked many of them. He also lacked the willingness to recruit individuals into the leadership of the party who would provide them. As a result, his party was far from being a government in waiting. The fundamental problem was that between 2017 and 2019 Corbyn inspired a large part of his party's membership but only a small segment of the electorate. When the electorate is many times larger than the party membership, this is not a winning strategy. In the next section we examine how the wider electorate reacted to Corbyn's leadership and discuss how these reactions help to explain Labour's electoral defeat in 2019.

Corbyn and the 2019 general election

We have already made the point that Corbyn was a relatively unpopular leader among the wider public from the start of his tenure. Figure 3.3 goes into more detail by showing what the public thought of the Labour leader

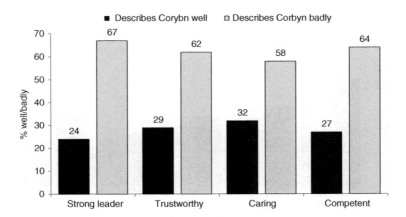

Figure 3.3 Corbyn's image
Source: 2019 Essex–UTD General Election Survey. Responses to: 'How well do these words describe Jeremy Corbyn?'

just before the 2019 election. It identifies some of the more important attributes of leadership and so provides more detailed information about his public image than Figure 3.2. The data in Figure 3.3 come from an Essex–UTD survey that asked respondents to indicate how well (or badly) they thought various desirable leadership traits described the Labour leader.

The results reveal that by the time of 2019 general election campaign Corbyn was seen as weak, untrustworthy, uncaring and incompetent by most voters. Fully two thirds thought he was weak, and almost as many judged him to be incompetent and untrustworthy. A solid majority also believed that he was unresponsive. Despite the opportunities to oppose the government provided by Theresa May's lack of a parliamentary majority and multiple defeats in the House of Commons, Corbyn had clearly failed the test of effective leadership in the eyes of many voters.

Responses to these survey questions about leadership attributes closely correlate with a summary measure of attitudes to leaders obtained by asking respondents to use an 11-point scale to indicate how much they like or dislike a leader. On this scale a zero score means 'strongly dislike' and ten means 'strongly like'. Figure 3.4 shows the average likeability scores for the Labour leader among different age cohorts during the 2017 and 2019 general-election campaigns. It identifies the extent to which Corbyn's image changed between the two elections.

It is evident that the relationship between age and Corbyn's likeability scores was strong in both instances. In 2017 the youngest age cohort gave him an average score of 6.2, roughly twice as big as the score of 3.2 given

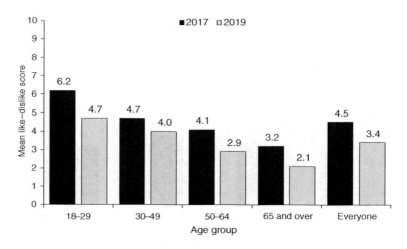

Figure 3.4 Likeability scores for Corbyn by age group in 2017 and 2019
Source: 2017 and 2019 Essex–UTD General Election Surveys.

by the oldest cohort. These age rankings did not change very much in 2019, with the youngest liking him most and the oldest liking him least. What did change between the two elections, however, were the overall scores that the Labour leader received from the different cohorts. It is striking that his 2019 scores were much lower than in 2017 in every age group. Moreover, the largest reduction in likeability occurred among the youngest group (18–29-year-olds), with their average likeability scores for him falling from 6.2 to 4.7.

Clearly, by 2019 disillusionment with the Labour leader had set in, particularly among the young. Most of the factors that helped to improve his image in 2017 had disappeared by 2019. There was widespread exhaustion with the Brexit issue, making the Conservatives' 'get Brexit done' slogan in 2019 considerably more effective than their 'strong and stable' mantra had been in 2017. Above all, Corbyn was no longer a fresh face saying something that young voters had not heard from previous Labour leaders.

Figure 3.5 identifies Corbyn's average likeability scores among various groups. It is clear that low-income voters liked him more than well-heeled

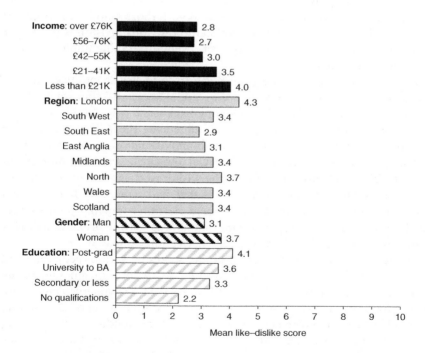

Figure 3.5 Corbyn's likeability by income, region, gender and education
Source: 2019 Essex–UTD General Election Survey.

voters. In addition, he was relatively well liked in London, but much less so in the South East of England. It is also noteworthy that his popularity in London (a mean score of 4.3) was significantly higher than it was in the North of England (3.7) and in the Midlands (3.4), where many of the seats in the 'red wall' of Labour strongholds could be found.

The most interesting finding in Figure 3.5 is the difference between the education and income scores for the Labour leader. Highly qualified people liked him much more than the less well educated. In contrast, people in higher-income groups liked him less than those with lower incomes. These results suggest that the traditional class-based politics which has been the backbone of Labour support over the years has bifurcated into separate economic and cultural dimensions, a point made earlier in relation to party members. Voters who are rich in financial capital were much less supportive of Corbyn and Labour more generally than were voters with fewer financial assets. This is the traditional division in two-party politics in Britain, with the well-off supporting the Conservatives and the less well-off backing Labour.

The new division is between those who are rich in human and cultural capital and those who are not. Both are closely linked to education and give rise to distinctive political values.[44] Individuals with these values were more supportive of the Labour leader, compared with those who lack substantial human and cultural capital. One explanation for this division is the Brexit issue, but as we will see below this exists even after taking public attitudes to Brexit into account.

By 2019 Corbyn was no longer a new face in British politics, and the divisions in Labour continued, with the scandal over anti-Semitism bubbling to the surface and more rebellions among backbench MPs. In the event, one such rebellion played a crucial role in influencing the 2019 election. This took place in October, when nineteen Labour MPs ignored a three-line whip and supported Boris Johnson's withdrawal agreement, enabling him to win the vote. They did this even though the withdrawal agreement was almost the same as Theresa May's earlier deal that had repeatedly failed to win parliamentary approval. In the subsequent election campaign Johnson was quick to claim that this victory meant that he was 'getting Brexit done'. This argument was crucial to the Conservative election campaign.

Figure 3.6 examines Corbyn's likeability scores by various economic and political attitudes held by the public during the 2019 campaign. One of the most striking differences is between Leavers and Remainers. There were sharp divisions on this issue, with Corbyn scoring a mere 2.2 among respondents who had voted Leave in the 2016 EU referendum and 4.8 among those who had voted Remain. This huge difference in attitudes towards Corbyn among the two groups was particularly evident among younger voters.[45]

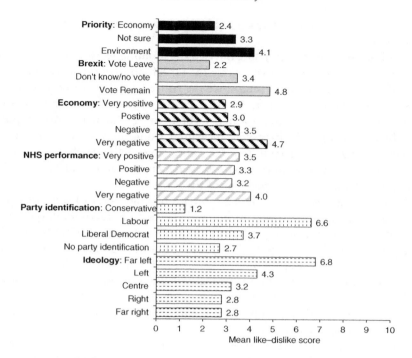

Figure 3.6 Corbyn's likeability by economic and political attitudes
Source: 2019 Essex–UTD General Election Survey.

These differences would have appeared in Labour's private polling during the election campaign. It would have been clear that he was doing badly among Brexiters but that there was an opportunity to do better among Remainers, However, the Labour leader failed to exploit the full potential of the Remain and 'Bregret' support by sitting on the fence on the issue. This was all the more surprising because the May 2019 European Parliament elections, where the fence-sitting strategy first appeared, was a disaster for the party. Labour took only 13.6 per cent of the vote and came third in that election. There might have been a case for ambiguity about the Brexit issue before the European elections, but that result put paid to it.

It is likely that had Labour come out as a Remain party, by asking voters to reconsider EU membership in a second referendum, something that party members, most Labour MPs and a clear majority of the party's supporters wanted, it could have won more of this vote. The result was that instead of rallying strongly to Labour, Remain voters were divided among Labour, the Liberal Democrats, the Greens and the Scottish and Welsh nationalists. The effect of this splintering was compounded by the fact that support for Nigel

Farage's Brexit Party collapsed and the Leave vote rallied round the Conservatives.

In addition to the Brexit issue, the two outstanding features of Figure 3.6 are strong support for Corbyn among the far left and Labour partisans. The role of ideology is not surprising since the entire Corbyn project was aimed at shifting Labour to the left. As an electoral strategy, however, it was of limited value since there are not many voters on the far left in British politics. In our survey, ideology was measured using another 11-point scale varying from zero (far left) to ten (far right). If we define far left generously as the number of respondents who scored between zero and two on the scale, they made up only 9 per cent of the total.

Labour partisanship was a much more promising source of support when it came to electoral strategy. Corbyn had successfully recruited large numbers of grassroots members; although many of them were not on the far left, he could nonetheless rely on their support.[46] But only 24 per cent of respondents in our survey were Labour identifiers, down from 26.5 per cent in 2017. In addition, the number of 2019 Labour identifiers compared unfavourably with the 30 per cent who identified with the Conservatives. When it came to rallying support from partisans among voters, the Conservatives had a big advantage.

There is important evidence of valence voting in Figure 3.6. Voters preferred Corbyn and Labour if they were dissatisfied with the performance of the government in delivering on the economy and the National Health Service. Valence issues are those on which there is little division of opinion among the voters about objectives – the great majority of people want a prosperous economy and efficient and effective health care. Disagreement occurs about which party and party leader are most likely to deliver the desired outcomes. Typically, these issues exert a strong influence on electoral choice in Britain.[47]

In 2019 Corbyn's average likeability score was 4.7 among those who were very negative about the performance of the economy, compared with only 2.9 among those who were very positive. Corbyn was more warmly received among people who judged NHS performance negatively than those who evaluated it positively. However, these differences were quite small – this despite Labour's repeated promises that they would improve the health service. Finally, Corbyn did better than average among voters who attached a high priority to the environment, and, in that respect, he probably took votes away from the Greens.

A multivariate statistical model enables us to gauge the relative importance of the various factors that explain differences in Corbyn's likeability.[48] The results of this analysis appear in Figure 3.7, which displays the statistically significant effects. It shows that the most powerful predictor was

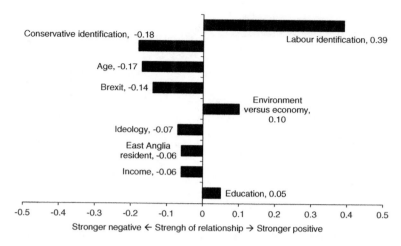

Figure 3.7 Statistically significant predictors of Corbyn's likeability
Source: 2019 Essex–UTD General Election Survey.

Labour partisanship. This was just over twice as strong as the negative effect of Conservative identification on Corbyn's likeability scores. The next most powerful predictor was age – the young liked him much more than the old. In addition, attitudes to Brexit played a significant role, as we observed earlier, and although ideology was important, it was much less so than the Brexit issue. Environmentalists liked him more than others. Both education and income were significant predictors, but in opposite directions, reinforcing the point made earlier about the emergence of a class-related bifurcation in Labour support.

In this chapter we have focused closely on the role of Jeremy Corbyn in explaining support for Labour in both the 2017 and subsequent 2019 general-election campaigns, and Figure 3.8 illustrates why the Labour leader was so important in the latter. It shows the relationship between liking (or disliking) Jeremy Corbyn and the probability of an individual voting for the Labour Party in the 2019 general election.[49] As Corbyn's likeability scores increased among different voters in our survey, the likelihood that they would vote Labour increased dramatically, so this made a huge difference to the Labour vote.

Post-election developments

Labour suffered a major defeat in the 2019 general election, and this chapter has examined factors associated with Labour's poor performance,

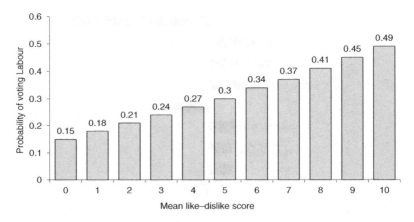

Figure 3.8 Probability of voting Labour by Corbyn's likeability score
Source: 2019 Essex–UTD General Election Survey.

focusing on the role of party leader, Jeremy Corbyn. Several factors influenced what the voters thought about him. When he won the leadership contest in 2015 it was a surprise for everyone, and it triggered a civil war in the parliamentary party. However, attempts to oust him were prevented by enthusiastic grassroots party members who supported him throughout the whole period.

A common assumption is that party members and activists are 'extremists' in comparison with voters.[50] The implication is that this extremism bears a lot of the responsibility for Labour's defeat in the 2019 election, but events since the election tell a rather different story. In the past, some election defeats have forced Labour into major rethinks – for example, after the 1983 election, when Neil Kinnock replaced Michael Foot as leader, and again after the 1992 election, when Tony Blair became leader (in 1994).[51]

What was unusual about Labour's 2020 leadership contest is that the party's individual members opted for a real change of direction. In the past changes were initiated by leaders like Kinnock and Blair after they were elected. But in the 2020 leadership contest Sir Keir Starmer, who is a very different politician from Jeremy Corbyn, won a decisive victory among the grassroots membership. Whereas 50 per cent of party members voted for Jeremy Corbyn in the leadership contest in 2015, just five years later 56 per cent voted for Starmer. In contrast, Rebecca Long-Bailey, who was endorsed by Jeremy Corbyn and was his heir apparent, won only 28 per cent of the vote.

This suggests that although Labour endured its worst electoral defeat since the 1930s in 2020, the party appears keen to chart a new course for the future and to put factional fighting behind it. The party members defended Jeremy Corbyn during the infighting that occurred after he became leader, but the 2019 debacle has made many of them change their minds. The result is that both the parliamentary and grassroots parties appear united behind a new leader. This is a starting point for Labour to rebuild its support over the next few years, which – as a result of the coronavirus pandemic – is shaping up to be the most turbulent period in British politics since the 1930s.

Notes

1 Corbyn entered the House of Commons after the 1983 general election. He had served for thirty-two years when he became leader.
2 The Manifesto Research on Political Representation (MARPOR) group is a long-standing collaborative research project with political scientists in many countries measuring the policy commitments made by political parties in their election manifestos. It systematically codes a whole range of policies using a technique known as content analysis to create numerical scales. These measure how left-wing or right-wing political parties are in different elections across the world's democracies. See Manifesto Project, available at: https://manifesto-project.wzb.eu/, last accessed 26 June 2021.
3 Anthony Downs, *An Economic Theory of Democracy* (New York: Harper and Row, 1957).
4 Michael Foot, *Aneurin Bevan: A Biography, vol. 2 1945–1960* (London: Faber and Faber, 1973).
5 The election of Ed Miliband as leader in 2010 was an example of a leftward movement. In the event, Miliband disappointed the left by emphasising economic credibility. See Thomas Quinn, 'Revolt on the left: Labour in opposition', in Nicholas Allen and John Bartle (eds), *None Past the Post: Britain at the Polls, 2017* (Manchester: Manchester University Press, 2018), pp. 34–57.
6 Across all post-war elections there is a moderate correlation of -0.6 between these two variables.
7 Sharp-eyed readers will note that Labour's move to the left in February 1974 was not associated with a rise in the Conservative share of the vote. This may be because the incumbent Heath government had presided over increased inflation and industrial disputes. This election saw a rapid rise in support for the centrist Liberals and an increased seat share for Labour as a result of the electoral system. See Ivor Crewe, Bo Sarlvik and James Alt, 'Partisan dealignment in Britain, 1964–74', *British Journal of Political Science*, 7 (1977), 129–190.
8 See Tim Bale, Paul Webb and Monica Poletti, *Footsoldiers, Political Party Membership in the 21st Century* (London: Routledge 2020).
9 The NEC, made up of elected representatives, is responsible for the strategic direction of the party. The two largest groups on it are the trade unions and the constituency parties.

10 See Quinn, 'Revolt on the Left'.

11 Patrick Wintour, 'Jeremy Corbyn: I would never use nuclear weapons if I were PM', *Guardian*, 30 September 2015, available at: www.theguardian.com/politics/2015/sep/30/corbyn-i-would-never-use-nuclear-weapons-if-i-was-pm, last accessed 26 June 2021.

12 BBC News, 'Labour MPs pass no-confidence motion in Jeremy Corbyn', 28 June 2016, available at: www.bbc.co.uk/news/uk-politics-36647458, last accessed 26 June 2021.

13 Patrick Seyd and Paul Whiteley, 'Why did Labour's grassroots switch from Jeremy Corbyn to Keir Starmer?', Political Quarterly blog, available at: https://politicalquarterly.blog/2020/05/08/labour-switch-corbyn-starmer/, last accessed 26 June 2021.

14 Mark Pack, 'Latest general election voting intention opinion polls', available at: www.markpack.org.uk/155623/voting-intention-opinion-poll-scorecard/, last accessed 26 June 2021.

15 Young people disproportionately voted Remain in the referendum. See Harold D. Clarke, Matthew Goodwin and Paul Whiteley, *Brexit: Why Britain Voted to Leave the European Union* (Cambridge: Cambridge University Press, 2017), pp. 80–85.

16 Paul Whiteley, Harold D. Clarke and Matthew Goodwin, 'Underpaid, overworked and drowning in debt: You wonder why young people are voting again?', The Conversation, 6 October 2020, available at: https://theconversation.com/underpaid-overworked-and-drowning-in-debt-you-wonder-why-young-people-are-voting-again-85298, last accessed 26 June 2021.

17 Philip Cowley and Dennis Kavanagh, *The British General Election of 2015* (London: Palgrave Macmillan, 2015).

18 This was an internet-based two-wave panel survey conducted just before and after the 2017 general election by DeltaPoll with a quota sample of 5,134 respondents.

19 The 2019 Essex–UTD election survey was a two-wave panel conducted just before and after the general election by Deltapoll with a quota sample of 3,236 respondents. The survey showed that 49 per cent of respondents under the age of 26 said that they used the internet for information about the election 'a great deal' or 'a fair amount'. In contrast, only 19 per cent of respondents over the age of 65 did this.

20 Cowley and Kavanagh, *The British General Election of 2017*, pp. 308–312.

21 Cowley and Kavanagh, *The British General Election of 2017*, p. 433.

22 'What UK thinks, "In hindsight, do you think Britain was right or wrong to vote to leave the EU?"', available at: whatukthinks.org/eu/questions/in-highsight-do-you-think-britain-was-right-or-wrong-to-vote-to-leave-the-eu/, last accessed 26 June 2021.

23 Robert Saunders, *Yes to Europe* (Cambridge: Cambridge University Press 2018).

24 James Tapsfield, '"I won't pretend Brexit isn't a catastrophe": Labour MPs condemn Jeremy Corbyn's fence-sitting on whether to leave the EU – as leader's allies threaten to stage a walkout during keynote speech by Remainer deputy Tom

Watson', MailOnline, 24 September 2019, available at: www.dailymail.co.uk/news/article-7498051/Labour-MPs-condemn-Jeremy-Corbyns-fence-sitting-Brexit.html, last accessed 26 June 2021.

25 Labour Party, *For the Many, Not the Few* (London: Labour Party, 2017), pp. 23–32.

26 Patrick Seyd and Paul Whiteley, *Labour's Grassroots: The Politics of Party Membership* (Oxford: Clarendon Press, 1992). See also Bale *et al.*, *Footsoldiers.*

27 In the membership surge the party also recruited a group of returnees – old hands who for decades had been on the fringes of the party or in other left-wing factional groups but returned to the party to vote for and support Corbyn. See Paul Whiteley, Monica Poletti, Paul Webb and Tim Bale, 'Oh Jeremy Corbyn! Why did Labour membership soar after 2015?', *British Journal of Politics and International Relations*, 21 (2019), 80–98.

28 See Polly Toynbee and David Walker, *The Verdict: Did Labour Change Britain?* (London: Granta Books, 2011).

29 In the pre-election Essex–UTD 2019 survey we found that 31 per cent of respondents thought that the Conservatives would be best at handling the three most important issues in the election compared with only 24.6 per cent who thought this about Labour.

30 Clarke *et al.*, *Brexit.*

31 Labour Party, *It's Time for Real Change: The Labour Party Manifesto 2019* (London: Labour Party, 2019), pp. 70, 71.

32 Ian Austin was adopted by Jewish parents. All three MPs were under threat of deselection at the time of their resignation.

33 Oliver Wright, 'Jeremy Corbyn "absolutely resolute" about tackling anti-Semitism in Labour Party', *Independent*, 10 April 2016, available at: www.independent.co.uk/news/uk/politics/jeremy-corbyn-absolutely-resolute-about-tackling-anti-semitism-in-labour-party-a6977876.html, last accessed 26 June 2021. See also *The Shami Chakrabarti Inquiry* (London: Labour Party, 2016) available at: https://labour.org.uk/wp-content/uploads/2017/10/Chakrabarti-Inquiry-Report-30June16.pdf, last accessed 26 June 2021.

34 Jenni Frazer, 'Labour overwhelmingly backs anti-Semitism rule change', *Jewish News*, 27 September 2017, available at: https://jewishnews.timesofisrael.com/labour-backs-anti-semitism-rule-change-as-corbyn-denies-he-leads-a-nasty-party/, last accessed 26 June 2021.

35 Eric Shaw, *Discipline and Discord: Politics of Managerial Control in the Labour Party, 1951–86* (Manchester: Manchester University Press, 1988).

36 Between 2016 and 2018, 170 cases of anti-Semitism were reported to the party as warranting investigation but were not acted on. See *The Work of the Labour Party's Governance and Legal Unit in Relation to Antisemitism, 2014–2019* (London: Labour Party, 2020), p. 240.

37 Labour Party, *The Work of the Labour Party's Governance and Legal Unit in Relation to Antisemitism, 2014–2019.*

38 In Labour's past proof of 'a party within the party' was grounds for a faction's proscription and the expulsion of its members from the party. See Shaw, *Discipline and Discord.*

39 The organisational power of this slate was demonstrated in 2018 when Ann Black, a long-standing Left member of the NEC who had been first elected as a constituency party representative on the NEC in 2000, and had been party chair in 2009–2010, was removed from the list and not re-elected. Her failure to oppose the expulsion of various individuals from the party for their supposed activities against the party prompted her removal from the slate.

40 Under the new rule the reselection process would only be triggered if one third or more of local party branches or affiliated organisations demanded it. Previously the process was only triggered if 50 per cent of either demanded it. The rule change made it slightly easier for party activists to deselect their MP, but this modest change did not satisfy the hardline Corbyn supporters who wanted the introduction of an automatic reselection procedure as a means to rid the PLP of Corbyn opponents.

41 Patrick Seyd, 'Corbyn's Labour Party: managing the membership surge', *British Politics*, 15 (2020), 1–24.

42 Labour Party, *Democracy Review* (London: Labour Party, 2018), available at: https://labour.org.uk/wp-content/uploads/2018/09/Democracy-Review_.pdf, last accessed 26 June 2021.

43 Archie Brown, *The Myth of the Strong Leader* (London: Bodley Head, 2014), pp. 1–2.

44 See Ronald Inglehart, *Cultural Evolution* (Cambridge: Cambridge University Press, 2018).

45 See Clarke *et al.*, *Brexit*.

46 See Whiteley *et al.*, 'Oh Jeremy Corbyn!'.

47 See Harold D. Clarke, David Sanders, Marianne Stewart and Paul Whiteley, *Performance Politics and the British Voter* (Cambridge: Cambridge University Press, 2009).

48 The coefficients in Figure 3.7 are produced by a multiple-regression model. Larger absolute values of the coefficients indicate stronger relationships between feelings about Jeremy Corbyn and a given predictor variable.

49 Note this figure derives from a binomial logit analysis, showing the probability of voting Labour as feelings about Corbyn vary from 0 (strongly dislike) to 10 (strongly like) with other predictor variables held at their mean values.

50 This has been formally expressed in May's Law, which argues that members have more extreme views than both voters and leaders. See John D. May, 'Opinion structure of political parties: The special law of curvilinear disparity', *Political Studies*, 21 (1973), 135–151.

51 The immediate response of the party after 1992, however, was to elect John Smith, a moderate figure on the traditional social-democratic wing of the party.

4

The two-party system: 'all else is embellishment and detail'

John Bartle

The 2019 general election provided the UK electorate with the same fundamental choice as at every other general election since 1931: a choice between a Conservative and a Labour government.[1] When it came to choosing their local MPs, voters had other options, of course. In England, Scotland and Wales, the Liberal Democrats and Greens fielded candidates in most constituencies, and in Scotland and Wales, the two nationalist parties provided voters with even more choice.[2] In 2019 these four established challengers were joined by two new parties that had emerged in the context of the deadlocked parliament: the Independent Group for Change (or Change UK), formed by dissident Labour and Conservative MPs, and the Brexit Party, a populist vehicle formed by those who had campaigned to leave the EU and who felt this decision was being frustrated by 'the elite'. In some constituencies these challengers mattered a great deal. In the overall scheme of things, they were embellishments and details.[3] The two-party system was not on the ballot paper anywhere in 2019 but it triumphed again over challenger parties old and new.

The two-party system was a key element of Britain's traditional constitution that minimised the demands on the people but gave them great power of choice.[4] The winning party could almost always claim a 'mandate' for the programme set out in its manifesto and be held accountable for its actions at subsequent elections. General elections thus provided the people not only with the power to select their government but also to decide the broad direction of policy. Many elements of the traditional constitution have changed but the two-party system largely endures. That is does so represents something of a puzzle. The class and religious bases of the historic party coalitions – a centre-left Labour Party representing the unionised industrial working class, non-conformists and city dwellers, and a centre-right Conservative Party representing the middle class, the established church, the English core and rural dwellers – have waned. New social conflicts based on age, education, identity and geography have emerged, exacerbated in some respects by the outcome of the 2016 Brexit referendum. In Scotland, Wales,

Northern Ireland and London, new devolved assemblies have been established based on proportional representation, which has increased the number of parties contesting and winning seats. The multi-party modernism of the devolved assemblies stands in marked contrast with Westminster's two-party traditionalism.

Some commentators have wondered whether contemporary conflicts can be contained in the present two-party system or, indeed, any possible two-party system.[5] Some reformers have demanded a more plural House of Commons and cooperation in place of competition.[6] Others have pressed for the electorate to have a more direct say over policy via referendums. Voters too have started to be affected directly by changes in the party system. The 2010 general election produced a hung parliament and the first peace-time coalition since 1939.[7] The 2017 election resulted in another hung parliament and a minority Conservative government propped up by a confidence and supply agreement with the DUP.[8] The relative simplicity of post-war politics, in which the Conservatives or Labour could claim a clear mandate to govern, seemed long gone.

This chapter analyses party competition in Britain from a systemic and long-term perspective. It explores how the party system has changed over time but continues to be dominated by two parties. It introduces the other parties that featured in the 2019 election, albeit as supporting actors. Above all, it explains why, despite all the political tumult of the preceding years, the electorate in 2019 was ultimately faced with the familiar choice between a Conservative or Labour government, and why challenger parties – both old and new – continued to be held in check.

The party system, 1918–2019

The current two-party system was firmly established at Westminster and in the popular psyche by 1931. Historically, Britain had two other identifiable two-party systems. From the late seventeenth to the early nineteenth century, politics was dominated by the Tories, who supported monarchical or aristocratic rule, farming interests and the Church of England, and the Whigs, who opposed monarchical power, championed the middle classes and advocated religious freedoms. Around the mid-nineteenth century both parties split and reformed as a result of disagreements and the challenges associated with the extension of the franchise.[9] The Tories split over the repeal of the Corn Laws in the 1840s and formed the new Conservative Party, which championed traditional values, the established church and imperial power. The Whigs split and largely moved towards the new Liberal Party, which stressed personal freedom, non-conformism and free trade.

These two parties co-existed for around sixty years, slowly adapting to new demands. By 1918 an increasingly assertive Labour Party, formed less than two decades earlier, sought to replace the Liberals rather than continue cooperating with them in an electoral pact. Helped by an expanded electorate, trade-union support and changing public expectations about the role of the state, Labour adopted a socialist programme. This move coincided with a fatal split in the Liberal Party that made it difficult for the older party to respond – though the Liberals could not have fended off Labour's challenge without radical policy change.[10]

Since 1918 all but four governments have been either Conservative or Labour single-party administrations. Three of the four exceptions were Conservative-dominated coalitions. The 1918 coalition government, led by David Lloyd George, a Liberal, relied on the support of 379 Conservative MPs. The National Governments that existed between August 1931 and May 1940 were formally a coalition of Conservative, National Labour and National Liberal MPs, but the Tories supplied 470 of the 554 National MPs after the 1931 election and 387 of the 429 National MPs after 1935. The Conservatives also dominated the 2010 coalition government with 310 MPs to the Liberal Democrats' fifty-seven. The remaining exception was Churchill's wartime coalition, in which the Conservatives and Labour genuinely shared power.

Figure 4.1 shows how the two major parties have alternated in power and the number of continuous days that each has been in office. It excludes Churchill's wartime coalition. The periods of Conservative government include the three Tory-dominated coalitions. If the governments are simply

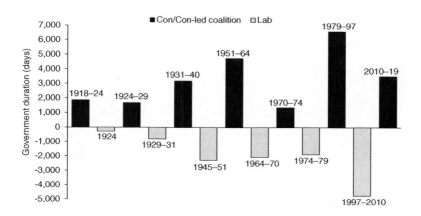

Figure 4.1 Government duration (days in office), 1918–2019
Source: Author's calculations based on dates of government formation. Negative scores refer to the duration (in days) of Labour governments.

presented in chronological order there seems to be a pendulum swinging between Conservative-right and Labour-left. Yet, this pendulum is far from regular. Including the three coalitions they led, the Conservatives have been in government for almost twice as long as Labour: 22,899 days to 12,096. Even if we exclude the periods of coalition, the Tory advantage (16,475 days to 12,096) is pronounced. British politics might have been dominated by collectivist and egalitarian ideas – but it was dominated by Conservative governments.

The two major parties have also dominated elections. The broken line in Figure 4.2 displays the combined Conservative and Labour share of the vote since 1918.[11] From 1918 to 1929 the two parties jointly won on average 69 per cent of the vote. From 1931 to 1970 they won on average over 90 per cent of the vote. In February 1974 the two-party vote suddenly dropped by 14 points and subsequently drifted downwards. Its post-war nadir came in the 2010 general election, when it plumbed 65 per cent. The two-party domination of the vote seemed re-established in 2017, when it returned to 82 per cent. The subsequent fall in 2019 to 76 per cent suggested otherwise.

Despite the diminished two-party share of the vote, the Conservatives and Labour remained completely dominant in Parliament. The solid line in Figure 4.2 displays the two-party seat share in the House of Commons.

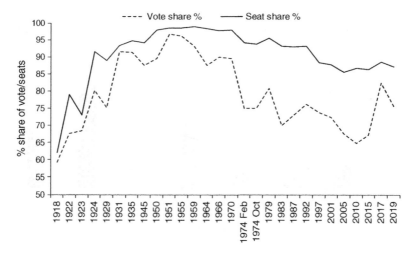

Figure 4.2 Two-party seat and vote share, 1918–2019
Source: Lukas Audickas, Richard Cracknell and Philip Loft, *UK Election Statistics: 1918–2019 – A Century of Elections*, House of Commons Library, Briefing Paper CBP7529, 27 February 2020, available at: https://commonslibrary.parliament.uk/research-briefings/cbp-7529/, last accessed 26 June 2021.

This always exceeded vote share because the electoral system over-rewarded the two major parties. From 1931 to 1997 the two-party seat share never fell below 90 per cent, topping out at nearly 99 per cent in 1959. Its lowest ebb was the 86 per cent recorded in 2005. These trends in vote and seat share produced a visible gap between the two parties' hold over seats and their hold over voters.

Figure 4.3 displays the vote shares for the individual parties since 1918. Several phases are evident: 1918–1929, 1931–1970, 1974–2010 and 2015–present. The years from 1918 to 1929 witnessed a period of intense three-party competition for votes and the emergence of the present two-party system. From 1931 to 1970 the Conservatives and Labour competed on (more or less) even terms. Across the whole period the Tories enjoyed a slight advantage over Labour in vote share (48 to 44 per cent). Across the 1945–1970 period, which excludes the complicating effects of the National Governments, Labour enjoyed a slight advantage over the Tories (46 to 45 per cent). Whichever of the two major parties was behind in terms of the vote in this period was rarely very far behind the winner. The average lead for the winner was a mere 3.9 points. In a distant third place, the Liberals averaged just 7 per cent. No other party received a significant share of the vote. Despite having lasted only forty years – twenty-five years if you focus narrowly on post-war politics – this period of two-party domination is often characterised as the 'traditional' party system. Fifty years after it ended, it continues to influence understandings of how party politics should operate.

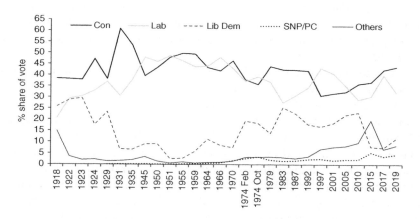

Figure 4.3 Parties' vote shares, 1918–2019

Source: Lukas Audickas, Richard Cracknell and Philip Loft, *UK Election Statistics: 1918–2019 – A Century of Elections*, House of Commons Library, Briefing Paper CBP7529, 27 February 2020, available at: https://commonslibrary.parliament.uk/ research-briefings/cbp-7529/, last accessed 26 June 2021.

From 1974 to 2010 both major parties received far smaller shares of the vote. The Conservatives averaged 37 per cent and Labour 35 per cent. At the same time, the average lead for the winning party, 7.4 points, was far larger than in the previous twenty-five years. The traditional system characterised by intense two-party competition gave way to one characterised by 'alternating predominance', with the Conservatives winning four successive elections from 1979 to 1992 and Labour winning three from 1997 to 2005.[12] A related development was a surge in support for the Liberals, later the Liberal Democrats. The 'third party' secured on average around 20 per cent between 1970 and 2010. In 1983 the Liberals in alliance with the Social Democrat Party (SDP), with whom they merged in 1988, won 26 per cent of the vote and came within 2 points of second-placed Labour. Meanwhile, support for other parties crept up slowly and from a very low base. The Scottish National Party (SNP) won 30 per cent of the vote in Scotland in October 1974, but its remarkable success proved short-lived. Nationalist sentiment in neither Scotland nor Wales challenged the two-party system.

In the three general elections from 2015 to 2019 the Conservatives averaged 41 per cent of the vote and Labour averaged 34 per cent, suggesting another period of Conservative predominance. The most significant developments, however, occurred among the challenger parties. In 2015 the Liberal Democrat's vote share collapsed from 23 to 8 per cent. The nationalists' share of the vote rose dramatically as a result of the SNP's surge in Scotland, where it won 50 per cent of the vote. At the same time, there was a spike in support for other parties. Eurosceptic right-wing UKIP won 13 per cent of the vote, and the Greens picked up 4 per cent. In 2015 challenger parties other than the Liberal Democrats and nationalists picked up nearly 20 per cent of the vote.

The vote shares documented in Figure 4.3 were rarely reflected in seat shares. As Figure 4.1 demonstrates, the two-party share of the vote went down after 1970 but the two-party share of seats did not. Instead, the electoral system alternately flattered the two major parties, as shown in Figure 4.4. Small shifts in support for the Tories and Labour were translated into tidal waves of gains and losses. Governments on both sides secured landslide majorities. The growth in support for the Liberals after 1970 did not translate into seats until 1997, when the party won forty-six seats, but its seat share still lagged behind its vote share. The growing support for most of the challenger parties produced few seats. In 2015 UKIP's 13 per cent of the vote translated into just one MP. The single and hugely important exception to this rule has been the SNP. The surge in its support in 2015 was translated into a tidal wave of gains in Scotland, where it won 56 out of 59 seats. The SNP has been the 'third party' at Westminster ever since.

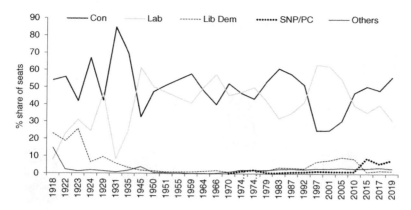

Figure 4.4 Parties' seat shares, 1918–2019
Source: House of Commons Library, Lukas Audickas, Richard Cracknell and Philip Loft, *UK Election Statistics: 1918–2019 – A Century of Elections*, House of Commons Library, Briefing Paper CBP7529, 27 February 2020, available at: https://commonsli-brary.parliament.uk/research-briefings/cbp-7529/, last accessed 26 June 2021.

Pendulum politics

The balance of advantage in the two-party system varies over time. In general, when the Conservatives are up, Labour are down. When Labour is up, the Tories are down. There are, of course, exceptions. In 1924, 1951 and 2015 both major parties' vote shares rose as the Liberals' declined.[13] In February 1974 and 1983 both major parties' votes fell as the Liberals' shot up. Nevertheless, in most cases the two parties' vote shares have moved in the opposite direction. Broadly speaking, there are three explanations of this pendulum-like tendency of the two major parties' shares of the vote.

Policy thermostats

The first explanation of pendulum politics is a consequence of the fact that governments control policy and voters have preferences about policy. Labour tends to expand government activity, in the form of regulation and higher levels of taxation and public spending, while the Conservatives tend to pursue reductions in government activity. Both tendencies are strong because party ideology is important to members and because inertial forces make it difficult for governments to reverse course.[14] Voters, on the other hand, are ambivalent about government activity. They want government to provide public services, reduce unemployment and tackle poverty. They also want lower taxes, less bureaucracy, lower inflation and personal benefits.[15]

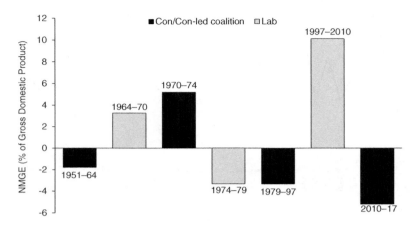

Figure 4.5 Change in non-military government expenditure, 1951–2017
Source: Author's calculations (see note 17).

The result of this ambivalence is that as the government supplies more activity, the electorate wants less; and as it supplies less, the electorate wants more. Public policy preferences respond like a thermostat, signalling when things are 'too hot' and 'too cold'.[16] At some point government policy tends to 'overshoot' the electorate's ideal point and, after a time, policy gets out of line with preferences.

Figure 4.5 displays non-military government expenditure (NMGE) as a proportion of Gross Domestic Product (GDP) from 1951 to 2017.[17] This can be thought of as a simple indicator of government activity. Labour governments should be expected to increase NMGE over time and Conservative governments to reduce it. Three of the four Conservative governments and two of the three Labour governments fit this pattern. The two exceptions are in the economically unstable 1970s. Rising unemployment compelled the 1970–1974 Tory government to increase spending, whereas rising inflation compelled the 1974–1979 Labour governments to reduce spending. Otherwise, Labour has tended to engage in 'more' and the Conservatives in 'less' government activity.

Figure 4.6 displays shifting responses to a British Social Attitudes (BSA) question that asks whether the government should increase or decrease taxes and spending. Responses to such questions reflect social desirability biases. In every year since 1983, for example, the BSA has asked this question and a majority have preferred increasing taxes and spending. Nevertheless, these responses change over time, and these changes are inversely related to government activity as measured by NMGE. From 1983 to 1997, for example, preferences moved left as the Tories reduced government activity. From

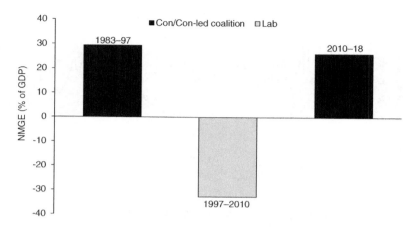

Figure 4.6 Changes in public preferences about tax and spending, 1983–2018
Source: British Social Attitudes.

1997 to 2010 preferences moved right as government activity increased under Labour. Preferences again moved left from 2010 to 2018 as the Conservative-led coalition and then single-party Tory governments reduced government activity. Similar thermostatic responses are observed in a wide variety of survey questions relating to welfare, public spending and inequality.[18]

Evaluations of party competence

Voters want policies that honour their values, and governing competence in the achievement of consensual outcomes like a healthy economy, well-managed public services and corruption-free government. Figure 4.7 displays quarterly estimates of the public's overall assessments of the three major parties' competence based on responses to a wide range of survey items that ask which party is best able to deal with an issue or problem.[19] The estimates suggest that the two major parties have had comparable reputations for competence. They also suggest the Liberals and their successors, who have had no experience of governing, have been regarded as far less competent.

The estimated competence scores suggest that the Conservatives enjoyed a significant advantage over Labour from the 1950s to the early 1960s, after which Labour moved ahead. From the late 1960s the Tories gained an advantage that was eliminated in the early 1970s, around the time of the oil-price shocks that destabilised Western economies. The Conservatives moved ahead of Labour yet again from 1975 and remained there until the mid-1990s. The sharp decline in assessments of Labour competence from

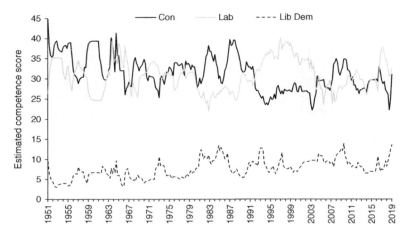

Figure 4.7 Evaluations of party competence, 1951–2019 (quarterly estimates)
Source: Author's estimates (see note 19).

1981 to 1983 coincided with a collapse in support for the party. From around 1993 until 2005 the positions were reversed, with Labour enjoying a competence advantage. The sharp decline in evaluations of Tory competence after 1992 and 'Black Wednesday' – when the UK was forced out of the European Exchange Rate Mechanism – preceded New Labour's triumph in 1997.[20] The Conservatives moved ahead around 2008 but lost their advantage once in government. Following the 2017 general election, Labour's evaluations improved then fell. In the quarter before the 2019 general election the parties were tied.

Over the full sixty-eight years the Conservatives on average scored slightly higher than Labour on competence, by 31.3 to 30.8. Such evaluations have a powerful effect on party vote shares at general elections, net of policy considerations. The patterns displayed in Figure 4.7 suggest that the pendulum swings in part because governments lose their reputation for competence. This implies that the parties have their fates in their own hands. There is, however, one additional consideration that qualifies this proposition.

The costs of ruling

Ruling parties tend to lose a portion of their support, net of all other factors – such as economic conditions – between successive elections. This phenomenon has been labelled the 'costs of ruling'.[21] Evidence across time and space suggests that parties lose somewhere in the region of 2–3 points in vote share for every four years they are in government. In a multi-party system, the effects of the costs of ruling can be extremely complex. In a simple two-party system, the votes lost by the governing party are transferred to the other party, leading eventually to a turnover of power.

Although the evidence is clear, the reasons for the costs of ruling are unclear. It may simply be that governments are punished for bad times but not rewarded for good times. It may also be that the electorate has unrealistic expectations of what government can achieve. It may simply be that voters believe that party alternation is desirable in itself.[22] Yet while the costs of ruling provide hope to opposition parties, they would be unwise to rely on them. The old adage that 'oppositions do not win elections, governments lose them' needs to read 'Governments are capable of losing elections – but only if there is an Opposition party available that people are willing to vote for.'[23] A party that advocates policies out of line with public preferences will struggle.

Causes of the two-party system

It is now time to consider the puzzle noted in the introduction and explain why the two-party system has been so resilient over the last century. The explanations overlap and there is no obvious place to start. Nevertheless, it makes some sense to examine the most abstract and most easily missed explanation first.

Party systems

The term 'party system' trips off the tongue so easily that it is all too easy to overlook its significance. A 'system' consists of recurring interactions between component parts. The component parts in a party system are the electorate and political parties. Both have goals that they pursue within the system. Voters are motivated by considerations of policy and competence, as noted.[24] Ideally, voters would get policy that honours their values and beliefs, *and* governing competence, but this is not always available. In some cases, the party that has the most attractive policies also enjoys the best reputation for competence. In other cases, the party that has the most attractive policies is thought incompetent. The electorate may have to choose between a party with preferable policies and another that is more competent.

Parties also have mixed motivations: they want to achieve their vision of the good society and enjoy the fruits of office.[25] In some cases these motivations coincide. In others policy motivations overwhelm office-seeking objectives. In general party members have strong policy motivations. A party may be pulled towards its polar position. If most voters are located to the centre this move is likely to cost votes. A party might still win elections if it has a competence advantage but if it does not, it will be punished. The feedback from elections and office-seeking motivations are likely to produce pressure to moderate by moving away from a polar position. These competitive forces compel the parties to adapt or fail.

The Conservatives and Labour have long dominated Britain's party system. This simple fact has provided both parties with numerous advantages, including party memberships, finance and extensive organisations that can recruit and train candidates and mobilise potential voters. Because the two parties are fixtures, voters are familiar with them and have impressions of their basic stances and reputations. Most voters have developed a generalised sense of 'being' supporters of one party or another.[26] Indeed, the two parties represent such familiar points of reference that it is difficult to think about political choices other than as being organised by them. As one observer noted, 'The principal explanation for the existence of a two-party system is ... that we have a two-party system.'[27]

Dominating the party system has also enabled the Conservatives and Labour to advantage themselves in other ways. Since they alternate in government, they naturally choose laws and rules that benefit their collective interests. Not surprisingly, some challenger parties and the public see the two major parties as a cartel that stifles competition.[28] Populist politicians use the terms 'the establishment', 'the Westminster establishment' and 'the liberal elite' to describe those that they believe are arrogantly unresponsive to 'the people'.[29] The notion that the two major parties have – in some sense – become part of the state is not wholly unfounded.

The constitution

Two-party politics has long characterised British politics. Before the present Conservative–Labour configuration, as we have seen, there were other two-party systems. Both the Whig–Tory and Liberal–Conservative systems predated the adoption of a uniform model of single-member constituency representation, in 1948. This suggests that there is something about the British constitution beyond the voting system that tends towards two-party politics.

One of the reasons for the longevity of the two-party system may be the peculiar importance that its parties and people attach to the goal of 'strong government'. Britain's most important constitutional rule is parliamentary sovereignty: Parliament enjoys supreme legal authority, and no other institution can constrain it.[30] By convention, a prime minister can only become prime minister if they command the confidence of the House of

Commons. This rule of government formation is crucial. Historically, it encouraged the formation of organised parties in Parliament to control the executive.[31] Today, it means there are few limits on a government's power other than periodic elections. The House of Lords is weak. The courts uphold parliamentary sovereignty. For all practical purposes parliamentary sovereignty means government-of-the-day sovereignty.[32] The government dominates the parliamentary agenda. It proposes and the opposition opposes. This 'power hoarding' mindset extends beyond Westminster. It encourages voters to think of elections as a chance to select a government rather than a local representative.

The opposition is hugely important in this context because it provides competition. While the larger of the two main parties forms the government of the day, the other becomes 'her majesty's most loyal opposition', or the 'official' opposition. Its leader is entitled to a salary paid for by public funds and appoints a shadow cabinet that scrutinises ministers, serves as a credible alternative government and, most importantly, provides voters with choice. The work of all opposition parties in Parliament is supported by the system of 'Short money'. The funding formula advantages the official opposition. In 2018–2019, for example, some £7.9m was allocated to Labour, £645,000 to the Liberal Democrats and £809,000 to the SNP.[33]

The balance of power in the House of Commons is determined by the electorate and the electoral system. Until recently voters have relied on the news media for most of their information about political matters. The principle of a free press is well established and newspapers can be as biased as their proprietors allow. There is an identifiable 'party in the media' on both sides. Broadcasting is potentially more impactful and heavily regulated. All broadcasters are required to be impartial even if they do not receive public funds. The Communications Act 2003 and Ofcom guidelines basically define impartiality by reference to the status quo. While 'both sides' in political arguments are given opportunities to express their views, it is largely assumed that there are only two sides. The two major parties spend most of their time attacking each other and rarely engage with challenger parties. Most stories are framed around the government's and official opposition's lines because of their established positions. In election campaigns, broadcasting regulations also advantage the two major parties. Challenger parties find it difficult to cut through. In 2019 the Liberal Democrats were excluded from a two-headed televised debate between the prime minister and leader of the opposition. Neither the courts nor Ofcom were willing to stop it going ahead.[34] The rise of social media has reduced the major parties' advantages to a degree. Nevertheless, traditional – or 'legacy' – media, like the constitution, are still largely organised around the logic of two-party politics.

Electoral system

The most obvious reason why Britain's two-party system endures is its plurality, or first-past-the-post, electoral system. The simple rule that the winning candidate in each constituency needs more votes than any other candidate profoundly influences the behaviour of electors and parties.[35] If there were two candidates, voters could cast a sincere vote for their preferred candidate since it would also enable them to stop their least preferred candidate. If there are more than two candidates, voters may cast a tactical vote in order to elect their second-choice candidate and/or to prevent their least preferred candidate from winning. In short, their vote depends on their relative preferences for the candidates, the number of candidates and each candidate's likelihood of winning. If a party is unlikely to gain a plurality, voting for it will be a 'wasted vote'. Over time, such parties will have their vote 'squeezed'. After the 2017 election the two major parties were in first and second place in 522 out of 650 seats.[36] The Liberal Democrats were second in just 35 constituencies and the Greens runners-up in just one. Casting a ballot for these challenger parties might help them build on that vote in later elections. It might represent a symbolic rejection of the major parties. In terms of choosing a representative, however, it would be largely pointless. Parties know that too. The cost of fighting a losing campaign – in terms of effort and lost deposits – can deter them from investing resources into seats or even fielding candidates.

National considerations increase the squeeze on challenger parties. The old adage that a Westminster election is really 650 individual contests is misleading. General elections are, above all, opportunities to choose a government, and that choice is either Labour or Conservative. Unless there are strong forces in their favour, challenger parties are subject to a double squeeze: X will not win here; X will not form the government.[37] The collapse of the Liberal Party documented in Figures 4.2 and 4.3 illustrates this well. In 1924 the Liberals fielded 339 candidates and won 18 per cent of the vote and forty seats. In 1929 they fielded 513 candidates and won 23 per cent of the vote and fifty-nine seats. In 1931 the party fielded just 119 candidates, won 7 per cent of the vote and took thirty-nine seats. By 1931 it was clear to all that the party was no longer a serious competitor for government.

Most accounts suggest that the electoral system is an exogenous cause of the two-party system, but the form of voting system is chosen by the two major parties. The two-party system predated the universal adoption of the single-member plurality system for Westminster elections. Since Parliament is sovereign and only Labour and the Conservatives are likely to govern, the voting system is unlikely to change. Some in the Labour Party toyed with electoral reform immediately after its fourth consecutive general-election defeat in 1992. Ahead of the 1997 election the party leadership promised an inquiry and then a referendum that would allow voters to choose between the plurality system and a proportional alternative. True to its word, the incoming Labour government established an independent commission on electoral reform. In 1998 this body recommended a hybrid system called 'alternative vote plus', which would use the alternative vote in constituency elections and a regional top-up to reduce disproportionality.[38] The promised referendum never happened. Labour made progressively weaker commitments to review the system in subsequent manifestos. It then resurrected the issue of electoral reform in 2009 ahead of an anticipated hung parliament. As a sweetener for potential coalition partners, its 2010 manifesto promised a referendum on introducing the alternative-vote system (AV) but without any regional top-up. As sweeteners go, it was somewhat soured by the fact that AV can be more disproportional than the plurality system.[39] In the event, the 2010 election led to a hung parliament with the Conservatives as the largest party. The Tories matched Labour's offer of a referendum on AV in their coalition agreement with the Liberal Democrats but left themselves free to campaign against it. The 2011 poll elicited little interest and voters emphatically rejected AV with 68 per cent voting 'No' and 32 per cent 'Yes' on a turnout of just 42 per cent.

Party adaptation

The present party system's resilience owes much to the constitution and the electoral system. It also owes a great deal to the underlying social conflicts and political issues that it embodies. The system is rooted in Labour's adoption of a socialist programme in 1918.[40] Its advocacy of massive increases in public spending to provide healthcare, education and welfare appealed to the interests of the newly enfranchised and majority working class. It was so popular that it compelled the Conservatives to accept that government should play a greater role in the economy and society. From that point on, elections were structured around a choice between 'more' government activity with Labour and 'less' with the Tories.

In any system, outputs in one period feed back as inputs into the next. The expansion of the state after 1945 modified party coalitions. It created a new middle class employed by the state with a vested interest in government activity. Many voters also came to rely on the state for health, education and transport. These groups tended to coalesce around Labour. Workers in the private sector and homeowners were usually less willing to pay taxes to fund this activity and tended to coalesce around the Conservatives. From the 1960s onwards immigration from the Commonwealth added another distinct social group to the coalition in favour of government activity. In more recent years, younger voters have increasingly looked to government for assistance with tuition fees, low wages and housing. Over time the electoral coalitions have evolved as society has evolved.

Policy tends to track public preferences because the electorate generally rewards moderation and punishes extremism. Labour's lurches to the left in February 1974 and 1983, for example, were associated with reductions in its vote share. Its move to the centre in 1997 was rewarded with a 9-point increase in its vote share (Figure 4.2). Likewise, the Conservatives' moves to the right in 1983 and 1987 reduced their vote share, though not enough to prevent victory. The two major parties' distance from the centre during this time even created space for the Liberals to grow their support. Other factors can lessen the effects of moderation and extremism. Labour's centrism helped it sustain its vote share in 2001 but not in 2005, when anger over the Iraq war cost it support. In 2017 the collapse of UKIP, the continued toxicity of the Liberal Democrats and a disastrous Conservative campaign help to explain why Labour's vote share shot up by 8 points even as the party moved further to the left.[41] Net of these factors, however, moving left almost certainly cost Labour votes.

The occasional lurches of the parties to their polar positions are something of a puzzle given the parties' office-seeking motivations. One explanation is that the parties do not appreciate the impact of these moves. This is unlikely but cannot be altogether excluded. Parties may be able to move towards their preferred polar positions if the enjoy other advantages as a result of enduring party loyalties, assessments of party competence or the operation of the plurality electoral system. The signals sent by voters may be misinterpreted as indicating a preference for radical policies. Parties sometimes fall into the hands of individuals for whom ideological convictions outweigh the pursuit of office. The Labour Party in particular is prone to periodic lurches towards its polar position.

Despite the centrality of economic issues, the two-party system has always incorporated issues associated with other social conflicts. The Conservatives historically defended the established Church of England, whereas Labour was founded by non-conformists who were keen to free themselves from the Church's orthodoxies. The 1964–1970 Labour government did much to ensure a more 'permissive society', making divorce and abortion easier and legalising homosexual relations.[42] The Conservatives generally resisted these changes, though some Tory MPs supported liberalisation. Many working-class voters held more traditional views but remained tied to Labour out of loyalty or because they attached more importance to economic issues.

In recent years party loyalties have been strained by new cross-cutting issues. Some relate to personal freedom, sexuality and recreational drugs. In general, younger and better educated voters support liberalisation while older and less educated voters oppose it. The most impactful issues, however, relate to immigration. The fault lines are again age and education, as Maria Sobolewska explains in Chapter 5. Younger and better educated voters tend to view immigration positively; older and less educated voters view it negatively. In the mid-2000s the influx of workers from Eastern Europe strained the loyalties of many Labour voters who felt threatened by migrants. Both Labour ministers and activists – who tend to be younger and better educated – largely welcomed this influx. The issue drove a wedge between Labour and its traditional supporters. Some defected to minor parties like the British National Party (BNP) or UKIP. Others abstained. When David Cameron announced an 'in–out' referendum on EU member-ship, the issue of immigration became bundled up with EU membership and concerns about national sovereignty. The 2016 referendum gave people the chance to register their concerns about immigration and 'take back control'.

The 2016 referendum produced two groups of voters whose party loyal-ties were out of line with their positions on Brexit: Conservative Remainers and Labour Leavers. Large portions of both groups switched between the two main parties in 2017, but both the Conservatives and Labour were suf-ficiently ambiguous to retain some voters in the respective groups. After two years of Brexit delay both major parties resolved the tensions by prioritising party unity and following their members' preferences. The Tories adopted a policy of leaving even without a deal. Labour adopted a policy of renegoti-ating a deal and then putting it to the people in a second referendum.

In the aftermath of Brexit, a new coalition of the young, the educated, ethnic minorities and sizeable portions of Remainers coalesced around Labour. This group supports government activity, personal freedoms and a closer relationship with Europe. The new Conservative coalition consists of the old, the less educated and many white voters and Leavers in former Labour areas. This group supports traditional values and looser links with the EU. When it comes to government activity, the Tories' new recruits are out of line with the party's commitment to a smaller state. The Conserva-tives promised Leavers in former Labour seats that they would 'level up' variations in wealth. Boris Johnson has allegedly described himself as a 'Brexity Hezza'.[43] This allusion to Lord Heseltine, a former Conservative deputy prime minister and advocate of state intervention, implies a commit-ment to continued public spending in 'left behind' areas. Tories of a free-market disposition may resist these policies. These contradictions may cause tensions in the Conservative coalition.

Voters and the party system

The system of alternating single-party rule represents one way of governing Britain, but there are alternatives. Other countries – and the devolved authorities in Scotland, Wales and Northern Ireland – provide their electorates with more choice by adopting a proportional electoral system. Such systems almost invariably lead to power-sharing coalitions. The policies that emerge are often demonstrably closer to public opinion, but the direct link between election outcomes and government formation is broken.[44]

Most individuals do not have strong preferences between single-party or coalition government. As is the case with many abstract issues, individuals are ambivalent and their responses often reflect misunderstanding. Nevertheless, when preferences are aggregated, they become intelligible. Over the last three decades, BSA has asked respondents whether it would generally be better to have a government formed by 'one political party on its own' or 'two political parties together – in coalition'. Figure 4.8 shows that, on balance, there was a clear preference for single-party government from 1983 until the early 1990s, when the public became more evenly divided on the merits of the two options. The public's experience of coalition from 2010 to 2015, however, seems to have put the cause of power sharing back. Support for single-party government shot up in 2011 and support for coalition government fell back. There is no data for 2019, but it seems unlikely that the public's experience of the Brexit deadlock advanced the cause for power sharing.

Evidence from the BES provides further evidence of popular support for single-party government. Between 2014 and 2017 respondents consistently tended to agree that 'it is more difficult to know who to blame when parties govern in coalition' or that 'parties cannot deliver on their promises when they govern in coalition'. Conversely, respondents consistently tended to

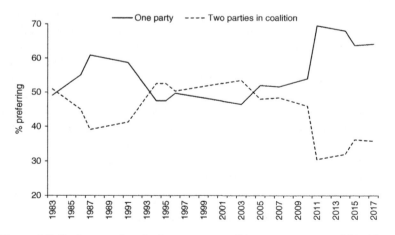

Figure 4.8 Preferences for single-party or coalition government, 1983–2017
Source: British Social Attitudes.

disagree that 'coalition governments are more effective than single party governments' or that 'coalition governments are more in tune with the public than governments formed of one party'.[45]

Traditional claims about the virtues of the two-party system still seem to be widely accepted. Even in the unlikely event that one of the two parties – presumably Labour – were to adopt the cause of proportional representation, it seems that they would be hard put to convince a sceptical public in a referendum. Public opinion towards coalitions provides another reason why the two-party system is likely to endure.

Embellishments and details: the challenger parties in 2019

British general elections continue to be a choice ultimately between a Conservative or a Labour government. Yet, voters also have other options, even if these are 'wasted votes' when it comes to choosing a government. From a systemic perspective, voters can back one of the challenger parties to send a message that the two major parties need to pay more attention to neglected issues, such as regional government or the environment. Voters can also signal their dissatisfaction with the two major parties and use challenger parties as 'a bucket to spit in'.[46] Such behaviour can be hugely consequential at a local level. High levels of support for one of the challenger parties can make it harder for one or both of the two major parties to win a seat. What are embellishments and details at the macro level can be hugely important at the micro level. It is to these embellishments and details that we turn now.

The Liberal Democrats

The Liberal Democrats are the oldest of the challenger parties. Their long history provides clues about what drives behaviour in the party system since it was their growing support between 1950 and 2010 that was intimately related to the decline of the two-party vote. In principle, these developments could represent voters being pushed away from the two major parties or being pulled to the centre party. There are good reasons, however, for believing that 'push' rather than 'pull' factors best explain the Liberal Democrats' growth.[47] While the party has long fretted about what it can do to increase its vote share, it has ultimately relied on one or other, or both, of the two major parties to push voters towards them.[48]

The growth in centre-party vote is associated with three systemic factors. The first is social change, specifically an increasing middle class, increasing levels of education, an expanding public-sector workforce and a consequent increase in liberal values. Since the centre party was out of office between 1922 and 2010, it cannot have contributed in any way to these changes; it was simply the beneficiary. The second factor underlying Liberal Democrat growth was the behaviour of the Conservatives and Labour. When either of the major parties vacated the centre, parts of the electorate found themselves closer to the Liberal Democrats and some switched despite 'wasted vote' arguments. In some cases local-election successes helped convince voters that they could win the seat.[49] In February 1974 Labour lurched to the left and the Liberal vote share increased by 12 points. In 1983 Labour and the Conservatives simultaneously moved to their polar positions and the SDP–Liberal Alliance shot up by 12 points.

The third factor pushing voters to the centre party was comparative assessments of party competence, such as those displayed in Figure 4.7. In February 1974, for example, the Conservatives' diminished reputation pushed voters to the Liberals. Assessments of Liberal Democrat competence were not directly affected by economic conditions since it was never in power; they were driven almost entirely by evaluations of the two major parties. The only thing the party did to influence assessments of its competence was to join a coalition in 2010. As Figure 4.7 shows, this decision damaged its reputation for competence.

The Liberal Democrats' decision to enter a coalition also had a direct impact on the party's vote, reducing it by around 15 points.[50] It continued to cost them in 2017 and 2019. The reasons for this are simply stated. One consequence of the Conservatives' relative electoral success was that over time the Liberal Democrats acquired a reputation as a centre-left party. By the mid-1990s at a constituency level they were largely in competition with the Tories. The party signalled its unwillingness to form a coalition with the Conservatives.[51] This encouraged non-Conservative voters to vote tactically against the Tories from 1997 to 2010 and netted the Liberal Democrats extra seats (Figure 4.4). When the party joined a Conservative-led coalition in 2010, many voters felt duped. Support for the party halved within a few months.[52] The sense of betrayal was heightened by the coalition government's cuts to public spending that appalled many of the left-of-centre voters who had 'lent' the Liberal Democrats their votes. At the 2015 general election the Liberal Democrats experienced their own 'costs of ruling'. The magnitude and speed of this reversal of fortune was astonishing.

After the 2015 debacle the Liberal Democrats tried to restore their fortunes by electing a new leader, Tim Farron, who was untainted by personal association with the coalition. The result of the 2016 referendum on EU membership boosted the party's membership. Many Liberal Democrats hoped that its consistent pro-European views would remove the stain of coalition and attract back many Remain voters who were disappointed by

Labour's timidity in opposing Brexit. These hopes were dashed in 2017. The party gained two seats but lost votes. The Liberal Democrats looked to their own actions to explain their failure. Some blamed Farron's failure to cut through to voters and allegations that Farron – as an Evangelical Christian – believed that gay sex was a sin. In the wake of the disappointing result Farron resigned and was replaced by the 74-year-old Sir Vince Cable.

The Liberal Democrats' reduced number of MPs meant that the party was a bit player in the drama that unfolded at Westminster following the 2017 general election. The breakaway Independent Group of Labour MPs, later known as Change UK, initially appeared to represent a threat to the Liberal Democrats, especially when they were joined by three moderate Conservative MPs. But that new group soon imploded. Some of its more prominent MPs, including Luciana Berger and Chuka Umunna (formerly Labour) and Heidi Allen and Sarah Wollaston (formerly Tory), later joined the Liberal Democrats, as did two Tory rebels, Sam Gyimah and Antoinette Sandbach. The chaos surrounding the Brexit negotiations and Labour's reluctance to support a second referendum provided the Liberal Democrats with an opportunity to unite Remain voters in Remain seats. The party was buoyed by its second place in the May 2019 European Parliament elections, when it received 20 per cent of the vote. It was further buoyed by polling evidence that suggested the party was poised to win 73 seats.[53] Cable stepped down in July 2019 and was replaced by Jo Swinson. The youthful new leader suggested that she was a candidate for prime minister and that a Liberal Democrat victory would provide a mandate for revoking Brexit without a further referendum.

After the European elections, events moved quickly and worked against the Liberal Democrats. The Conservatives replaced the unpopular Theresa May with Boris Johnson. Labour adopted its second-referendum policy, enabling it to claw back some of its lost support among Remainers. The Liberal Democrats then played a crucial role in ensuring a December general election by voting for the Early Parliamentary General Election Bill. The party claimed that an election was necessary to halt the passage of the Withdrawal Bill, but others believed that the party was simply cashing in on its new-found support. Once the campaign got underway it was clear that the Liberal Democrats had lost momentum. When Swinson was given a platform to appeal directly to voters, such as on the BBC's *Question Time* programme, her messages fell flat. Her promise that a Liberal Democrat victory would allow them to cancel Brexit provoked anger from Leavers. Swinson was also challenged about her support for austerity as a minister in the 2010 coalition government.[54] As ever, the 'wasted vote' argument was deployed against the Liberal Democrats at the local level, and support for the party fell back in the campaign. Overall, the party increased its vote share by 3.8 points but suffered a net loss of one seat, reducing it to just 11 MPs. The party's 11.6 per cent share of the vote was lower than in any general election between 1974 and 2010. Although the Liberal Democrats recorded spectacular increases in some southern Remain seats, such as Surrey South West, Esher and Walton, Buckingham, Finchley and Golders Green, and Hitchin and Harpenden, it was rarely enough. To cap a bad election night, Jo Swinson lost her own seat in East Dumbartonshire to the SNP by 149 votes.

In the wake of their defeat some Liberal Democrats found comfort in the fact that they were in second place in ninety-two seats, eighty of which were Conservative held. This might provide a springboard for future success. Yet their fortunes will continue to be driven by public responses to the two major parties. If the past is any guide, one or both of the major parties will move away from the centre or lose their reputation for competence. Yet even this may not restore the Liberal Democrats' fortunes. Other parties may take up their mantle as the main challenger party.

The Brexit Party

The Brexit Party that contested the 2019 general election was the inheritor of UKIP, originally formed in 1993 to oppose the UK's membership of the EU. UKIP had performed poorly in general elections until 2015, when a series of developments boosted its support (Table 4.1). The most important of these was increasing public concern – particularly among older and less educated voters – about the economic and cultural consequences of immigration from Central and Eastern Europe. This issue had previously been exploited by the far-right BNP, which campaigned primarily in working-class constituencies in the early 2000s. When the BNP fell apart in a bitter internal struggle, UKIP took the opportunity to link the issue of immigration with withdrawal from the EU.[55] UKIP argued that the UK could not control immigration while being in the single market. The party's prospects were boosted by the formation of a Conservative-led coalition government in 2010. Those voters who were generally disgruntled could no longer spit in the Liberal Democrat bucket because that party was now in government. Those voters who were disgruntled about the specific issue of immigration turned to UKIP. The Tories had promised to reduce net migration 'to the tens of thousands'.[56] They failed to keep this promise – partly because the economy needed migrant labour and partly because the Liberal Democrats resisted 'tougher' policies. Support for this challenger party was again driven by the failures of the major parties.

UKIP contributed to its own success by moving away from its narrow fixation on the EU and using immigration to grab attention. It also adopted

Table 4.1 UKIP/Brexit Party performance in general elections, 2001–2019

	UKIP					Brexit Party
	2001	2005	2010	2015	2017	2019
Vote (%)	1.5	2.2	3.1	12.6	1.8	2.0
Candidates (number)	428	496	558	624	378	273
Deposits lost (number)	422	458	459	79	337	167
Seats (number)	0	0	0	1	0	0

Source: House of Commons Library.

a successful populist approach, drawing on dissatisfaction with 'the system' and the seeming unresponsiveness of elected representatives.[57] These themes resonated after the 2007–2008 financial crisis and the 2009 MPs' expenses scandal.[58] Nigel Farage, the party's leader, characterised the two major parties as part of a 'Westminster elite' and claimed to speak for 'the people'. His rhetoric found a ready audience among those who had grown disillusioned with the major parties.

UKIP came first in the 2014 European Parliament elections and followed that with success at the 2015 general election. The party fielded 624 candidates and received 13 per cent of the vote. Although it won only one seat, it lost only seventy-nine deposits, showing that it had widespread support.[59] Its success from 2010 onwards contributed to David Cameron's decision to hold an in–out referendum. UKIP subsequently provided some of the more controversial contributions to the 2016 referendum campaign, including the 'breaking point' poster that claimed to show a hoard of migrants heading for Britain. Arron Banks, one of UKIP's most prominent financial backers, styled the party as 'the bad boys of Brexit'.[60]

Support for UKIP collapsed after the 2016 referendum. Many voters and members regarded their mission as accomplished. Farage stepped down as leader, and those who remained tried to rebrand UKIP as an anti-Muslim party. The party failed miserably in the 2017 general election and was riven by bitter personal battles. Yet, as the Brexit process dragged on, many Eurosceptics began to worry that Theresa May's government would produce a 'Brexit in name only' or no Brexit at all. Farage and others launched the new Brexit Party in April 2019. It scored an immediate success by coming first in the European Parliament elections with 31 per cent of the vote. The electoral threat posed by the new party was one of the factors that persuaded Conservatives to replace May with Boris Johnson. The new prime minister rejected a proposed 'Leave alliance' and dealt with the Brexit-Party threat by expressing a noisy intention to leave the EU with or without a deal. Support for the Brexit Party evaporated. In November 2019 the party decided to field candidates only in the 337 seats not held by the Conservatives. Having failed in his previous seven attempts to enter Parliament, Farage declined to stand himself.

In the general election the Brexit Party obtained 2 per cent of the vote. Its influence on both the campaign and outcome was limited. It did well in Leave-voting former mining constituencies like Barnsley East, Barnsley Central, Wentworth and Dearne, Doncaster North, Don Valley, Rother Valley, Easington and Blaenau Gwent, where a Conservative vote was socially unacceptable. Otherwise its intervention did little to alter the outcome.

From a systemic perspective, however, both UKIP and the Brexit Party have been impactful. They have influenced the direction of policy, even though they came nowhere near government. UKIP's success in the late 2000s persuaded the Conservatives to hold a referendum. Hardline Tory Eurosceptics used the threat of the Brexit Party to strong-arm their party to 'get Brexit done'. Voting for – or threatening to vote for – these parties was not a 'wasted vote'. There are other targets – such as human-rights legislation – that might motivate future campaigns.[61] The issue of immigration is also likely to provide further opportunities. Centre-right parties can suppress populist parties but only by mimicking their policies.[62] Authoritarian populist parties are likely to remain a fixture of Britain's party system.

The Greens

Britain is unusual among Western European countries in having a weak Green party.[63] This is at least in part because other parties – particularly the Liberal Democrats and Labour – have incorporated environmental concerns in their programmes. Nevertheless, support for the Greens has increased over recent elections, as displayed in Table 4.2.

Increased support for the Greens in part reflects the declining significance of old class-based issues and the rise of cultural issues. Green voters tend to be young, better educated and have post-material concerns – chiefly about the environment, but also democracy, human rights and freedom.[64] Support for the Greens has risen as a result of the expansion of educational opportunities, increasing concerns about climate change and – as always with challenger parties – disillusion with other parties.

Like all other challenger parties, the Greens find it difficult to convert votes into seats under the plurality voting system. The party does better where proportional electoral systems are used, such as in the Scottish and Welsh Parliaments and especially in London. Success in these elections has

Table 4.2 Green Party performance in general elections, 1992–2019

	1992	1997	2001	2005	2010	2015	2017	2019
Vote (%)	0.5	0.2	0.6	1.0	1.0	3.8	1.6	2.7
Candidates (number)	256	95	145	203	335	573	467	497
Deposits lost (number)	256	95	135	179	328	442	456	466
Seats (number)	0	0	0	0	1	1	1	1

Source: House of Commons Library.

encouraged the party to field more candidates in general elections. Despite the costs of fighting losing campaigns, the Greens have never fielded fewer than 300 candidates since 2010 (Table 4.2). In 2015 they fielded a record 573 candidates, losing 442 deposits, or £221,000. For all its efforts the party has just one seat at Westminster. It has held Brighton Pavilion since 2010, partly as a result of a strong personal vote for its lone MP, Caroline Lucas. The Greens remain vulnerable to being squeezed. In 2017, when the Labour campaign attracted younger and better educated voters, the party's share of the vote fell. In 2019 its share of the vote rose as voters turned away from Labour.

For the moment the Greens appear unlikely to pose a serious electoral threat to the other parties. Despite their massive efforts in the 2019 general election, the party came second in just Bristol West and Dulwich and West Norwood, both seats with massive Labour majorities. They have few obvious 'target' seats. If the environment rises up the agenda, they are likely to prosper. Comparative studies suggest that if mainstream parties respond by emphasising their environmental credentials, they tend to increase the importance of the issue and boost support for the Greens still further because they are assumed to 'own' that issue.[65] Environmental issues have not yet reached that level of public concern. Such a development would pose difficulties for Labour, particularly if it seeks to claw back working-class voters who are more concerned with jobs than post-material issues.

The nationalist parties

In addition to the challenger parties that contest almost every seat are those nationalist parties that cannot hope to form a government at Westminster since they only contest seats in their region. The goal of these parties is to break the union of Great Britain and Northern Ireland, creating an independent Scotland and Wales and, in the case of Northern Ireland, a united

Ireland. Sinn Féin's Irish nationalist MPs never take their seats in Parliament because they do not recognise its legitimacy. Nevertheless, all these parties can matter a great deal in their respective regions and may influence the behaviour of parties and voters in England where upwards of 86 per cent of the population live.

The historical relationship between Scotland and England was one of suspicion punctuated by conflict. Scotland united with England in 1707 but retained its distinctive legal and educational systems. The SNP was established in the early twentieth century with the goal of breaking the union. It attracted little support until the late 1960s, when a growing sense of difference north of the border led first to a decline in support for the Conservative Party. Labour came to be seen as the defender of Scottish interests. Nevertheless, in the 1974 general elections the SNP used the issue of North Sea oil to campaign to keep the benefits of 'Scotland's oil'.[66] The SNP vote share in Scotland rose to 30 per cent in October 1974 but it won only 15 per cent of the seats (Table 4.3). Labour responded by offering a measure of devolved government. These proposals were supported by a narrow majority of Scots in a referendum in early 1979. Nevertheless, the plans for devolution were shelved because 40 per cent of the electorate did not support the proposals, a requirement set out in the referendum's paving legislation.

Support for the SNP fell during the eighteen years of Conservative rule after 1979, but support for devolution did not. In 1997 the Scots voted in another referendum in favour of establishing a new Scottish Parliament with wide primary law-making powers. Labour won the first two Scottish Parliament elections and governed in coalition with the Liberal Democrats. Since the elections were fought under a proportional system, the SNP was unhindered by the 'wasted vote' argument and fared much better than at Westminster. It rebranded itself as a centre-left party that stood up for Scotland and portrayed Scottish Labour as London's representatives in Scotland. By 2007 it had won enough seats to the Scottish Parliament to form the government in Edinburgh. However, the SNP still struggled to convert its support in Scottish Parliament elections into votes and seats at Westminster. In the 2010 general election it gained a mere 20 per cent of the vote.

After winning an overall majority in the 2011 Scottish Parliament elections, the SNP felt strong enough to call a referendum on Scottish independence. The Scots rejected independence by 55 per cent to 45 per cent in the 2014 vote, but the referendum forged strong identities for 'Yes' and 'No' to independence. The referendum also compelled Labour to defend the union in alliance with the Conservatives and Liberal Democrats. Labour's claim to represent Scottish interests was cast into doubt. In the 2015 general election the SNP won fifty-six of the fifty-nine seats in Scotland, and Labour was reduced from forty-one to just one seat.

Table 4.3 Scottish National Party performance in general elections, 1974–2019

Year	1974 Feb	1974 Oct	1979	1983	1987	1992	1997	2001	2005	2010	2015	2017	2019
Vote	21.9	30.4	17.3	11.8	14.0	21.5	22.1	20.1	17.7	19.9	50.0	36.9	45.0
Seats	9.9	15.5	2.8	2.8	4.2	4.2	8.3	6.9	10.2	10.2	94.9	59.3	81.4

Source: House of Commons Library and author's calculations. Vote is share of vote in Scotland.

The SNP suffered a reverse in the 2017 general election, when its vote share fell back by 13 points. Labour won seven seats, the Conservatives won thirteen and the Liberal Democrats won four.[67] The nationalists remained in first place with 35 per cent of the vote and thirty-five seats. In 2019 the SNP raised the prospect of a second referendum on independence. By then it was clear that the UK was likely to leave the EU. The Scots had been told by the main parties in the 2014 independence referendum that they might not be able to join the EU as an independent nation. Now Scotland was being taken out of the EU, despite having voted overwhelmingly to remain. Together with the prospect of a Conservative government in London, Brexit was enough to tip the balance in favour of the SNP. Labour was again reduced to one seat, the Tories to six and the Liberal Democrats retained their four seats. The SNP won forty-eight of the fifty-nine seats in Scotland. The party immediately demanded a second referendum on independence and the Conservative government in London immediately rejected it.

The SNP's victories north of the border have had systemic implications. They have been used as campaign weapons by the Tories in England. In 2015 Conservative general-election posters portrayed Ed Miliband, the then Labour leader, as someone in the pocket of the SNP in the event of a hung parliament. Such claims may have influenced a small number of voters in the last two general elections. They may have a greater impact in the future.

Plaid Cymru, the Welsh nationalist party, has been unable to match the success of the SNP in Scotland (Table 4.4). Wales has been integrated with England far longer than Scotland, and it has been more fully integrated. There is no distinctive legal system, as in Scotland, and the Welsh education system is less distinctive. Its politics have also long been dominated by Labour. Welsh nationalists have never had an issue such as North Sea oil to generate a sense of difference or grievance. Whereas a narrow majority of Scots supported devolution in 1979, nearly 80 per of voters in Wales opposed it in their referendum. The 1997 referendum on the creation of a Welsh assembly was also much closer than the equivalent poll in Scotland. The measure was approved by just 50.3 per cent. Labour has governed in Cardiff, either by itself or in coalition with another party, ever since.

Welsh national identity is based around the Welsh language, which is spoken by a small minority. Nevertheless, the Welsh Parliament, or Senedd, has been running for over twenty years and has established its reputation. In 2011 voters in Wales agreed to extend its powers. Wales, like England, voted narrowly to leave the EU in 2016, and UKIP and the Brexit Party have performed well there. On election night in 2019 the Conservatives gained six seats and Labour lost six. Labour's grip on Wales looked more fragile than at any point since 1945.

Table 4.4 Plaid Cymru performance in general elections, 1974–2019

Year	1974 Feb	1974 Oct	1979	1983	1987	1992	1997	2001	2005	2010	2015	2017	2019
Vote	10.8	10.8	8.1	7.8	8.3	8.9	9.9	14.3	12.6	11.3	12.1	10.4	9.9
Seats	5.6	8.3	5.6	5.3	7.9	10.5	10.0	10.0	7.5	7.5	7.5	10.0	10.0

Source: House of Commons Library and author's calculations. Vote is share of vote in Wales.

Conclusions

The outcome of the 2019 general election confirmed that the two-party system is likely to remain in place for the foreseeable future. Anywhere but in Scotland – a statement that covers around 90 per cent of the electorate – voters who wish to eject the Conservatives at the next general election must hope that Labour can build an electoral coalition and develop a programme that unites a broad swathe of the left and centre left. Those who wish to prevent a Labour government must place their trust in the Conservatives.

Neither of the two major parties are likely to disappear any time soon.[68] Neither is likely to embrace a more cooperative politics based on proportionality and coalitions. If the past is any guide, governments will disappoint and the pendulum will swing to the opposition. If the current opposition is unattractive, other parties may well gain votes but are unlikely to gain seats. It is possible that there may be more hung parliaments and that minor parties could demand electoral reform as the price for coalition. The major parties, however, are likely to govern as minorities. And even if one of the parties were to accede to such demands, there would be one final obstacle. It is now widely accepted that any change to the electoral system must be endorsed by voters in a referendum. Recent experiences have damaged public perceptions of coalitions. This, together with all the other forces that reduce politics to a binary choice, means that challenger parties are unlikely to bring down the two-party system.

Notes

1 Leslie Lipson, 'The two-party system in British Politics', *American Political Science Review* 47 (1953), 337–358; Paul Webb, *The Modern British Party System* (London: Sage, 2000).
2 Northern Ireland is largely detached from the rest of the UK party system. It has traditionally returned a very small number of MPs. The developments in the province are beyond the scope of this chapter.
3 The phrase comes from Peter Pulzer's famous comment on the social basis of electoral competition in Britain: 'class is the basis of British party politics; all else is embellishment and detail'. See Peter G. J. Pulzer, *Political Representation and Elections in Britain* (London: George Allen and Unwin, 1967), p. 98.
4 Anthony King, *The British Constitution* (Oxford: Oxford University Press, 2007), pp. 39–62.
5 Patrick Dunleavy, 'Facing up to multi-party politics: How partisan dealignment and PR voting have fundamentally changed Britain's party system', *Parliamentary Affairs*, 58 (2005), 503–532.

6 Power Commission, *Power to the People: The Report of Power – An Independent Inquiry into Britain's Democracy* (London: The POWER Inquiry, 2006).

7 Philip Norton, 'The politics of coalition', in Nicholas Allen and John Bartle (eds), *Britain at the Polls 2010* (London: Sage, 2011), pp. 242–265.

8 Rosie Campbell, 'A coalition of chaos', in Nicholas Allen and John Bartle (eds), *None Past the Post: Britain at the Polls 2017* (Manchester: Manchester University Press, 2018), pp. 190–213.

9 Alan R. Ball, *British Political Parties: The Emergence of a Modern Party System* (London: Macmillan, 1987).

10 Paul Adelman, *The Decline of the Liberal Party, 1910–1931* (London: Longman, 1981).

11 The choice of 1918 as a start date is based on more than historical convention. The 1918 general election marked the first election that can be said to have taken place on the basis of almost universal suffrage. The working class and women over thirty could vote. The 1928 election was the first election when women could vote on the same basis as men.

12 Thomas Quinn, 'From two-partism to alternating predominance: The changing UK party system, 1950–2010', *Political Studies*, 61 (2012), 378–400.

13 In 1931 and 1951 this was in part the result of the decision not to contest many seats.

14 Ian Budge, *Politics: A Unified Introduction of How Democracy Works* (London: Routledge, 2019).

15 John R. Zaller, *The Nature and Origins of Mass Opinion* (Cambridge: Cambridge University Press, 1992).

16 Christopher J. Wlezien, 'The public as thermostat: Dynamics of preferences for spending', *American Journal of Political Science*, 39 (1995), 981–1000.

17 This is calculated simply by subtracting defence expenditure as a proportion of GDP from total managed expenditure. The defence spending estimates from SIPRI from 1951 are available at: https://sipri.org/databases/milex, last accessed 26 June 2021. Total managed expenditure estimates are from the Office for Budget Responsibility, available at: https://obr.uk/public-finances-databank-2019-20/, last accessed 26 June 2021. Ideally, we would also deduct other 'right-wing' spending on law and order, the courts and so on, but these data are not readily available.

18 John Bartle, Sebastian Dellepiane-Avalleneda and James A. Stimson, 'The moving centre: Preferences for government activity in Britain, 1950–2005', *British Journal of Political Science*, 41 (2011), 259–285.

19 Estimates are based on responses to multiple questions that ask which party is best able to deal with issues and problems. See John Bartle, Nicholas Allen and Thomas Quinn, 'Modelling British post-war general elections, 1945–2017: Party position, policy mood and party competence'. Paper prepared for delivery at the Elections Public Opinion and Political Parties Conference at the University of Strathclyde, 13–15 September 2019. See also Jane Green and Will Jennings, *The Politics of Competence: Parties, Public Opinion and Voters* (Cambridge: Cambridge University Press, 2017).

20 Anthony King, 'Why Labour won – at last', in Anthony King (ed.), *New Labour Triumphs: Britain at the Polls* (Chatham: Chatham House, 1998), pp. 177–208.

21 See Peter Naanstead and Martin Paldam, 'The costs of ruling', in Han Dorussen and Michael Taylor (eds), *Economic Voting* (London: Routledge, 2002), pp. 17–44.

22 David Butler and Donald Stokes, *Political Change in Britain: The Evolution of Electoral Preference* (London: Macmillan, 1974).

23 King, 'Why Labour won', p. 205.

24 Robert S Erikson, Michael B. Mackuen and James A. Stimson, *The Macro Polity* (Cambridge: Cambridge University Press, 2002).

25 Kaare Strøm, 'A behavioural theory of competitive political parties', *American Journal of Political Science*, 34 (1990), 565–598.

26 John Bartle and Paolo Bellucci (eds), *Political Parties and Partisanship: Social Identity and Individual Attitudes* (London: Routledge, 2009).

27 Ivor Jennings, *The Queen's Government* (London: Pelican, 1964), p. 62.

28 Richard S. Katz and Peter Mair, 'The cartel party thesis: A restatement', *Perspectives on Politics*, 7 (2009), 753–766.

29 Jan-Werner Müller, *What Is Populism?* (London: Penguin Books, 2017).

30 A. V. Dicey, *Lectures Introductory to the Study of the Law of the Constitution* (London: Macmillan, 1885).

31 Gary Cox, *Making Votes Count: Strategic Coordination in the World's Electoral Systems* (Cambridge: Cambridge University Press, 1997), pp. 181–202.

32 Anthony King, *Does the United Kingdom Still Have a Constitution?* (London: Sweet and Maxwell, 2002), p. 29.

33 Richard Kelly, *Short Money*, House of Commons Library, Briefing Paper 01663, 16 November 2020, available at: https://researchbriefings.files.parliament.uk/documents/SN01663/SN01663.pdf, last accessed 26 June 2021.

34 Owen Bowcott, 'Lib Dems and SNP lose high court bid over TV election debate', *Guardian*, 18 November 2020, available at: www.theguardian.com/politics/2019/nov/18/lib-dems-and-snp-lose-high-court-bid-over-tv-election-debate, last accessed 26 June 2021.

35 Maurice Duverger, *Political Parties: Their Organization and Activity in the Modern State* (London: Methuen, 1954).

36 Ron Johnston, David Rossiter, David Manley, Charles Pattie, Todd Hartman and Kelvyn Jones, 'Coming full circle: The 2017 UK general election and the changing electoral map', *Geographical Journal*, 184 (2018), 100–108.

37 Thomas Quinn, 'Third-party strategy under plurality rule: The British Liberal Democrats and the New Zealand Social Credit Party', *Political Studies*, 65 (2017), 740–763.

38 Independent Commission on the Voting System, *The Report of the Independent Commission on the Voting System*, Cm 4090–1 (London: The Stationary Office, 1998).

39 Independent Commission on the Voting System, *The Report of the Independent Commission on the Voting System*, para. 87.

40 Judith Bara and Albert Weale, 'Introduction', in Judith Bara and Albert Weale (eds), *Democratic Politics and Party Competition* (London: Routledge, 2006), p. 4.

41 See John Bartle, 'Why the Conservatives lost their majority – but still won', in Allen and Bartle, *None Past the Post*, pp. 160–189.

42 Clive Ponting, *Breach of Promise: Labour in Power, 1964–70* (London: Hamish Hamilton, 1989).

43 Tom Newton Dunn, 'Brexit backstab', *Sun*, 11 September 2019, available at: www.thesun.co.uk/news/9903205/boris-johnson-spears-in-my-back-tory-eurosceptics-hints-push-compromise-brexit-deal/, last accessed 26 June 2021.

44 Thomas Quinn, Judith Bara and John Bartle, 'The coalition agreement, who won? The verdict of the content analyses', *Journal of Elections, Public Opinion and Parties*, 21 (2011), 295–312.

45 British Election Study Internet Panel. In May 2017, for example, 56 per cent agreed that 'it is more difficult to know who to blame' and 16 per cent disagreed; 60 per cent agreed that 'parties cannot deliver on their promises' and 14 per cent disagreed; 14 per cent agreed that 'coalition governments are more effective' and 47 per cent disagreed; and 29 per cent agreed that 'coalition governments are more in tune with the public' and 34 per cent disagreed.

46 Austin Mitchell, 'Opposition tied in a tag-wrestling knot – a Labour view of third-party tangles', *Guardian*, 22 January 1988.

47 Bartle *et al.*, 'Modelling British post-war general elections, 1945–2017'.

48 Don MacIver, 'Political strategy', in Don MacIver (ed.), *The Liberal Democrats* (London: Prentice Hall/Harvester Wheatsheaf, 1996), pp. 173–90.

49 Jack H. Nagel and Christopher Wlezien, 'Centre-party strength and major party divergence in Britain, 1945–2005', *British Journal of Political Science*, 40 (2010), 279–304.

50 Bartle *et al.*, 'Modelling British post-war general elections, 1945–2017'.

51 Quinn, 'Third-party strategy under plurality rule', pp. 756–757.

52 John Curtice, 'Remaining in the doldrums', in Allen and Bartle, *None Past the Post*, pp. 58–77.

53 Liberal Democrats, *2019 Election Review Report* (London: Liberal Democrats, 2020), p. 7, available at: www.libdems.org.uk/2019-election-review, last accessed 26 June 2021.

54 Peter Walker, 'BBC Question Time leaders special: Who came out on top?' *Guardian*, 22 November 2019, available at: www.theguardian.com/politics/2019/nov/22/question-time-leaders-special-who-won-johnson-corbyn-swinson-sturgeon, last accessed 26 June 2021.

55 Robert Ford and Matthew Goodwin, *Revolt on the Right: Explaining Support for the Radical Right in Britain* (London: Routledge, 2014).

56 Conservative Party, *The Conservative Manifesto 2010: Invitation to Join the Government of Britain* (London: The Conservative Party, 2010), p. 29.

57 Steve Richards, *The Rise of the Outsiders: How Mainstream Politics Lost Its Way* (London: Atlantic Books, 2018).

58 See Michael Moran, 'The financial crisis and its consequences', in Allen and Bartle, *Britain at the Polls 2010*, pp. 89–119; Oliver Heath, 'The great divide: voters, parties, MPs and expenses', in Allen and Bartle, *Britain at the Polls 2010*, pp. 120–146.

59 Candidates pay a £500 deposit that is forfeit if they do not receive at least 5 per cent of the votes cast in the constituency.

60 Arron Banks, *The Bad Boys of Brexit: Tales of Mischief, Mayhem and Guerrilla Warfare in the EU Referendum Campaign* (London: Biteback Publishing, 2016).

61 John Bartle, David Sanders and Joe Tywman, 'Authoritarian populist opinion in Europe', in Ivor Crewe and David Sanders (eds), *Authoritarian Populism and Liberal Democracy* (Basingstoke: Palgrave Macmillan, 2019), pp. 49–72.

62 Tarik Abou-Chadi, 'Niche party success and mainstream party policy shifts – how green and radical right parties differ in their impact', *British Journal of Political Science*, 46 (2014), 417–436.

63 Or, more accurately, parties, since the Greens in England and Wales, in Scotland and in Northern Ireland are independent entities.

64 Sarah Birch, 'Real progress: Prospects for Green party support in Britain', *Parliamentary Affairs*, 62 (2009), 53–71.

65 Abou-Chadi, 'Niche party success and mainstream party policy shifts'.

66 Iain McLean, 'The politics of fractured federalism', in John Bartle and Anthony King (eds), *Britain at the Polls 2005* (Washington, DC: CQ Press, 2006), pp. 97–123.

67 Rob Johns, 'Squeezing the SNP', in Allen and Bartle, *None Past the Post*, pp. 100–120.

68 There is one example that provides more hope for reform. New Zealand chose to abandon the plurality system in the mid-1990s. See Jack H. Nagel, 'Social choice in a pluralitarian democracy: The politics of market liberalization in New Zealand', *British Journal of Political Science*, 28 (1998), 223–267.

5

A changing electorate: new identities and the British 'culture war'

Maria Sobolewska

In the run-up to the 2016 Brexit referendum, Jo Cox, a Labour MP, was brutally murdered. The words from her maiden speech in Parliament – 'we have more in common than that which divides us' – were repeated often in the aftermath but increasingly felt like wishful thinking.[1] The referendum result itself was a moment of reckoning. Since then, signs of political division have saturated the media, and 'identity politics' and 'culture wars' have become part of the new lexicon of politics. As Robert Johns explains in Chapter 6, identity and culture played a significant role in the outcome of the 2019 general election. Yet, what these terms mean, the divides they signify and when and where these divides originated is still largely unknown. While it is tempting to speak of 'the Brexit division', the truth is that those divisions were present in the electorate years before the referendum and cover a range of social and political attitudes that are not directly related to the question of EU membership.

Two long-term demographic trends helped to drive these divisions: higher levels of education, especially university-level education, which have been responsible for new political values and priorities, and an increase in ethnic diversity, which has introduced an enduring division over immigration and race. Within two generations these twin developments have changed Britain almost beyond recognition. Someone born in the 1950s was raised in an almost entirely white society and with little prospect of going to university.[2] Their grandchild born in 2019 will go to a school in which over a third of their peers might be of ethnic minority origin, and have an odds-on chance of going to university.[3] Education matters so much because it changes people's political outlook on issues of identity and belonging. University graduates tend to have more open attitudes towards migrants and other ethnic groups and are generally more tolerant and accepting of different lifestyle choices, sexual orientations, cultural practices and non-traditional family roles. While people with lower levels of education cling to tradition and narrower ideas of who 'belongs' and how to live one's life, those with degrees are usually more comfortable with change. These differences are exacerbated by growing diversity. The presence of many different groups with different traditions tends to challenge those who left full-time education at eighteen or earlier, whereas those who received a higher education are often unconcerned and sometimes excited about this diversity.

Responses to diversity do not always have the power to influence politics. They have become influential in recent years because of a combination of factors. First, the relative size of the two 'opposing' groups – those with a university degree or of minority ethnic origins, and the traditional white working class with lower qualifications – has shifted. From the 2015 general election onwards, the former 'cosmopolitical' group has outnumbered the latter, creating within the second group a sense of existential threat and nostalgia for the times when they wielded more significant political power.[4] Second, the increased political salience of immigration since the mid-2000s has mobilised traditional white working-class voters. Without the salience of this issue, it is very likely that the tensions between cosmopolitan and traditional lifestyles would have remained latent in political debate. The third factor increasing the political impact of diversity was the collapse in support for the Liberal Democrats after 2010. This resulted in a clearer partisan sorting, with cosmopolitan voters supporting Labour and traditionalists supporting the Conservatives. Such clear-cut partisan divisions make it easier for conflicts to be organised into cleavages and channelled into electoral politics. Without clear partisan sorting, there is an incentive for parties to de-emphasise those issues that cut across established dividing lines.

Finally, the 2016 Brexit referendum gave these two opposing groups of voters a sense of self: they united around Leaver or Remainer labels and became aware of their underlying differences. These labels neatly captured the diverging worldviews of the more cosmopolitan, liberal and ethnically diverse (and accepting of diversity) Remainers, and the more traditional, nativist Leavers. I will expand on these points in the remainder of the chapter, before reflecting on how these identity divides set the scene for the 2019 election.

Culture wars and identity politics in the UK

First, however, I need to clarify what is meant when commentators talk of 'culture wars' and 'identity politics'. A 'culture war' can refer to any significant value conflict. It was first used to describe a nineteenth-century conflict between the German Kingdom of Prussia and the Catholic Church. Even then it was recognised that education promotes fundamental and lifelong values. For this reason, the Prussian state wanted to limit the powers of the

Church and assert control over schooling. In modern times the term is most strongly associated with the US, where the clash between the religious right and liberal progressives has been a recurring feature of politics since at least the 1960s.[5] The idea of an American culture war was popularised in the 1990s.[6] It originally centred on the religious–progressive conflicts around abortion, gay rights and the traditional family structure, but from the beginning it also subsumed issues such as gun control and attitudes towards race. These issues were a dominant influence on US politics in the 1960s and have become so again since the election of Barack Obama in 2008. Most electoral commentary has moved on from the mantra of 'it's the economy, stupid', which dominated politics in the 1990s and early 2000s, to focus on values and identity.[7]

Many of the issues that drive the American culture wars have religious overtones. But the role of women, sexual and gender orientation and especially immigration and race are issues that also resonate in countries significantly less religious than the US. Britain, where religious conflict is largely historical, is a good example.[8] Britons are far less religious than their US counterparts.[9] While issues such as gun ownership and abortion, so strongly associated with the US culture wars, are not remotely salient, the struggle over values and identity is familiar. Questions around the multi-ethnic and multicultural nature of the nation, its place in the world and the related issue of immigration go to the heart of Brexit itself and the value divide that underpins it.[10] It is race and immigration that form the main front in the British culture wars, and it is the attitudes towards these two issues that link culture wars and Brexit with broader politics.[11]

Attitudes towards immigration and racial minorities are shaped by a powerful human tendency to see oneself as being inside or outside social groups. This tendency to 'ethnocentrism' underlies feelings of national belonging, xenophobia and identity, and forms part of a broader political or cultural unity – for instance, a sense of 'being European'. Ethnocentric conflict underlies most of human history. Elites have justified wars of aggression, as well as defence, as necessary struggles to protect 'us' and defeat 'them', whether 'we' and 'they' have been defined by religion, nationhood, race, culture or language. Ethnocentrism also underpins the less consequential tribal identities people tend to hold, such as supporting a political party or a football club. Most evolutionary biologists and some social psychologists believe it is ingrained in our species, and that it perhaps conferred a genetic advantage at times when groups and tribes fought to defend the scarce resources necessary for survival.

US sociologists at the turn of the twentieth century concluded that ethnocentrism underpinned most human cultural practices and was a universal human tendency.[12] This conclusion was reinforced by research that aimed to explain the horrific and inhuman treatment of some ethnic and social groups during the Second World War. US political science subsumed the notion of ethnocentrism under the broader notion of an 'authoritarian personality'.[13] A dislike of the 'other' and a strong need to protect the in-group was synonymous with 'conventionalism', compliance towards authority, dislike of change and a preference for traditional ways of life. This was the first time that social scientists recognised that not all individuals might share the same level of ethnocentrism. Some people were more likely to display this type of 'personality', just as some were more open-minded and accepting of alternative traditions and behaviours and 'others'.

The importance of this tendency lies in the way that the sense of threat among more strongly ethnocentric individuals can be activated when they perceive the in-group's interests are challenged.[14] Since these individuals think that difference and change are inherently threatening, social change, and especially the sudden social changes associated with large-scale immigration, can activate such beliefs. It is a short step from activation to political mobilisation against immigration and ethnic minorities and in favour of limiting civil rights and liberties.[15] Culture-war issues can activate this sense of threat because they involve disputes about the boundaries of what is acceptable, as well as who is 'us' and 'them'.

Other US research, focusing predominantly on attitudes towards race, concluded that while levels of ethnocentrism vary between individuals, they are extremely stable. Strongly ethnocentric people tend to remain strongly ethnocentric. Weakly ethnocentric likewise tend to remain so. This finding suggests that ethnocentrism is either a type of 'personality' or something learnt early in life during 'formative periods'. Just as the nineteenth-century Prussian state assumed, education is one such major formative period. Education correlates with ethnocentrism. In Britain, the sustained expansion of educational opportunities since the 1970s created a large social group with lower levels of ethnocentrism. It also set up a conflict between this group and others with much higher levels of ethnocentrism and kick-started the British brand of culture wars.

Educational expansion and the rise of the liberals

The first social change that helped to fire up Britain's culture wars was the expansion of the education system. Accessible and affordable mass education for children over the early teenage years is a relatively new phenomenon. The UK only raised the compulsory school leaving age to sixteen in 1972. Before then, most people left school with no qualifications at all, and only around 20 per cent of young people stayed in formal education beyond fifteen. Afterwards, more and more people achieved CSEs and O-Levels, later GSCEs, and then left school with A-Levels. However, it was the expansion of the higher-education sector that really changed the face of British society. In the 1960s university attendance was around 10 per cent for any cohort. The university sector grew steadily through the 1970s and 1980s, with a 50 per cent increase in students earning degrees by the late 1980s. By this time, around 40 per cent of young people were staying on at school beyond 16. The 1992 Education Act further expanded access to tertiary education. It gave many technical colleges university status and transformed the image of the 'typical' student. In 1999, Tony Blair, the then Labour prime minister, set a target of half of all young adults going into higher education in the next century. This goal was achieved twenty years later: 2019 marked the first year in which half of those turning eighteen went to university.[16]

The political impact of this social change is largely mediated by values, and in particular the value that is central to identity politics: ethnocentrism.[17] The impact of social change on political values has been well documented among generations growing up after the Second World War.[18] Rising prosperity caused a shift from 'materialist' values, which had dominated politics for those generations that grew up worrying about survival, towards 'postmaterialist' values, held by more affluent 'baby boomers', who were free to worry about self-actualisation and civil liberties. Much of this social change was generationally structured because generations share formative experiences and reflect, to an extent, the political climate of their youth.

For similar reasons, social changes resulting from higher levels of education and rising levels of diversity have also been generational. While not everyone has benefited from wider access to higher education or had first-hand experience of racial diversity, everyone has grown up in an era when these were becoming the norm. They have been socialised into new norms and expectations, influenced by those in their generation who have enjoyed a university education and/or experienced diversity. They often think in radically different ways about the world from their parents. Such political learning creates stable political values that last a lifetime and are resistant to change.[19] This generational structure also helps to explain the apparent delay between social changes and their political effects: it takes time for the younger generations to replace the old.

One of the biggest differences between younger generations of British voters and their parents' and grandparents' generations is that they have become more liberal and supportive of personal freedom. Virtually all British voters under fifty now hold more racially liberal views than those born immediately after the Second World War.[20] However, two things are

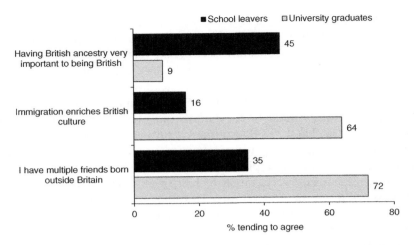

Figure 5.1 Ethnocentric attitudes among white Britons, by level of education
Source: British Social Attitudes.

important to note. First, although these liberal views are present among all educational levels, this development has been led by those with the first-hand experience of diversity and university. The gap between graduates and/ or those who belong to an ethnic minority and white school leavers remains significant. Second, this difference is politically consequential, particularly where attitudes towards race and ethnicity are concerned. Parallel liberalisation on gender, gay rights or religion has not had a political impact. As I show later, the value of ethnocentrism has been activated by immigration. Other issues associated with liberal–conservative contestation elsewhere have not been especially salient in UK politics.

Unlike in the US, there is no standard set of measures of ethnocentrism in Britain. Nevertheless, Figure 5.1 presents a selection of attitudes that are typical of ethnocentric voters. Such people are usually more insular, have fewer contacts outside their ethnic in-group, do not value diversity and difference and are more protective of their in-group status. They also prefer to make it harder for people to meet the criteria for group membership. Survey data from 2013 suggest stark differences between those with a uni-versity degree and those with few or no qualifications. While only a very small minority of graduates believe that one must have British ancestry to be British, almost half of those with no qualifications agree with this proposi-tion. Two thirds of those with a degree report having friends from an out-group and more than two thirds say that immigration enriches British culture. By contrast, only one third of school leavers have friends from an out-group and just 15 per cent agree that immigration has a positive impact on British culture. Insofar as there is evidence of polarisation around ethnocentrism, it is very much along educational lines.

Racial diversity and the racially liberal coalition

So how does ethnocentric polarisation map on to the second of the transformative social changes of the post-war era: a more racially diverse society? Britain has always been an ethnically and religiously diverse country.[21] It has had some non-white residents for centuries, reflecting Britain's Roman, trading and colonial history.[22] Nevertheless, the rise in racial diversity since the 1950s has been on a wholly different scale.[23] In 1948, the arrival of the HMT Empire Windrush with around 800 immigrants of Caribbean origin made the national newsreels for its perceived rarity.[24] Over the intervening sixty-three years, Britain became a truly multiracial country, particularly in cities. By 2011, the census estimated that 14 per cent of all Britons had non-white origins. But even in places that remain predominantly white, most people experience the UK's diversity through an increasing number of non-white people in very visible positions, from MPs and ministers, to television, film and sports stars and even archbishops.[25] The Britain in which almost no one had any contact with a person of colour has become a country in which almost half of white Britons report having friends of an ethnic minority background.[26] This change – as with education – has occurred within a single lifetime and is again generationally structured, with older people being more likely to report that all or most of their friends have the same ethnic background as themselves.[27] The rate of intermarriage and interracial relationships has also increased.[28] The fastest growing ethnic group in Britain is those with a mixed racial heritage.[29] The 2011 census found that 6 per cent of children under ten had mixed heritage, seven times higher than those over fifty. With continuing immigration and fast-growing populations of British-born ethnic minorities, diversification is set to continue.

The rise in ethnic diversity intersects with the change in values brought about by wider access to higher education. A new electoral coalition has emerged comprising educated white Britons, for whom ethnic, religious and racial tolerance is a badge of their liberalism, and ethnic minorities, for whom tolerance is a matter of self-defence. The so-called 'Windrush scandal', in which Britons of Caribbean descent were wrongly deported as part of the Conservatives' 'hostile environment' policy, is just the latest example of why ethnic minorities might want to join such a coalition.

This coalition has held even though racial tolerance among white educated liberals is wedded to social liberalism in a way that it is not for many ethnic minority voters. The latter group are on average more religious than

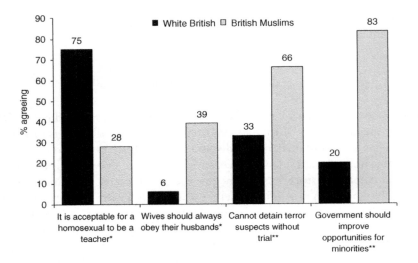

Figure 5.2 Liberal and conservative gaps between white and Muslim Britons
Source: * ICM for Channel 4, 2015 and **Ethnic Minority British Election Study and
British Election Study face to face, 2010.

white Britons and often hold quite traditional views on gender, sexuality
and family roles. Yet, some white liberals will compromise on their socially
liberal positions if they contravene their principles of racial tolerance. This
suggests that tolerance of racial difference is the dominant principle for
them. One example that is often mentioned in this context is the apparent
willingness of liberals to compromise on gender equality in order to accommodate some Muslim communities' cultural traditions.[30] This suggests that
any coalition between the two groups is to a large extent situational, and
largely reliant on the dominance of the principle of racial equality among
white liberals.

The liberal electoral coalition in British politics can thus be divided into
'conviction liberals', educated white voters who hold liberal values across
the board, and 'necessity liberals', ethnic minority voters for whom liberalism on racial tolerance and equality is a matter of essential need, rather than
personal values.[31] Figure 5.2 illustrates this division by looking at attitudinal
differences between Muslim and white Britons. On the one hand it shows
that Muslim Britons are on average much more socially conservative than
the majority of white Britons. They tend to believe, for instance, that wives
should obey their husbands and that homosexuals should not be teachers.
On the other hand, Muslim Britons are much more liberal on issues relating
to civil liberties and equal opportunities' policies that affect them

personally: they are much more likely to be accused of terrorist offences and are the beneficiaries of government equality policies. This figure does not account for education levels, which are generally higher among white Britons. Controlling for education brings white Britons closer to Muslims by about 15 percentage points on the civil-liberties and equal-opportunities questions, but even further away from Muslims on the social-conservatism items.[32] Data on non-Muslim minorities' social conservatism are not available, but given the relatively high levels of religiosity among all minorities, it is likely that they are also on average more socially conservative than white Britons.[33]

Disagreement on the non-racial aspects of liberalism is obviously a potential source of political division. If the electoral coalition between educated white Britons and ethnic minorities is to be maintained, it is crucial that racial equality and tolerance remain politically salient and the political consensus around other issues tied to social liberalism endures. Both conditions are likely to hold for the time being. Labour and the Conservatives, the two main political parties, are committed to gender equality and gay rights and passing relevant legislation.[34] The absence of polarising party competition on these issues makes them less likely to become a salient political division. The all-important issue of immigration, moreover, shows no sign of going anywhere. Attitudes towards other racial groups are strongly linked to attitudes towards immigration, and both are related to an ethnocentric worldview. The political salience of immigration and the active party competition around it activate other ethnocentric views, including positive biases towards perceived in-groups, and generalised biases against 'others'. Ethnocentrism is a particularly powerful political value, but it can be deactivated and made effectively dormant if there is no issue to activate and mobilise it. I will describe how the growing salience of immigration has led to the political activation of the new identity divides later in this chapter.

From social change to a changing electorate

While both education and ethnic diversity cause very large differences in political outlook, they make a very small impact on the electorate between each election. It is their cumulative effect over many electoral cycles that produces a very different kind of electoral competition. When Margaret Thatcher as Conservative leader faced the voters for the third time in 1987, seven out of ten people had left formal education at sixteen or earlier and only 8 per cent were university graduates.[35] In contrast, when the Tories under David Cameron narrowly won the 2010 election, more young people were leaving school with post-sixteen qualifications than were leaving

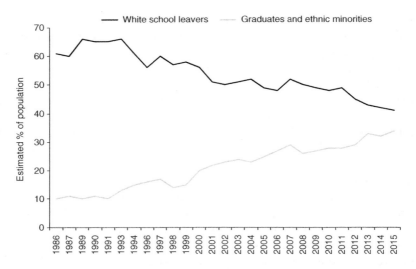

Figure 5.3 White school leavers and graduates/ethnic minorities in England
Source: British Social Attitudes. The data are representative of England only because of
the sample design.

school with just GSCEs or no qualifications at all.[36] The ethnic minority
population had tripled between these elections, and by 2010 constituted
almost 10 per cent of the electorate.[37] In 1979, Thatcher notoriously said
that people were afraid that 'this country might be rather swamped by
people with a different culture'.[38] In 2005, by contrast, Cameron included
'the people living in our inner cities of all races and religions' as one of the
demographics he wanted to attract to the Conservative Party.[39]

These demographic trends are set to continue. Generations for whom
ethnic diversity and higher education are the norm are replacing those for
whom diversity and higher education were the exception. As a result, there
is a gradual but relentless process of population replacement. This change is
amplified because graduates are more likely to vote than school leavers. On
current trends, graduates and ethnic minorities will soon outnumber white
school leavers with only GSCEs (Figure 5.3).

Geography also influences the political effect of rising levels of education
and ethnic diversity.[40] The concentration of universities, graduate employment and ethnic diversity in cities and larger towns leads to them diverging
from small towns and rural areas in their values as well as demographic
make-up. As young people leave the smaller towns for larger towns and
cities, those who stay behind are generally white school leavers. The areas of
outflow do not have the economic incentives to draw in newcomers and

balance out the outward migration. Over time, the shrinking areas become more socially homogenous and older.[41] The growing economic gap compounds the values gap: the older, whiter and poorer towns remain wary of diversity, whereas the younger, richer and more diverse cities become more open-minded and cosmopolitan.[42] Since the British electoral system is based on single-member constituencies, geographic concentration increases the political impact of any social group. This makes it more likely that university towns will vote differently from ageing and declining post-industrial towns, which contributes to political polarisation.[43]

No amount of polarisation, however deep, can have an electoral impact if it is not organised into party politics, particularly in a largely two-party system such as that operating in Westminster elections. One question we need to ask is why these different attitudes were not visible and influential in party politics before the 2016 Brexit referendum. Another is how they became so influential afterwards. The answers lie with the political salience of different issues. Because questions of race and immigration are so closely related to ethnocentrism, and the history of the UK's ethnic diversity is so closely related to immigration from the former empire, it was the issue of immigration that linked ethnocentrism and politics. The first time in postwar British history when immigration became one of the most important political issues was in the late 1960s and 1970s. This was an era associated with the inflammatory politics of Enoch Powell and the localised successes of the National Front. These developments helped the Conservatives into power in 1970 but simultaneously scared British elites, who still had first-hand memories of Nazi atrocities. Conservative leaders, like Edward Heath, steadied the ship and largely organised immigration out of politics and electoral competition.

The issue of immigration returned with a vengeance following the EU's enlargement into Central and Eastern Europe in 2004. This led to an influx of large numbers of migrants from the eight new accession countries. Since the UK was the largest economy that did not implement a transition period to limit the new entrants' freedom of movement, net migration doubled almost immediately.[44] The political importance of immigration grew rapidly. In 2006 it topped the list of public concerns, with almost 40 per cent naming immigration as the 'most important issue' in polls.[45]

The increasing importance of immigration had two effects. First, ethnocentric people became less influenced by economic considerations. Up to that point the electoral orthodoxy had maintained that voters' economic perceptions drove their electoral choices.[46] Those who thought the economy was doing well rewarded the government, while those who thought the economy was not doing well punished it by voting for an opposition party. In the 2015 general election, however, many voters switched to support

UKIP. This challenger party won 12.6 per cent of the vote based on appeals to non-economic considerations of national sovereignty and immigration.[47] Second, the increased salience of immigration initially favoured the Conservatives. Of the two major parties, they had the strongest anti-immigrant reputation, a legacy in part of Enoch Powell's and Margaret Thatcher's xenophobic rhetoric in the late 1960s and 1970s. This boost for the Tories started the slow and initially barely visible party realignment on the issue that led, even before the 2016 referendum, to a new type of politics influenced by identity divisions. The story of this largely pre-Brexit realignment is told next.

Identity politics before the Brexit referendum

The realignment driven by the new identity politics saw previously loyal voters shift their support away from one party towards another in line with their ethnocentric views. Ethnocentric Labour voters, for example, increasingly left the party over the issue of immigration. Some switched to UKIP, some to the Conservatives and some simply chose not to vote at all.

It is the movement of former Liberal Democratic voters, however, that best illustrates how identity politics drove a realignment in British party politics. These voters shifted their support largely according to their values, rather than economic perceptions. It took a political shock to start this process. This was provided by the collapse in support for the Liberal Democrats following their entry into coalition with David Cameron's Conservatives in 2010 (Chapter 4). Their support collapsed because they were seen to have compromised on their values and electoral promises by joining the coalition. Unlike UKIP, the Liberal Democrats had enjoyed some degree of success in winning Westminster seats and in many places were the main challenger to the sitting Conservative or Labour MP. The redistribution of their support to other parties, therefore, had the potential to alter the party balance in the House of Commons. As the Liberal Democrats' platform is generally centre-left and progressive, it is easy to assume that former Liberal Democrat voters should have moved to Labour. The sources of the party's support, however, were diverse. The party drew on residual loyalties to a Liberal tradition but also attracted a variety of 'protest votes'. The switching of support away from the Liberal Democrats was complex, and ethnocentrism played a major role in influencing which party voters switched to.

Figure 5.4 draws on BES data to compare the 2015 voting patterns of 2010 Liberal Democrat voters by their ethnocentric views, measured here by a question on whether equal-opportunity rights for ethnic minority Britons had gone too far or not far enough. While those who voted Liberal

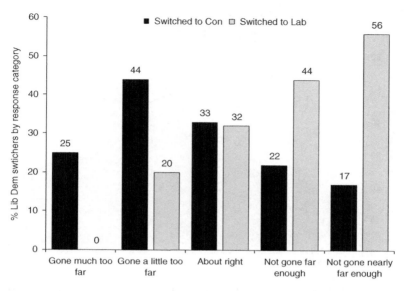

Figure 5.4 Liberal Democrat switchers in 2015 by attitudes towards minority rights
Source: British Election Study 2015, face-to-face survey. Percentages are the proportions of Liberal Democratic switchers (i.e. voted for another party in 2015) by each response category who voted either Conservative or Labour.

Democrat in 2010 and who felt that these rights had not gone far enough predominantly switched to Labour in 2015, those who felt the rights had gone too far tended to switch to the Conservatives. Those who had voted Liberal Democrat in 2010 and who opted for the 'about right' option switched evenly to Labour and the Tories. A relatively large proportion of 2010 Liberal Democrat voters who believed that equal rights had gone much too far switched to UKIP (not shown), while a small number of those on the more liberal end of the spectrum switched to the Greens (also not shown).[48]

This pattern of switching shows that attitudes towards race, a classic culture-war issue, had begun influencing elections before the 2016 referendum, even if awareness of this effect was low. It also means that while these changes went largely unnoticed at the time, both main political parties' electoral coalitions were slowly and steadily changing. Educated white liberals were becoming increasingly numerous among Labour voters, while the Conservatives were attracting a higher share of strongly ethnocentric voters.

At the same time, ethnic minorities, the other part of the wider liberal electoral coalition, abandoned the Liberal Democrats and flocked back to the Labour Party. In particular, Muslim Britons, who switched their votes

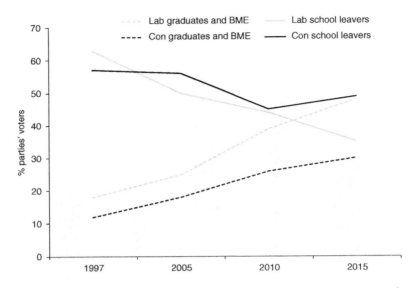

Figure 5.5 Changing composition of Labour and Conservative voters in England
and Wales
Source: British Election Study face-to-face surveys. 2001 is omitted as the survey had an
unusual distribution of the relevant demographics.

from Labour to the Liberal Democrats following the 2003 invasion of Iraq,
returned to the fold.[49] Since the vast majority of the other ethnic minority
groups remained loyal to Labour – and saw an increase in their overall numbers – they represented an increasingly important part of Labour's electoral
coalition.[50] By the 2015 election, Labour held sixty-seven of the seventy-five
Westminster seats in England and Wales where over 25 per cent of residents
were from non-white backgrounds.[51]

Figure 5.5 shows the changing composition of Labour and Conservative
voters between the 1997 and 2015 general elections. The proportion of
Labour voters from the new liberal electoral coalition – white graduates and
ethnic minorities (BME) – grew especially fast between 2005 and 2015. At
the 2015 election, even before the 2016 referendum revealed the new values
divide, just under 50 per cent of Labour voters came from this group. This
was the first general election in which white school leavers, the backbone of
Labour's traditional electoral coalition, were a smaller proportion of Labour
voters than members of the new coalition. The demographic changes among
Conservative voters followed a similar but less dramatic pattern. A higher
proportion of their support base now comprises graduates and ethnic
minority voters, a reflection of changes in the social profile of the electorate
as a whole, but school leavers still predominate. Indeed, the proportion of

Tory voters drawn from school leavers actually increased between 2010 and 2015.

Identity politics and the Brexit referendum

Although education and growing ethnic diversity were already changing the profiles of the two main political parties' supporters, the public's awareness of the political impact of these demographic changes arrived with a bang in 2016 and the referendum on Britain's membership of the EU. The Remain side failed to persuade British voters to focus on the economic benefits of EU membership, and most of the campaign focused on culture-war issues such as immigration and national sovereignty. Unsurprisingly, the demographic characteristics most associated with high levels of ethnocentrism – being white British, having few or no qualifications and being older – proved decisive. Table 5.1 shows that these demographics, and ethnocentric attitudes towards immigration and racial equality, had a big impact on whether people voted Leave or Remain. By contrast, economic evaluations had no apparent relationship with vote choice in the referendum.

Given the obvious importance of demographics and their associated ethnocentric values in explaining the referendum result, it is perhaps surprising that the two major parties waited until the 2019 general election to realign more clearly around the values that drove Brexit. One of the reasons why this did not occur sooner is that before the referendum the electorate itself had very little awareness of these divisions. When this awareness arrived, on the day when the referendum result was announced, the new labels and identities of Leave and Remain largely subsumed, rather than augmented, traditional party identities.

As the previous section made clear, the divisions that became visible around the 2016 referendum had existed in the population for a long time. But the referendum itself played a crucial role in how they developed. The result of the referendum transformed these divisions into new social and political identities. This is important, because an identity forges strong bonds and reasserts divisions between those who subscribe to it and those who do not. Identity is not just a label for oneself, however. It is also a sorting mechanism for categorising others and acts as a source of psychological bias. People may be positively biased towards others who identify with the same label, and negatively biased against those who do not. Once the ethnocentric tendency in some voters gets activated, a feedback loop develops. In the case of Brexit, powerful new political identities were created through self-awareness, positive in-group bias and negative out-group bias.

Table 5.1 The 2016 referendum vote by demographic group and attitudes (%)

	Leave	Remain	Leave lead
Age			
45 or over	57	42	+15
Under 45	39	60	−21
Race			
White	53	46	+7
Non-white	35	64	−29
Education			
Graduate	38	62	−24
Non-graduate	70	30	+40
Social class			
Middle class	44	55	−11
Working class	65	34	+31
Ethnocentric attitudes			
Immigration bad for culture	75	23	+52
Immigration good for culture	20	79	−59
Ethnic minority rights gone too far	71	29	+42
Ethnic minority rights not gone far enough	33	67	−34
Economic evaluations			
Economy getting better	57	43	+14
Economy getting worse	55	44	+11

Source: British Election Study Internet Panel 2016, wave 9.

The first of these elements, self-awareness, is the aspect of identity most frequently measured. Many surveys following the referendum asked the British public whether they identified with Leave or Remain, and how strongly. Just one year after the referendum, the BES found that 88 per cent of respondents volunteered such an identity, about 45 per cent for Remain and 43 per cent for Leave. This proportion was significantly larger than the number of respondents who said they identified with a political party. Indeed, as few as 54 per cent of respondents reported any identification with the Conservatives or Labour in the same survey. When the BES researchers asked how much people saw fellow Leavers or Remainers as 'we' or 'them', a classic measure of identity, they found that these feelings also outstripped the same feeling towards the parties (Figure 5.6). They also discovered that people had invested emotionally in these Brexit identities. Around 40 per cent of Brexit identifiers felt that any criticism of their referendum 'side' felt like an insult. This was almost twice the percentage of Conservative partisans who felt that any criticism of their party was an insult, and 10 points more than the proportion of Labour partisans who felt similarly.

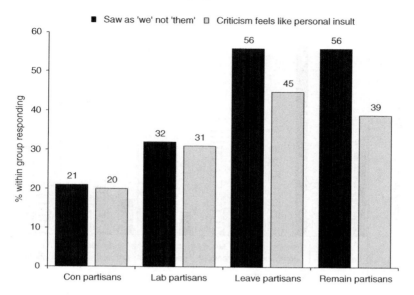

Figure 5.6 Expressions of emotional attachment to the two major parties and Brexit camps
Source: British Election Study Internet Panel 2014–2018, wave 10 (autumn 2016).

Leavers' and Remainers' self-awareness was coupled with a deeper knowledge of what their 'side' looked like more broadly in terms of its demographics. This gave them a wider positional awareness about their and others' place in society. Two years after the referendum, I asked the polling company YouGov to ascribe adjectives to the different Brexit 'camps'. People correctly said that Leavers were 'older' and more 'working class' and that Remainers were 'younger' and 'better off'. These responses were also reflected in Leavers' and Remainers' self-perceptions. Leavers perceived themselves to be more working-class and Remainers to be more well off than did Remainers (Figure 5.7).

The second and third elements of identity are positive in-group bias and negative out-group bias. Research conducted soon after the referendum found evidence of both: Leavers and Remainers thought of their own side as intelligent, open-minded and honest, but considered their opponents to be selfish, hypocritical and closed-minded.[52] These biases proved very stable over time. When similar questions were asked in 2018 both sides of the Brexit divide displayed strong biases towards their own group and against the other.[53] Figure 5.8 analyses four of these perceived characteristics: two positive traits – being reasonable and patriotic – and two negative traits – being selfish and intolerant. The numbers display a strong

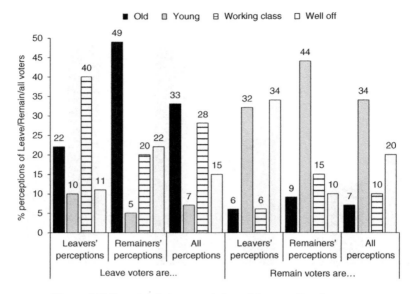

Figure 5.7 Perceived characteristics of the two Brexit camps
Source: YouGov, for the author.

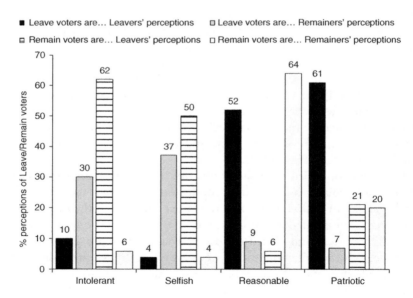

Figure 5.8 Leave and Remain voters' perceptions of the two Brexit camps
Source: YouGov, for the author.

pattern: Remainers believe fellow Remainers are more reasonable and less selfish and intolerant, and Leavers believe fellow Leavers are more reasonable and less selfish and intolerant. Both view their own side as the 'good guys' and the other side as the 'bad guys'.

The one interesting exception to this general bias seems to be the attribute 'patriotic'. Leavers believe that fellow Leavers are more patriotic than Remainers, something that can be interpreted in terms of positive in-group bias. Remainers, by contrast, believe that Leavers and Remainers are equally patriotic. This balance could be consistent with the holding of in-group and out-group biases, but it might reflect the fact that some of the more cosmopolitan Remainers dislike patriotism, while other Remainers believe that leaving the EU is not good for the country and thus unpatriotic.[54] Such heterogeneity would in effect even things out for this group.

Conclusion

Given that the electoral and party realignments around values had been happening at least since the mid-2000s and, further, that the 2016 referendum gave voters a new awareness of themselves as Leavers and Remainers, pitched on opposite sides of the identity-politics and the culture-wars divide, it was a surprise to all that the 2017 general election was not a 'Brexit election'. The referendum changed British political identities and seemingly upended existing loyalties, yet the 2017 election did not reflect this new political reality. Just as voting in the referendum cross-cut party choices in 2015, so voting in the 2017 election cut across referendum choices. One quarter of Remainers still voted for the Conservatives in 2017, despite the party's effort to recast themselves as the party of Brexit. A similar proportion of Leavers stayed with Labour, even though almost all the party's leading figures – with the notable exception of Labour's ambivalent leader, Jeremy Corbyn – campaigned wholeheartedly for Remain.[55] In fact, Corbyn's ambivalence, or 'Brexit Blairism', might have saved Labour in that election and denied the Conservatives a clear victory. Labour promised a softer Brexit in 2017 but otherwise sought to change the campaign conversation into one about austerity. This strategy enabled it to keep some of the Leave voters who might have doubted Labour's commitment to delivering on the referendum result. Its effects were clear at the constituency level. Because very few constituencies had overwhelming majorities for either Leave or Remain, and the majority were fairly evenly divided, the usual effects of the British electoral system and political geography moderated the impact of Brexit. Although the Conservatives gained some seats in Leave-leaning constituencies and lost ground in more Remain areas, there were no visible geographical patterns of gains or losses for Labour.[56] Yet, crucially, Labour's majorities shrunk in places where they still won, making many Northern and Midlands seats more likely to topple to the Conservatives the next time around.

Despite the seemingly moderate Brexit effect in 2017, the political identities associated with Brexit did not wane. The deadlocked 2017 parliament did not help either the Conservatives or Labour to persuade voters of their competence to deliver in the negotiations with the EU. In the 2019 European Parliament elections, it was the Liberal Democrats and Greens who rallied the Remainers, and the Brexit Party, the successor party to UKIP, which topped the poll and scooped much of the Leave vote. Both the Conservatives and Labour performed abysmally. Going into the 2019 election campaign, the Tories had reasons to fear a repetition of the 2017 campaign. It was largely for that reason that the party and its new leader, Boris Johnson, pushed hard the message of 'get Brexit done' in a bid to win over Leave partisans. Labour, despite still representing so many of the most Leave areas in the country, bent under pressure from the dominant Remainer majority in the party membership. It went into the 2019 election without the cover of Brexit Blairism and committed instead to a second referendum. The consequences of these decisions are explored fully in the next chapter.

It only remains here to reflect on the possible future of identity politics in the UK and the British culture wars. At the time of writing it seems likely that issues of racial equality are here to stay. During the summer of 2020 Britain was gripped by responses to the Black Lives Matter movement, imported largely from the US and spurred on by the racially motivated killing of an unarmed black man, George Floyd, by a Minneapolis police officer. The history of police mistreatment of black and Asian people in Britain is well documented, however.[57] The protests in the UK quickly turned from showing solidarity with the US movement into a wider questioning of Britain's colonial heritage and the treatment of British minorities. Statues of British slave traders were removed around the country, prompting cries of approval and disapprobation in equal measures. One of the most prominent critics was Priti Patel, the Conservative home secretary and the first British-Asian woman to hold the role. She also condemned the Black Lives Matter marches for contravening the government's 'stay at home' advice amid the coronavirus pandemic. Patel was widely accused by Labour MPs of 'gaslighting' ethnic minority people on racism, by which they meant that she used her own experiences to downplay the extent of racism in British society.

Other issues might yet join the growing value polarisation, particularly the heated topic of gender identity. 'Transphobia' is a touchstone issue for some young activists and has sparked a subsidiary debate, particularly on social media, about freedom of speech. It is also a potential dividing line within the new liberal electoral coalition. J. K. Rowling, the Harry Potter author, and an outspoken critic of Brexit, was widely denounced for making allegedly transphobic comments in June 2020 by suggesting 'people who menstruate' should be called women. If it becomes more salient, the issue of gender identity could yet drive a wedge between younger liberals and more socially conservative ethnic minority voters. Alternatively, with immigration having decreased in political salience since the 2016 referendum, identity politics could become dormant again. Nothing in politics is inevitable. Given the economic shock resulting from the 2020 coronavirus pandemic, politics after 2020 might be rewritten in wholly unexpected ways.

Notes

1 House of Commons Debates, volume 596, 3 June 2015, cols. 674–676.
2 David Willetts, *A University Education* (Oxford: Oxford University Press, 2018).
3 This will vary depending on where this child lives. In cities, especially London, this proportion will be higher, and in rural areas lower. In 2017 on average 32 per cent of primary school children in the state sector were already of ethnic minority origin. See Department for Education, *Schools, Pupils and Their Characteristics*, SFR 28/2017, 29 June 2017, available at: https://assets.publishing.service.gov.uk/government/uploads/system/uploads/attachment_data/file/650547/SFR28_2017_Main_Text.pdf, last accessed 26 June 2021.
4 Justin Gest, Tyler Reny and Jeremy Mayer, 'Roots of the radical right: Nostalgic deprivation in the United States and Britain', *Comparative Political Studies*, 51 (2017), 1694–1719.
5 Rick Perlstein, *Nixonland: The Rise of a President and the Fracturing of America* (London: Simon and Schuster, 2009).
6 James Davison Hunter, *Culture Wars: The Struggle to Control the Family, Art, Education, Law, and Politics in America* (New York: Basic Books, 1992).
7 First coined in 1992 by Bill Clinton's strategist James Carville.
8 James Tilley, '"We don't do God?" Religion and party choice in Britain', *British Journal of Political Science*, 45 (2015), 907–927.
9 Robert D. Putnam and David E. Campbell, *Amazing Grace: How American Religion Divides and Unites Us* (London: Simon and Schuster, 2010).
10 John Sides, Michael Tesler and Lynn Vavreck, *Identity Crisis: The 2016 Presidential Campaign and the Battle for the Meaning of America* (Princeton: Princeton University Press, 2018).
11 Maria Sobolewska and Robert Ford, *Brexitland: Identity Conflicts in British Politics* (Cambridge: Cambridge University Press, 2020).
12 William Graham Sumner, *Folkways: A Study of the Sociological Importance of Usages, Manners, Customs, Mores and Morals* (Hong Kong: Hesperides Press, 2006).

13 Theodor W. Adorno, Else Frenkel-Brunswik, Daniel J. Levinson and Nevit Stanford, *The Authoritarian Personality* (New York: Harper, 1950).

14 Karen Stenner, *The Authoritarian Dynamic* (New York: Cambridge University Press, 2005).

15 Leonie Huddy, Stanley Feldman, Charles Taber and Gallya Lahav, 'Threat, anxiety, and support of antiterrorism policies', *American Journal of Political Science*, 49 (2005), 593–608; Jennifer L. Merolla and Elizabeth J. Zechmeister, *Democracy at Risk: How Terrorist Threats Affect the Public* (Chicago: University of Chicago Press, 2009); Clem Brooks and Jeff Manza, *Whose Rights? Counterterrorism and the Dark Side of American Public Opinion* (New York: Russell Sage Foundation, 2013).

16 Sean Coughlan, 'The symbolic target of 50% at university reached', BBC News, 26 September 2019, available at: www.bbc.co.uk/news/education-49841620, last accessed 26 June 2021.

17 This value cleavage between degree holders and the rest of the population has been documented internationally. See Rune Stubager, 'Education-based group identity and consciousness in the authoritarian-libertarian value conflict', *European Journal of Political Research*, 48 (2009), 204–233; Rune Stubager, 'The development of the education cleavage: Denmark as a critical case', *West European Politics*, 33 (2010), 505–533; and Paula Surridge, 'Education and liberalism: pursuing the link', *Oxford Review of Education*, 42 (2016), 146–164.

18 Ronald Inglehart, *The Silent Revolution* (Princeton: Princeton University Press, 1977); Ronald Inglehart, *Culture Shift in Advanced Industrial Society* (Princeton: Princeton University Press, 1990); Ronald Inglehart, *Modernization and Postmodernization* (Princeton: Princeton University Press, 1997); Ronald Inglehart and Pippa Norris, *Sacred and Secular: Religion and Politics Worldwide* (Cambridge: Cambridge University Press, 2004); Ronald Inglehart and Pippa Norris, *Rising Tide: Gender Equality and Cultural Change around the World* (Cambridge: Cambridge University Press, 2003); Ronald Inglehart and Christian Welzel, *Modernization, Cultural Change and Democracy: The Human Development Sequence* (Cambridge: Cambridge University Press, 2005).

19 Karl Mannheim, 'The problem of generations', in *Essays on the Sociology of Knowledge* (London: Routledge, 1928), pp. 276–320; Larry M. Bartels and Simon Jackman, 'A generational model of political learning', *Electoral Studies*, 33 (2014), 7–18.

20 Sobolewska and Ford, *Brexitland*.

21 Linda Colley, *Britons: Forging the Nation* (Yale: Yale University Press, 1992); Tilley, 'We don't do God?'; Ben Clements, *Religion and Public Opinion in Britain: Continuity and Change* (Basingstoke: Palgrave Macmillan, 2015).

22 David Olusoga, *Black and British: A Forgotten History* (London: Pan, 2017).

23 Lucinda Platt and Alita Nandi, 'Ethnic diversity in the UK: New opportunities and changing constraints', *Journal of Ethnic and Migration Studies*, 46: (2020), 839–856; Anthony F. Heath, Stephen. D. Fisher, Gemma Rosenblatt, David Sanders and Maria Sobolewska, *The Political Integration of Ethnic Minorities in Britain* (Oxford: Oxford University Press, 2013).

24 The figure quoted most often is 802, but it is sometimes contested.

25 John Sentamu, born in Kampala, Uganda, became the archbishop of York in 2005.

26 Ethnic minority status in Britain is largely linked to race, following the standard-use Office of National Statistics question that makes a distinction between the various white and non-white ethnicities.

27 See *Community Spirit in England: A Report on the 2009–10 Citizenship Survey* (London: Department for Communities and Local Government, 2011), p. 68, available at: https://webarchive.nationalarchives.gov.uk/20120919214034/http://www.communities.gov.uk/documents/statistics/pdf/2056236.pdf, last accessed 26 June 2021.

28 Raya Muttarak and Anthony Heath, 'Who intermarries in Britain? Explaining ethnic diversity in intermarriage patterns', *British Journal of Sociology*, 61 (2010), 275–305.

29 Robert Ford, Rachel Jolley, Sunder Katwala and Binita Mehta, *The Melting Pot Generation* (London: British Future, 2012), available at: www.britishfuture.org/wpcontent/uploads/2012/12/The-melting-pot-generation.pdf, last accessed 26 June 2021.

30 Rafaela M. Dancygier, *Dilemmas of Inclusion: Muslims in European Politics* (Princeton: Princeton University Press, 2017); Eleanor Hill, Maria Sobolewska, Stuart Wilks-Heeg and Magda Borkowska, 'Explaining electoral fraud in an advanced democracy: Fraud vulnerabilities, opportunities and facilitating mechanisms in British elections', *British Journal of Politics and International Relations*, 19 (2017), 772–789.

31 Ethnic minorities can feel an ethnocentric dislike of white Britons and other ethnic minorities. See Ingrid Storm, Maria Sobolewska and Robert Ford, 'Is ethnic prejudice declining in Britain? Change in social distance attitudes among ethnic majority and minority Britons', *British Journal of Sociology*, 68 (2017), 410–434.

32 The data on the social conservatism of Muslims does not allow me to disaggregate by education.

33 Maria Sobolewska, Stephen D. Fisher, Anthony F. Heath and David Sanders, 'Understanding the effects of religious attendance on political participation among ethnic minorities of different religions', *European Journal of Political Research*, 54 (2015), 271–287.

34 Although Conservative Party policies seem to be detrimental to young women in particular, women are as likely to vote Conservative, without controlling for age. See Anna Sanders and Rosalind Shorrocks, 'All in this together? Austerity and the gender-age gap in the 2015 and 2017 British general elections', *British Journal of Politics and International Relations*, 21 (2019), 667–688. On the issue of gay rights, traditionally the Conservative party has been hostile party to any legal change, but this has changed more recently, and it was the Conservative led government that legalised gay marriage in England and Wales in 2013.

35 David Owen, *Ethnic Minorities in Britain: Patterns of Population Change 1981–1991*, University of Warwick Centre for Research in Ethnic Relations, 1991

Census Statistical Paper No. 10, available at: https://warwick.ac.uk/fac/soc/crer/ research/publications/nemda/nemda1991sp10.pdf, last accessed 26 June 2021.

36 As the proportion of people going to university continues to rise, the proportion of those who leave school at sixteen keeps falling, not just as an obvious conse- quence of the first trend, but also as a result of more and more people leaving school at eighteen or beyond to study for some form of non-degree qualification.

37 Heath *et al.*, *The Political Integration of Ethnic Minorities in Britain*.

38 Interview with Granada's 'World in Action' programme, January 1978. An extract is available at: www.youtube.com/watch?v=JR9X6FkkOeY, last accessed 26 June 2021.

39 *Guardian*, 'Full text: David Cameron's speech to the Conservative conference 2005', 4 October 2005, available at: www.theguardian.com/politics/2005/oct/04/ conservatives2005.conservatives3, last accessed 26 June 2021.

40 Will Jennings and Gerry Stoker, 'The bifurcation of politics: Two Englands', *Political Quarterly*, 87 (2016), 372–382; Will Jennings and Gerry Stoker, 'Tilting towards the cosmopolitan axis? Political change in England and the 2017 election', *Political Quarterly*, 88 (2017), 359–369.

41 Jennings and Stoker, 'The bifurcation of politics'.

42 Rahsaan Maxwell, 'Cosmopolitan immigration attitudes in large European cities: Contextual or compositional effects?', *American Political Science Review*, 113 (2019), 456–474.

43 Jennings and Stoker, 'The bifurcation of politics'.

44 Madeleine Sumption and Carlos Vargas-Silva, 'Love is not all you need: Income requirement for visa sponsorship of foreign family members', *Journal of Economics, Race, and Policy*, 2 (2019), 62–76.

45 It was briefly replaced as the most important issue by the economy following the global financial crisis from 2008, but returned to the top from about 2012. Concern peaked at around 45 per cent in 2015–2016.

46 Michael Lewis-Beck and Mary Stegmaier, 'Economic models of voting', in Russell J. Dalton and Hans-Dieter Klingemann (eds), *The Oxford Handbook of Political Behaviour* (Oxford: Oxford University Press, 2007), pp. 519–537.

47 See Paul Whiteley, Matthew Goodwin and Harold D. Clarke, 'The rise and fall of UKIP, 2010–17', in Nicholas Allen and John Bartle (eds), *None Past the Post: Britain at the Polls, 2017* (Manchester: Manchester University Press, 2018), pp. 78–99.

48 Sobolewska and Ford, *Brexitland*.

49 Nicole Martin, 'Are British Muslims alienated from mainstream politics by British foreign policy?', *Ethnicities*, 17 (2016), 350–370; John Curtice, Stephen D. Fisher and Michael Steed, 'Appendix 2: An Analysis of the Results', in Dennis Kavanagh and David Butler (eds), *The British General Election of 2005* (London: Macmillan, 2006); John Curtice, 'New Labour, new protest? How the Liberal Democrats profited from Blair's mistakes', *Political Quarterly*, 78 (2007), 117–127.

50 Although there is little evidence that ethnic minority candidates made a direct difference. See Nicole S. Martin, 'Do ethnic minority candidates mobilise ethnic

minority voters? Evidence from the 2010 UK general election', *Parliamentary Affairs*, 69 (2016), 159–180; they may have helped indirectly, by helping to repair the Conservatives' reputation with ethnic minorities. See Heath *et al.*, *The Political Integration of Ethnic Minorities in Britain*.

51 Sobolewska and Ford, *Brexitland*.

52 Sara B. Hobolt, Thomas J. Leeper and James Tilley, 'Divided by the vote: Affective polarization in the wake of the Brexit referendum', *British Journal of Political Science*, FirstView (2020), 1–18: doi:10.1017/S0007123420000125.

53 Sobolewska and Ford, *Brexitland*, p. 243.

54 Perhaps proving then prime minister, Theresa May, right, when she said they were the 'citizens of nowhere'.

55 John Bartle, 'Why the Conservatives lost their majority – but still won', in Allen and Bartle (eds), *None Past the Post*, p. 173.

56 Robert Ford, Matthew Goodwin and Maria Sobolewska, 'British politics', *EU Referendum: One Year on* (The UK in a Changing Europe: 2017), pp. 16–17, available at: https://ukandeu.ac.uk/wp-content/uploads/2017/06/EU-referendum-one-year-on.pdf, last accessed 26 June 2021.

57 William Shankley and Patrick Williams, 'Minority ethnic groups, policing and the criminal justice system in Britain', in Bridget Byrne, Claire Alexander, Omar Khan, James Nazroo and William Shankley (eds), *Ethnicity, Race and Inequality in the UK: State of the Nation* (Bristol: Policy Press, 2020).

6

Why did the Conservatives win?

Robert Johns

This was the Brexit election. The election happened because of Brexit. The short campaign was dominated, the long campaign utterly dominated, by Brexit. The dramatic results of the night had Brexit written all over them. The word 'Brexit' has already appeared dozens of times in this book. In this light, the answer to the question raised in the title to this chapter seems simple, even trivial. Surely it would be perverse to deny that Brexit was the key to the Conservative victory.

This chapter will be only somewhat perverse. It will not deny the central-ity of Brexit to the outcome of this election. But it will add two important qualifiers. The first is to reject the idea that this was somehow an interrup-tion to normal service, that it was 'the Brexit election, not a normal election'. In fact, the Conservatives won for just the kind of reasons that the *Britain at the Polls* series has long identified as the reasons why parties win British elections: they were closer to voters ideologically and they were seen as more competent than the alternatives. There was a strong Brexit flavour to both advantages, of course. Leavers, for instance, were much more likely than Remainers to see Boris Johnson as a capable prime minister. The point is that Brexit was a powerful influence – but it was a powerful influence on the usual judgements that voters make when choosing parties. And it was not the only influence on those judgements.

The other qualifier draws a distinction between what drives individual votes and what decides overall election outcomes. Studies of British voting behaviour in the 1950s and 1960s emphasised the strength and reach of party allegiances, providing a convincing answer to the question of why most peo-ple voted the way they did.[1] However, not everyone was a party loyalist, and it was the switching of these 'floating' voters between elections that decided the outcomes. We might say something similar here. Loyal Leavers and Remainers were always going to vote respectively for and against an incum-bent promising to 'get Brexit done'. Yet there are others whose opinions on Brexit did not override every other consideration in this election. Given the roughly 50:50 split between Leave and Remain in the electorate, the party that won the 'everything else' battle would win the election.

This chapter will say plenty about Brexit but plenty also about everything else – or, at least, the key parts of it. It begins with the election's vital statistics, including the flow of the vote and the social basis of the parties' support. Then it highlights the importance of both Brexit and the broader value conflict which, as Maria Sobolewska describes in Chapter 5, was not created but amplified by the EU referendum. The first pillar underpinning the Conservatives' victory was that Brexit made the election more about those values, and less about the economic left–right conflict on which Labour was more in tune with the electorate. The chapter then turns to the second pillar, the Conservatives' general advantage over Labour in terms of economic competence, leadership and moderation. If this sounds odd in the light of the chaotic lead-up to the election, it should be borne in mind that voting is a choice. On criteria like competence and unity, voters saw this election as something of a race to the bottom – a race that Labour 'won'.

Another consequence of focusing on the election outcome is that parties other than the two contenders for government get rather short shrift in this chapter. They have been given their due in Chapter 4 but are somewhat peripheral to the question of why the Conservatives won. This follows in part from the size of the Conservative majority. A tighter race would have prompted closer analysis of the impact of the Brexit Party's decision to contest only Labour-held seats. A stronger Labour showing would have renewed debate about whether the party can win a majority without reclaiming seats in Scotland from the SNP. In the Westminster electoral system, though, a 163-seat gap between the two major players leaves the rest of the cast looking like extras.

Votes and where they came from

The result of the 2019 general election is displayed in Table 6.1. Two things are clear from the top rows of the table: the Conservatives beat Labour by a large margin; and this was courtesy of Labour losses rather than Conservative gains. The contrast is all the starker when we consider that in 2017, as in 2019, the Conservatives held the same 12-point opinion-poll lead over Labour with around three weeks to go. In 2017, that lead narrowed dramatically as polling day approached. In 2019, it held steady.

The story of the 2017 campaign was of Labour squeezing support from the smaller parties as well as from undecided voters.[2] The story of the 2019 campaign was one of Labour failing to repeat the trick, while the Conservatives held their coalition together. The other gainers in Table 6.1 were the parties that resisted a Labour revival in 2019. The gains for the Liberal Democrats and the Greens do not look spectacular in percentage-point terms but represent a growth of more than 50 per cent in those parties' vote

Table 6.1 Results of the 2019 UK general election

| | Votes (%) | | Seats | |
	2019	Change	2019	Change
Con	43.6	+1.3	365	+48
Lab	32.1	−7.9	202	−60
Lib Dem	11.6	+4.2	11	−1
SNP	3.9	+0.8	48	13
Green	2.7	+1.1	1	0
Brexit Party	2.0	−	0	−
DUP	0.8	−0.1	8	−2
Sinn Féin	0.6	−0.2	7	0
Plaid Cymru	0.5	0	4	0
Others/ independents	2.2	+0.8	4	+2

Source: House of Commons Library.

tallies. Meanwhile, the SNP's 0.8-point gain across the UK amounted to an 8-point climb from 37 per cent to 45 per cent of the vote in Scotland. The party reclaimed all six of the constituencies that it had lost to Labour in 2017, as well as unseating seven Conservatives.

Altogether, eighty-one seats changed hands in 2019. Two thirds of these were Conservative gains from Labour (a large proportion that is even larger if we exclude the fifteen Scottish and four Northern Irish seats, with their very different party systems). It can be tempting to infer from this that votes must also have switched from Labour to the Conservatives. Switching between the two major parties, however, has been the exception rather than the rule in British elections. Gains and losses for the major parties were driven mostly by switching in and out of abstention or voting for other parties. But that changed somewhat in 2017, which saw the highest level of traffic between the Tories and Labour since BES records began.[3] This illustrated the disruptive potential of Brexit, which was already providing a powerful reason for Labour Leavers and Conservative Remainers to switch all the way across. Even then, however, many who had previously voted Labour seemed set to defect but, in the final weeks of the 2017 campaign, were drawn back from the brink.

Table 6.2 records the flow of the vote between 2017 and 2019 and shows that both of the two major parties lost more votes to the other parties combined than to their main rival. Nevertheless, by historical standards, Labour-to-Conservative switching continued at a brisk pace. It looks as if many Leavers who had been tempted by the Conservatives in 2017 took the plunge in 2019. By contrast, just 4 per cent of those who had voted Tory

Table 6.2 Flow of the vote, June 2017–December 2019

Vote in 2017	Vote in 2019 (%)							
	Con	*Lab*	*Lib Dem*	*SNP*	*Plaid*	*Green*	*Brexit Party*	*number*
Con	85	4	7	0	0	1	2	11,238
Lab	12	73	8	2	0	3	2	10,349
Lib Dem	13	18	60	1	0	4	0	2,180
SNP	4	5	2	88	0	1	0	913
Plaid Cymru	20	17	3	0	48	2	9	115
Green	13	27	20	2	0	35	1	566
UKIP	67	4	1	1	0	2	18	662
Did not vote	38	37	13	4	0	4	3	2,947

Source: British Election Study Internet Panel, waves 13 and 19.

in 2017 crossed to Labour. And Labour was much less effective than in 2017 – and not much more effective than the Conservatives – in picking up votes from erstwhile Liberal Democrats, Greens or Welsh or Scottish nationalists. If a Remainer had not been won over by Labour in 2017, there was little chance that he or she would be in 2019.

Of course, we can only infer the influence of Brexit on the patterns in Table 6.1. This inference is more direct, though, in the case of UKIP and Nigel Farage's new vehicle, the Brexit Party. Those results are obviously affected by the latter's decision to stand only in Labour-held seats. Even so, the mass migration from UKIP to the Conservatives is striking. These staunchest of Eurosceptics were much likelier to go with Boris Johnson than with Farage. Considering that Leavers already dominated among 2017 Conservative voters, the fact that only 2 per cent of that group defected to the Brexit Party is another sign of how effectively the Tories presented themselves as *the* party of Brexit.

Another sign of a Brexit effect is in the results for those who did not turn out in 2017. In recent elections, non-voters have leaned appreciably to Labour (if asked which party they *would have* voted for) and so the party usually gains when abstainers return to the polls.[4] This is because, over the past twenty years or so, non-voters in Britain have come disproportionately from the poorer, working-class backgrounds that tend to give more support to left-wing parties.[5] Yet those who voted in 2019 having abstained two years earlier split evenly between the two parties. The likely reason is that the Conservatives have made headway among voters of lower socioeconomic status – and the likely reason for that is Brexit.

To substantiate that speculation, and to examine the demographic and social basis of 2019 voting more generally, we can draw on the Ipsos MORI series 'How Britain Voted'. Table 6.3 first confirms the sheer scale of the age divide. The youngest and oldest age groups look almost like one-party states: the over-65s were as allergic to Labour as 18–24-year-olds were to the Conservatives. That youngest age group is the only group in the table to have swung to Labour from the Conservatives since 2017 – against a national swing the other way of 5 points.

Meanwhile, the differences across social classes, already meagre in 2017, narrowed even further in 2019.[6] Conservative gains and Labour losses were

Table 6.3 Voting and turnout by social groups, 2019 (%)

	Con	Lab	Lib Dem	Lab–Con swing	Turnout
Age					
18–24	19	62	9	−4	51
25–34	27	51	11	+3	60
35–44	36	39	13	+7	59
45–54	46	28	14	+8	69
55–64	49	27	11	+3	72
65+	64	17	11	+6	80
Gender					
Female	43	34	12	+4	65
Male	46	31	12	+6	68
Ethnicity					
White	48	29	12	+7	68
BAME	20	64	12	+5	54
Education					
No qualifications	59	23	7	+10	64
Other qualifications	47	33	10	+4	64
Degree or higher	34	39	17	+5	74
Occupational class					
AB	45	30	16	+3	75
C1	45	32	12	+5	70
C2	47	32	9	+6	65
DE	41	39	9	+6	58
Housing tenure					
Owned outright	57	22	12	+5	76
Mortgaged	43	33	14	+4	70
Social renter	33	45	7	+10	57
Private renter	31	46	11	+4	55

Source: Ipsos MORI, 'How Britain voted in the 2019 election', available at: www.ipsos. com/ipsos-mori/en-uk/how-britain-voted-2019-election, last accessed 26 June 2021.

largest among those in manual occupations (C2s and DEs) and, so, unlike in 2017, the Tories won across the social-class board. BES investigators, using an alternative (and probably superior) measure of class, reach a dramatic conclusion: the Conservative lead in 2019 was actually larger among the working class than among the professional and managerial middle class.[7]

The impact of age is visible elsewhere in Table 6.3. While it might be concluded that class voting lives on but via housing tenure rather than occupation, a more mundane explanation is that homeowners are older and renters are younger. A parallel argument can be made concerning educational qualifications. While much has been made of the positive correlations between education – especially university education – and Labour and Liberal Democrat voting, the differences look much less dramatic when age is held constant. Considering only the under-35s, Labour support was 56 per cent among those with a degree but barely lower, at 51 per cent, among those with no qualifications. By contrast, among those aged 55 and over with a degree, the Conservatives held a 25-point lead over Labour. While education thus had some impact over and above age, the latter was much the more potent influence in 2019.

It is worth pausing to reflect on just how sharp a break all this marks from even the relatively recent past. The 1987 election provides a useful comparison, being around a generation ago and seeing a similar margin of Conservative victory. Figure 6.1 shows how far the relative influence of social class and age over party choice has changed between the two elections. Despite the much discussed dealignment of the 1970s, during which it became more difficult to predict vote choice based on social class, in 1987 there was still a strong association between the two. The Conservatives were a long way clear among non-manual workers (ABC1s) but well adrift among semi-skilled and unskilled manual workers. In contrast, age was largely irrelevant for the Labour–Conservative battle in 1987, with only a hint of younger voters' tendency to be more Labour. By 2019, knowing someone's date of birth was far more useful in predicting their vote than knowing their occupation or, for that matter, their income. Famously, Peter Pulzer in 1967 wrote that 'Class is the basis of British party politics; all else is embellishment and detail.'[8] Yet the class differences in voting during the 1960s were no larger than the age differences shown in Table 6.3.

This break from the past was vividly illustrated on election night. It was studded with declarations of Conservative gains in seats that Labour had held, usually with thumping majorities, since 1945. Even during Labour's struggles in the 1980s, it would have been almost unthinkable for the party to lose seats like Leigh in Greater Manchester, Bolsover in Derbyshire, Don Valley in South Yorkshire and Bishop Auckland in County Durham. But what became known as the 'red wall' came tumbling down. This term was

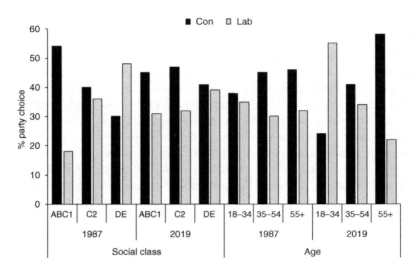

Figure 6.1 Social class, age and party choice in 1987 and 2019
Source: Ipsos MORI, 'How Britain voted in the 2019 election', available at: www.ipsos.
com/ipsos-mori/en-uk/how-britain-voted-2019-election, last accessed 26 June 2021; and
'How Britain voted since October 1974', available at: https://www.ipsos.com/ipsos-
mori/en-uk/how-britain-voted-october-1974, last accessed 26 June 2021.

coined to refer to the line of seats reaching from North Wales to South Yorkshire via Merseyside and Greater Manchester.[9] It was soon stretched to take
in any predominantly working-class constituency across the North and
Midlands in which Labour had a record of success.[10] In 2019 it became the
modish synonym for Labour's heartlands.

The term 'heartlands' was probably due for replacement. Affection for
Labour in these seats had been waning for a long time. This was partly
because the sociological soil in which Labour allegiance took root – heavy
industry, unionised workforces, council housing – had been eroded by industrial decline, social mobility and government policy. But it was not just the
voters who had changed. 'New Labour' under Tony Blair moved decisively
to the ideological centre ground, seeking a catch-all appeal, winning votes
but losing enthusiasm among those who had preferred the redder-blooded
outlook of 'Old Labour'. Moreover, it stopped looking and sounding like a
working-class party: Labour avoided referring to social class and both the
parliamentary party and party membership became dominated by middle-
class graduates.[11]

A growing number of former Labour supporters were therefore either
voting for the party out of habit or simply not voting at all. Even amid the
landslide victories in 1997 and 2001, there were warning signs for Labour

as turnout fell precipitously in its supposed heartlands. What very few disillusioned Labour voters were doing at the time, however, was switching to the Conservatives. Indeed, 'not the blue wall' is a better if less catchy label for these seats, because they were distinguished less by affection for Labour and more by an ongoing aversion to the Tories. The 'red wall' declarations were startling not so much because Labour lost but because the Conservatives won.

Dramatic though they were on the night, those results were really just an expression of what campaign polling (summarised in Table 6.3) had told us. Just as social class was proving little use in predicting whether a voter chose Conservative or Labour, so the proportion of working-class voters in a constituency proved not to be a statistically significant predictor of the gap between Conservative and Labour vote shares.[12] What did predict this gap, then? Table 6.3 again points the way. The Conservatives outpolled Labour where there were more pensioners, fewer minority ethnic voters, fewer graduates and more homeowners. One consequence was a strengthening of the familiar association between population density and party support. However, the divide is not a simple one between rural and urban areas. That profile of Conservative strongholds – older, whiter areas with less inward mobility – describes Britain's small and medium sized towns as much as its countryside.[13] In particular, it describes those four bricks in the 'red wall' listed above. Post-industrial towns like Doncaster, Leigh, Bolsover and Bishop Auckland had seen a pronounced ageing of their population in the past few decades, and that, coupled with the shift recorded in Figure 6.1, made them far more receptive to the Conservatives.[14] Since 56 per cent of the population of England and Wales lives in what the Office for National Statistics defines as towns, the electoral advantage is clear.[15] Labour cannot win by cities alone but was reduced to not much more than that in 2019.

Needless to say, the demographic drift that made towns more Conservative and cities more Labour dates back much further than 2016. We return to a recurring theme: that Brexit hastened processes that were already under way. A quicker way to summarise the redrawing of Britain's electoral map in 2019 is to say that the Conservatives gained most and Labour lost most in seats where more people voted Leave. However, these were also seats in which the Conservatives had gained at Labour's expense in the 2010 and 2015 elections.[16] And Labour had been strengthening its grip on urban areas long before the EU flags started flying over their younger, more educated and more ethnically diverse populations.

Another sign that this is not only about Brexit comes from the fate of the handful of Labour incumbents who in October 2019 had defied the party line and publicly backed Boris Johnson's revised Brexit deal. None of these MPs polled better than would have been forecast based on the estimated

Leave vote and demographic profile of their seat (and two – Ronnie Campbell in Blyth Valley and Melanie Onn in Great Grimsby – actually suffered bigger swings to the Conservatives than statistical models would have predicted). Of course, this is partly testament to the dominance of party over candidate in British voters' thinking. Leave supporters unhappy with Labour's Remain stance found little consolation in their local MP's defiance. Nevertheless, the lack of any bonus for that defiance suggests that the specifics of the issue were swept aside by a general incoming tide against Labour, even if Brexit triggered its biggest waves.

The Brexit factor

Analyses of the social basis of voting are instructive but incomplete. People do not vote for a party simply because they are a certain age or because they rent their home. In a landmark study of social cleavages and voting in Europe, it was shown that social groups would translate into political divisions only if, first, those groups had clearly different interests or issue positions and, second, parties or other campaigning organisations gave expression to these differences.[17] Class was the basis for voting in post-war Britain because working- and middle-class voters had diverging interests on left–right issues like redistribution and nationalisation, and because trade unions as well as the Labour Party made an explicit appeal to working-class voters.

Brexit did not bring about the differences in attitudes between young and old, or graduates and non-graduates, but it was crucial in politicising them. First, the 2016 referendum campaign and vote split the British electorate into two camps: Leavers and Remainers.[18] Then the subsequent politics, driven by the logic of Westminster's two-party system and adversarial institutions, brought the Conservatives and Labour slowly into line with those camps. So, even if Brexit deepened existing divides rather than created new ones, it would be silly to deny its centrality to the 2019 election.

In their seminal work on British voting, David Butler and Donald Stokes laid out four conditions that must be met if an issue is to have a significant effect on an election outcome: (1) the issue must matter to voters; (2) the leading parties must take different positions on the issue; (3) voters must choose the party that shares their position; and (4) opinion on the issue must be skewed in one direction or the other.[19]

Brexit passes the first test with flying colours. Every poll placed Brexit top or, as the campaign progressed, sometimes a close second to the NHS on voters' agendas. In Lord Ashcroft's exit poll of some 13,000 voters, 57 per cent said that either 'Getting Brexit done' or 'Stopping Brexit' was for them an important issue 'when it came to deciding how to vote in the general election'. Brexit was also by some distance the most talked-about issue in the press and especially on television.[20] Sky News even straplined it 'The Brexit Election' from the outset. The second condition was also fulfilled, and more clearly so than in 2017. BES respondents were asked after each election to place the parties on a scale from 0 ('unite fully with the EU') to 10 ('protect our independence from the EU'). In 2017, Labour was placed at 3.8 and the Conservatives at 6.6, neither all that far from the middle point. By 2019, the corresponding placements were 3.1 and 7.9, indicating that both parties were perceived as having moved towards opposing poles.

Table 6.4 confirms that the third condition was met too. Around four in five voters (77 per cent of Leavers and 80 per cent of Remainers) voted for a party that took their view on the issue. By that yardstick, 2017 had also been a Brexit election but not to the same extent. About a quarter of Leavers had voted Labour in 2017, and the same proportion of Remainers had voted Conservative. As the right-hand columns in the table show, at least one in three voters in those 'cross-pressured' groups – Labour Leavers and Conservative Remainers – resolved the inconsistency by switching in 2019 to a party that shared their Brexit preference.

The fourth condition is the stumbling block. Opinion on Brexit had been split almost 50:50 since the referendum, as Nicholas Allen describes in Chapter 1. If anything, Remain was slightly ahead by 2019. Table 6.4 further confirms that Remainers were just as determined as Leavers to vote along Brexit lines. The upshot is that in 2019, as in 2017, more British voters supported Remain parties than Leave parties. Under a proportional electoral system, the parliamentary wrangling over whether and how to leave the EU

Table 6.4 Voting in the 2017 and 2019 general elections by EU referendum vote (%)

	2017		2019		2019	
	All Leave	All Remain	All Leave	All Remain	Lab 2017 Leave	Con 2017 Remain
Con	65	24	73	19	32	66
UKIP/Brexit	4	0	4	0	6	0
Leave party	69	24	77	19	38	66
Lab	24	55	14	49	53	9
Lib Dems	3	12	3	21	4	21
SNP/Plaid	2	5	2	6	1	1
Green	1	2	2	4	2	2
Remain party	30	74	21	80	60	33

Source: British Election Study Internet Panel.

would still be in full swing. Under majoritarian Westminster rules, there is an alternative version of Butler and Stokes's fourth condition: 'Opinion on the issue must be skewed OR voters on one side must be more unified around a single party'. The second clause explains how the Leave side ended up with a majority of more than 80 seats: they were much more unified around the Conservatives.[21] Not even half of Remainers voted Labour in 2019.

The Conservatives had a built-in advantage because there were more parties on the Remain side all along. Moreover, the Liberal Democrats, the SNP and Plaid Cymru had purer Remain credentials than Labour. But the Conservatives could not take Leave votes for granted. UKIP's impressive performance in 2015 had already demonstrated that, warning the Tories against dismissing their humbling in the European Parliament elections of May 2019 as a flash in a proportional-representation pan. Only with an unambiguously pro-Brexit stance could the Tories be sure to hold off a damaging revolt on the right and tempt across those Leavers who in 2017 had drifted back to Labour.

The risk was that the Conservatives would lose Remainers. While campaign coverage and commentary focused obsessively on the threat to Labour incumbents in Leave-inclined seats, much less attention was paid to leafier Tory strongholds that were majority Remain. There was no talk of a 'blue wall'. Yet the Conservatives did lose Remainers – one in three of them – and, as a result, came too close for comfort to losing seats like Chingford and Woodford Green, Winchester and, most spectacularly, the foreign secretary Dominic Raab's seat of Esher and Walton, where a majority of nearly 29,000 in 2015 shrunk to less than 3,000. However, in an echo of Table 6.2, the Conservatives held on to more of their Remainers (66 per cent) than Labour did with its Leavers (53 per cent), and when they did lose them, it was rarely straight to their other side but more often to the Liberal Democrats.

How might we summarise all this? First, the Conservatives outperformed Labour when it came to securing votes on their side of the Brexit debate. Second, they also outperformed Labour when it came to winning votes from those on the other side of the debate. This one–two combination is hard to explain by Brexit alone. The Tories' hardline stance can account for the first but not the second. The same is true of Labour's more ambivalent stance. If the electorate was so polarised over Brexit that Labour was too Remain for all but 14 per cent of Leavers, then how did the Conservatives win 19 per cent of Remainers? The obvious explanation is that there were other factors that made the Conservatives more attractive than Labour in the 2019 election, factors unrelated to Brexit and relevant to both Leavers and Remainers.

Labour's strategy in the run-up to the election was the subject of constant debate, as discussed in Chapter 3. Some in the party called for a full-blown

Remain stance to keep voters from drifting to other Remain parties, notably the Liberal Democrats, whose slogan 'Bollocks to Brexit' planted their flag firmly at one pole of the debate. Others insisted that Labour needed an unambiguous acceptance of the referendum result if it was to shore up the 'red wall'. The truth was that either would have meant both gains and losses.[22] A different approach would have affected *which* Labour candidates were elected but not so much *how many* made it to Westminster. Certainly, no plausible scenario involved anything like the net gains needed to reverse the outcome. The reason is again that Labour's baseline popularity in 2019 was too low. The party was already unpopular among many of those Remainers who drifted off to the Liberal Democrats or Greens. Labour had also alienated much of the base that might otherwise have responded positively to hearing it say 'Bollocks to Remain'.[23]

The rest of this chapter is devoted to identifying those various factors that, independent of Brexit, gave the Conservatives a winning advantage in 2019. Before that, it is worth noting two more Brexit-specific contributions to that advantage. Both follow from the fact that Leavers have tended all along to care a little more about the EU issue.[24] In the Ashcroft exit poll, 64 per cent of those who had voted Leave in 2016 cited Brexit as one of the most important issues when they voted in 2019. Only 37 per cent of Remainers did so. First, then, we might expect Leavers to be more united around a 'get Brexit done' party than Remainers, who, while supporting an anti-Brexit party, drew on other considerations to decide on which one. An even more telling sign of Remainers' dwindling commitment to the Brexit issue comes from breaking down that issue-priority question by past vote. Of Remainers who had voted Conservative in 2017, an extraordinary 32 per cent actually endorsed 'Getting Brexit done' as one of the major issues for them when voting in 2019, more than the 23 per cent who mentioned 'Stopping Brexit'. If this was about quixotically accepting Brexit because the democratic contract required as much, then no one told 2017 Labour Remainers, only 4 per cent of whom cited 'Getting Brexit done'. Rather, those Remainers who had remained broadly pragmatic on Brexit were ready to admit defeat and get it over with. And the Conservatives looked a better bet than Labour to those voters who just wanted the Brexit issue swept quickly off the table.

Ideological proximity

The emotional intensity of the EU referendum and its aftermath stands in stark contrast to the indifference and inattention that characterised British public opinion on Europe for most of the preceding forty years. Whatever drives the ongoing feud between Leavers and Remainers, it is clearly not the details of fishing quotas or qualified majority voting. What is it about, then? A detailed answer to that question is provided in Chapter 5, by Maria Sobolewska. For the present purposes of mapping the ideological space and assessing how close the parties were to the voters in 2019, two points are worth picking out.

First, the Brexit issue is largely uncorrelated with the economic left–right spectrum that was the dominant divide in British politics for most of the last century. This is why it has created such havoc in a largely two-party system based around that economic dimension. Insofar as Leave and Remain are now seen as right- and left-wing respectively, it is because they have slowly become associated with the major parties of the economic right and left respectively. But this process happened because those parties changed, not because the issue has any more to do with left–right than it ever did.

Second, Brexit is instead much more closely aligned with a second ideological dimension. This cross-cutting spectrum has had more names than a royal baby: libertarian vs. authoritarian; social liberalism vs. conservatism; authoritarian populism vs. cosmopolitanism; 'somewhere's vs. 'anywhere's; nationalism vs. internationalism; open vs. closed; even, in one pioneering if eccentric 1950s study, tough-minded vs. tender-minded. Nevertheless, there is broad agreement about the kinds of values and outlooks that underlie this dimension and also that the dimension has long been needed to provide an adequate mapping of British public opinion. The proliferation of names just reflects the variety of issues that seem to align with the dimension. And Brexit has become pre-eminent among them. There is no logical reason why a Leaver would be keener on longer prison sentences or a Remainer more inflamed by gender inequality, but any observer of the Brexit debate would predict exactly that and be right much more often than not. These issues are ideologically intertwined.

Figure 6.2 shows where voters saw themselves and the six largest parties in 2019 as being located in this two-dimensional ideological space. The basis is four policy scales from the pre-election wave of the BES Internet Panel. Respondents placed themselves and the parties on 0–10 scales measuring attitudes to redistribution of wealth, taxes and spending, immigration and Britain's relationship with the EU.[25] The first two scales comprise the economic left–right dimension, the second two what is called here the nationalist–internationalist dimension. This label reflects not only the scales used but also, given the prominence of those issues, the way in which the vertical dimension is relevant in today's politics.

None of the parties was very close to the average voter. The Liberal Democrats were well placed in terms of economics but far too internationalist. The same was true of the Greens and the SNP (although, in the latter's

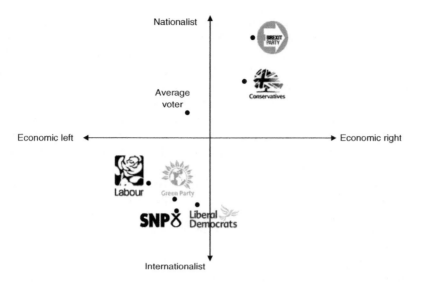

Figure 6.2 Mean placements of voters and parties on two ideological dimensions, 2019

Source: British Election Study Internet Panel, waves 17–18. Party positions are based on responses to questions posed in waves 17 and 18 of the British Election Study Internet survey. Positions on the economic dimension reflect respondents' perceptions of the parties' positions on two items relating to redistribution and tax and spending. Positions on the International dimension reflect perceptions of the parties' positions on two items relating to the EU and immigration.

defence, the average Scottish voter is a little further south west than the average British voter). The Brexit Party was widely seen as an extreme nationalist party. As for the two leading parties, the electorate was a lot tougher on Brexit and immigration than Labour, but well to the left of the Conservatives on economics. Overall, then, the 2019 election was not a triumph of policy representation. What matters here, though, is which of the two major parties was at least *closer* to voters. The answer is not obvious from the diagram but is easily calculated via Pythagoras's theorem. On these 0–10 axes, the Conservatives were 2.6 and Labour 3.2 points from the average voter. This greater ideological proximity is part of the reason why the Conservatives won in 2019.

In practice, however, the Conservatives' advantage here was greater than that. They were somewhat closer to voters overall but markedly closer on what *mattered* in 2019. The Pythagorean calculation gives both dimensions equal weight but, in the political world, their relative importance varies across voters and parties, and over time. The central claim here is that 2019 was a vertical more than a horizontal election. If voters were mainly looking up and down rather than left to right, then they will have seen the Conservatives as a good deal closer than Labour. In more concrete terms, if the 2019 election was about whether to 'get Brexit done' and reduce immigration, then the average voter preferred Conservative policy. The broadening of the vertical dimension beyond Brexit is important here. After all, Remain and Leave was still a 50:50 split. But Remainers were not all liberal internationalists. Many were more like Leavers when it came to other vertical issues, like immigration or gender equality.[26] These voters were ideologically closer to the Tories, and many went on to vote Conservative.

Why was 2019 a 'vertical election'? Part of the answer is obvious: Brexit's dominance of the agenda. However, as with the sociological realignment of voting, Brexit also accelerated existing trends towards more vertical competition in British party politics.[27] Historic immigration from the Commonwealth had already meant growing ethnic diversity; then there was an unexpectedly large influx of migration from the EU in the mid-2000s. Both of these brought immigration closer to the top of the agenda. Another was the expansion of university education, creating large cohorts of graduates who were typically more liberal and cosmopolitan in outlook than their parents and grandparents. Issues like immigration and crime began to figure more prominently on the agenda in British elections alongside perennial concerns like the economy and public services.

What limited the electoral importance of the vertical dimension before 2019 was the behaviour of the two major parties. Both represented voters from up and down that spectrum – there were authoritarian Labour supporters and liberal Conservatives – and so neither party was keen to commit to a position. This reluctance became palpable during the EU referendum campaign; it became unsustainable in its aftermath. Brexit thus made the 2019 election vertical in two connected ways: it brought issues relating to the nationalist–internationalist dimension to the top of voters' agendas *and* it obliged the parties to compete on that dimension. One striking feature of Figure 6.2 is that the parties are more spread out vertically than horizontally. Voters saw greater choice on that dimension than in the economic left–right options. Even Labour and the Conservatives, whose *raisons d'être* and competition over the past century had been based predominantly on the economic left–right battle, were placed just as far apart vertically as they were horizontally. This is all the more striking given that Labour was widely seen as obfuscating on Brexit while putting forward one of the most economically left-wing manifestos in the party's history.

Another Brexit effect here is worth highlighting. The referendum turned positions on the vertical dimension into allegiances. These Remain and

Leave identities are now at least as strong as party allegiances and at least as emotionally charged.[28] Divisions within the electorate are never as heated as their distorted online versions can imply. Nevertheless, the broader value conflict escalated by the Brexit referendum and Brexit process is one in which the other side is not just disagreed with but disparaged or even damned. Leavers are denigrated as racist boors on one side, Remainers as hypocritical snowflakes on the other, all just as ferociously as people hissed 'socialist' and 'fascist' at each other during the left–right conflicts of the 1980s.

A somewhat different question is: why was 2019 a more vertical election than 2017? A Brexit election had been widely heralded in 2017, too, but Labour's resurgence was based on refocusing the campaign from Brexit on to the classic horizontal issues of public services and austerity.[29] The fact that that resurgence won back Leavers as well as Remainers underlines the point.[30] Labour's strategy in 2019 was again to try to drag the agenda back on to left–right issues (on which it was advantaged), especially the NHS, and they enjoyed at least some success, with health climbing alongside Brexit in many issue-priority polls as election-day approached.[31] But 2019 still felt more of a Brexit election, a point widely cited by senior Labour figures as the reason for the heavy defeat.[32]

There are at least two reasons why we might have expected a more vertical election in 2019 than in 2017. One is that Brexit identities and enmities strengthened during the two and a half years of negotiations and parliamentary antics between the two elections. Far from receding into the distance, Brexit loomed ever larger. Another is the change of Tory leadership, in which Boris Johnson, a leading light from the Leave campaign, replaced Theresa May, an unenthusiastic Remainer. That change, described by Thomas Quinn in Chapter 2, was accompanied by the shift to a harder Brexit stance. However, there are also two reasons to question whether the two elections were really so different and whether the 2017 election was as horizontal as is often inferred from the Labour recovery. BES analysis confirmed that the cultural dimension (a similar combination of immigration, EU and liberal–authoritarian attitudes) was more or less as powerful as the economic dimension in predicting choices between Labour and Conservative.[33] This was a marked change from 2015, when the economic dimension had clearly predominated. Brexit is the obvious reason for the change. Second, there were reasons beyond ideology for Labour's rally. In 2017, to the surprise of many commentators, voters' evaluations of Labour and Jeremy Corbyn improved rapidly during the campaign: both party and leader became more widely seen as likeable and competent. The starkest contrast between 2017 and 2019 is the complete absence of this recovery in the latter election.

The competence question

The story on election night was one of Labour haemorrhaging votes in seats that had voted predominantly Leave. But there was no flip side of gains in Remain areas. Labour lost votes in 616 of the 631 seats that it contested. The same point can be made with polling data. Leave voters swung by 9 points from Labour to the Conservatives. There was no swing back to Labour among Remainers. If middle-class graduates in their 30s and 40s had swung to Labour while working-class non-graduates in their 60s and 70s swung to the Conservatives, little would have changed from 2017. But, as Table 6.3 has already confirmed, the Remainer rally to Labour did not happen.

This is the pattern we would expect if, while Brexit pulled Leavers towards the Conservatives and Remainers towards Labour, there was a separate force pulling both Leavers and Remainers towards the Conservatives. That force was the party's competence advantage. Everyone likes competence. Everyone wants the economy managed well. No one likes a divided or ideologically extreme party. Voters use these as danger signs about a party's likely performance in government.[34] Figure 6.3 shows the big advantage enjoyed by the Conservatives on various competence criteria in 2019. Their own scorecard was at best mixed but on every count was markedly better than Labour's. Not even three in ten voters saw Labour as fit to govern or trusted the party to handle the economy.

Leadership proved another problem for Labour. As Figure 6.3 shows, Boris Johnson maintained a sizeable lead on the standard polling question of 'who would make the best prime minister?'. Unlike last time around, Jeremy Corbyn's reputation did not improve during the campaign. By polling day in 2017, 48 per cent of BES respondents considered Corbyn a competent leader. By the same point in 2019, just 17 per cent did so. The Conservatives' change of leader improved their position. Admittedly, Boris Johnson did not enjoy especially wide acclaim. His own competence rating of 47 per cent was no higher than Corbyn's two years earlier. Nevertheless, it was enough for a big advantage over the Labour leader in 2019 and represented a noticeable improvement on Theresa May and her polling-day score of 37 per cent. It is worth noting, however, that even a campaign widely seen as calamitous for May still left her 20 points ahead of where Corbyn ended up in 2019.

Do people prefer a party because they think it more competent, or do they think a party is more competent because they already prefer it? There is doubtless plenty of the latter. Nothing but the most blinkered partisanship can explain any Conservative or Labour supporter denying that their party was divided in 2019! Moreover, whether people saw the Tories as

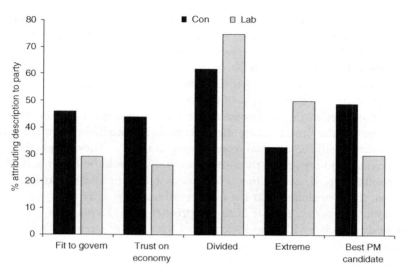

Figure 6.3 Conservative polling leads on competence criteria, November 2019
Source: Ipsos MORI, 'November 2019 political monitor: Topline results', 22 November 2019, available at: www.ipsos.com/sites/default/files/ct/news/documents/2019-11/november_2019_political_monitor_topline_221119.pdf, 26 June 2021, last accessed 26 June 2021. Responses to: 'Who do you think would make the most capable Prime Minister, the Conservatives' Boris Johnson, or Labour's Jeremy Corbyn?' and 'I am going to read out some things both favourable and unfavourable that have been said about various political parties. Which of these, if any, do you think apply to... a) the Labour Party b) the Conservative Party?'

economically competent or as extreme, for example, probably depended heavily on their view of Brexit in general and Johnson's revised withdrawal agreement in particular. But these evaluations, while clearly skewed by political sympathies, are more than just that. For one thing, a large and growing proportion of British voters have no great sympathy for any particular party, and not all voters are ardent Leavers or Remainers. Second, the more negative ratings on division than on extremity suggests that there was some objective assessment of the parties as particularly deeply split in 2019. Third, the Tory percentage-point lead on every one of the five criteria is wider than the margin by which they eventually won the election. Regardless of their own partisan leanings and Brexit preferences, many people saw a competence gap between the two main parties in 2019.

This gap mattered. Perceptions of competence – often referred to as 'valence evaluations' – are important in driving vote choice.[35] They are particularly influential on 'floating' voters, who lack strong partisan or ideological moorings. The valence evaluations of avid partisans, or passionate Remainers or

Leavers, were probably just another expression of those strong feelings and had no power to swing votes that were predetermined anyway. But the voters who decide election outcomes are those who assess the parties afresh each time, and their assessments in 2019 clearly favoured the Conservatives. The advantage shown in Figure 6.3 is thus another important part of the answer to the question posed in the title of this chapter.

It is worth reiterating at this point that there was always a strong valence component to the Brexit debate. Remainers were not all liberal internationalists, ideologically committed to remaining in the EU. They simply thought that Britain, and especially the British economy, would be better served by EU membership. If, conducting a similar cost–benefit analysis at the 2019 election, they concluded that the Conservatives were more likely to deliver economic prosperity, then it is no surprise that they voted for the party despite disagreeing with it on Brexit. The Conservative retention of Remainers due to their fear of the economic consequences of a Labour government was an important reason why the 'blue wall' never came under serious threat.

How do voters judge this capacity to govern? The answer is obviously different for government and opposition parties, since the incumbent party typically has a record by which to be judged. However, the Tories' record was hard to pick out in 2019 given the occlusion of normal politics by Brexit, the hung parliament and the change of prime minister. It somehow felt surprising that there had been a Conservative-led government for nine years: the last few of those years had been so tumultuous and, at times, it had been hard to discern all that much government anyway. Moreover, Boris Johnson had been in office for less than four months when the election campaign began. There was little sense of assessing whether his government had fulfilled its contract with the people. Rather, the election was about whether voters wanted to sign a fresh contract – primarily to 'get Brexit done' – with this administration. This is not to say that the Conservatives paid no 'costs of ruling' for their near decade in office.[36] Both the bumpy political ride of the preceding few years and the definite turn against austerity in the public's policy mood will have contributed to an underlying fatigue with Conservative rule, and the party was not especially popular in absolute terms in 2019.[37] Its handsome victory was won by being more popular than Labour.

As for oppositions, valence evaluations are of necessity based in part on general impressions or images of parties and their leaders: do they *look* competent? Words like 'impression' and 'image' confirm that this is also about how the parties present themselves and are presented by the media. In 2019, as in 2017, there was particular controversy about the coverage of Jeremy Corbyn, which in both elections amounted to a barrage of fierce negativity.[38] For many, the portrayal of Corbyn as an incompetent and probably anti-Semitic leader of an extreme party was the malicious distortion of a hostile media. For many others, it was self-evident truth. While the power of the media is easily overstated, there is sufficient evidence to suggest that this kind of sustained negative coverage has some effect on voters' perceptions of leaders and, in turn, on parties. It is unlikely to have turned the 2019 election but it almost certainly made Labour's task harder and its final result worse.

Exhibit A in the case *against* Labour's claim for damages against the media is what had happened two years earlier. The Conservative press had dished up the same treatment to Jeremy Corbyn during the 2017 campaign, yet his ratings improved sharply in the run-up to polling day. It is hard to argue that the Tory tabloid onslaught, however vitriolic, was the reason why there was no such resurgence in 2019. What, then, were the reasons?

First, there was no longer an element of surprise. For less politically attentive voters, Corbyn was a largely unknown quantity in 2017. Perhaps the one thing they did know about him was that he was widely thought incapable even by many within his own party. It was not hard to surpass expectations in that context. By 2019, voters were more likely to have made up their minds about him, and most had made up their minds in a strongly negative direction. The anti-Semitism scandal hardly helped, but Corbyn's handling of Brexit was probably a more important factor. Always a good deal less popular with Leavers, Corbyn's surge in popularity in 2017 had been primarily among Remainers, but they grew less forgiving of his non-committal approach.[39] The upshot was that he started the 2019 campaign from an appreciably lower base, as shown in Figure 6.4, which follows the likeability ratings of the major parties and leaders into, during and out of the campaigns in 2017 and 2019. The contrast in the two Corbyn trends confirms that the task of changing hostile minds proved much harder than impressing those whose minds were not yet made up.

Figure 6.4 also provides a broader reminder that 2017 jolted what has been called one of the 'truisms' of election campaigns:

> The party ahead in the polls at the beginning is almost always ahead at the end, often by roughly the same amount, and when this is not true, it is usually because of errors in the polls rather than any change in the standing of the parties. All the things that obsess journalists and excite politicians – the leaders' tours, the debates, any 'gaffes', the parties' manifestos – are electorally trivial. When a party wins or loses an election, it is not because of what it did in the weeks of the campaign, but because of more fundamental perceptions about the parties, their policies and the leaders which have built up over the preceding years.[40]

Should we conclude from the right-hand side of the graph that normal service resumed and that the 2019 campaign did not matter? This is a questionable interpretation. The 2017 election served as a reminder that

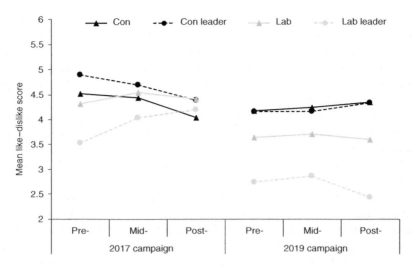

Figure 6.4 Campaign trends in likeability ratings of major parties and leaders, 2017 and 2019
Source: BES Internet Panel, waves 11–13 and 17–19. Responses to: 'How much do you like or dislike each of the following party leaders?'

campaigns always *can* matter; whether they do or not depends on how the campaign evolves. To invoke a footballing analogy, if the two leading contenders for the Premier League play out a draw, then that match, with hindsight, made no difference in the title race – but we would not conclude that such matches do not matter. Another perspective is offered by this chapter's predecessor in the 2017 volume. Explaining why the Tories won but lost their majority, its author argues that the 'trends in both major parties' poll ratings suggest that their vote shares were returning to their long-term levels based on the policy mood, economic conditions and satisfaction with the government's record'.[41] This reasserts the orthodoxy that it is the fundamentals that matter. Campaigns serve to activate them. The problem for Labour in 2019 was that those fundamentals were against the party. There are again signs of this in Figure 6.4: while Labour entered both the 2017 and 2019 campaigns on a similar poll rating, the party's underlying popularity was markedly lower in the latter election. The poll rating never really recovered.

Where next?

The Conservatives' competence advantage was described in the introduction as one pillar underpinning their victory in 2019. While it was indeed important, the word 'pillar' implies a misleading solidity. Valence reputations can crumble quickly. In particular, as the author of the next chapter puts it, the line between 'they're doing the best they can' and 'this is a shambles' can be a fine one.[42] With covid-19 and its economic aftermath to contend with, the new Conservative administration faces stiff tests of its governing competence. The early signs are that the handling of the pandemic has dented both the prime minister's and his party's ratings but has not written them off in the way that 'Black Wednesday' in 1992 did the Conservatives' reputation, especially for economic competence.[43] Conversely, Labour's new leader Sir Keir Starmer has enjoyed improving evaluations since taking the job, overtaking Boris Johnson on perceived competence within six months of the election, but has had no transformative effect on his party's ratings.[44]

One reason why the major parties' poll standing may not move fast, even in a volatile political environment, is the brake applied by Brexit. The continuing effect of this issue, and the wider realignment that it crystallised, is still visible in the polls just cited. Boris Johnson's ratings have taken a hit but, for all the talk about covid-19 hitting the new Tory seats particularly hard, he remains markedly more popular among working-class voters outside London and among non-graduates – in short, among Leavers.

But what about the consequences of the UK finally leaving the EU and negotiating a post-Brexit trade deal with the bloc? Will that prompt British electoral politics slowly to rotate back towards the horizontal? Much will depend on the relative importance of new identity conflicts in British politics, conflicts that 'pit graduates against school leavers, ethnic minorities against white nationalists, old against young'.[45] Given that Brexit escalated rather than created those conflicts, there is no reason to suppose that they will go away. Attention will turn to other issues that scratch the same ideological itches, as already seen with the Black Lives Matter protests and the ensuing arguments about statues of historic figures with racist pasts.[46] All that said, as the heat of Brexit very slowly subsides, there will at least be more bandwidth for economic issues. What this means for voting depends in part on whether the Conservatives can fulfil their commitments to 'levelling up' those poorer regions and communities disproportionately affected by covid-19. That shift to the left would offer the party some insurance against a resumption of horizontal competition.

Insofar as politics remains more vertical than horizontal, there will remain an advantage for the Conservatives, at least in the short-to-medium term. What of the long term? The answer depends on a question invariably raised by age divides like that shown in Table 6.3: is this a life-cycle or a generational difference? Are today's older people more Conservative because, as per the old adage, people get more conservative as they get older? Or are they more Conservative because their generation was brought up with more conservative values and will slowly be replaced by generations brought up with more liberal values? The latter implies a steady shift of the average voter down the vertical spectrum – and, other things remaining the same, closer to Labour and the other more internationalist parties. The evidence on this question paints a subtle picture. There is a generational drift down the spectrum towards more liberal or 'socially progressive' attitudes, but the psychological process of ageing shifts individuals upwards, increasing the appeal of parties that appeal to nostalgia and pledge to defend the status quo.[47] The Conservatives have prospered when they have moved slowly with the liberalising tide but remained clearly the more conservative option to attract the (ever growing) older age groups. This is a delicate balance. In 2019, a combination of the reliable support of Leavers and the perceived unfitness of Labour gave them ample margin for error. If Brexit recedes and Labour strengthens, however, it will be a harder balance to maintain.

Notes

1 David Butler and Donald Stokes, *Political Change in Britain: The Evolution of Electoral Preference* (Basingstoke: Macmillan, 1974).
2 Jonathan Mellon, Geoffrey Evans, Edward Fieldhouse, Jane Green and Christopher Prosser, 'Brexit or Corbyn? Campaign and inter-election vote switching in the 2017 UK general election', *Parliamentary Affairs*, 71 (2018), 719–737.
3 Mellon *et al.*, 'Brexit or Corbyn?'.
4 David Denver, Christopher Carman and Robert Johns, *Elections and Voters in Britain* (Basingstoke: Palgrave Macmillan, 2012), pp. 28–52.
5 Geoffrey Evans and James Tilley, *The New Politics of Class* (Oxford: Oxford University Press, 2017), pp. 170–190.
6 John Bartle, 'Why the Conservatives lost their majority – but still won', in Nicholas Allen and John Bartle (eds), *None Past the Post: Britain at the Polls, 2017* (Manchester: Manchester University Press, 2018), pp. 160–189.
7 Geoffrey Evans and Jonathan Mellon, 'The reshaping of class voting', British Election Study, 6 March 2020, available at: www.britishelectionstudy.com/bes-findings/the-re-shaping-of-class-voting-in-the-2019-election-by-geoffrey-evans-and-jonathan-mellon/#.Xv5AYy2ZPOR, last accessed 26 June 2021.
8 Peter G. J. Pulzer, *Political Representation and Elections: Parties in Britain* (London: George Allen and Unwin, 1967), p. 98.
9 James Kanagasooriam, 'How the Labour Party's "red wall" turned blue', *Financial Times*, 14 December 2019, available at: www.ft.com/content/3b80b-2de-1dc2-11ea-81f0-0c253907d3e0, last accessed 26 June 2021.
10 As Lewis Baston irately notes, some commentary also lumped in seats that belonged geographically in that original wall but were not in any sense Labour

fortresses – many were marginal and had been won by the Conservatives in 1992 (e.g. Bury South) or even as recently as 2015 (e.g. Colne Valley). See 'The myth of the red wall', *The Critic*, 18 December 2019, available at: https://thecritic.co.uk/the-myth-of-the-red-wall/, last accessed 26 June 2021.

11 Oliver Heath, 'Policy representation, social representation and class voting in Britain', *British Journal of Political Science*, 45 (2015), 173–193.

12 David Cutts, Matthew Goodwin, Oliver Heath and Paula Surridge, 'Brexit, the 2019 General Election and the realignment of British politics', *Political Quarterly*, 91 (2020), 7–23.

13 Will Jennings and Gerry Stoker, 'The divergent dynamics of cities and towns: Geographical polarisation after Brexit', *Political Quarterly*, 90 (2019), 155–166.

14 Ian Warren and Will Jennings, 'Addressing the needs of towns is key to winning this election', *Conservative Home*, 22 November 2019, available at: www.conservativehome.com/platform/2019/11/ian-warren-and-will-jennings-addressing-the-needs-of-towns-is-key-to-winning-this-election.html, last accessed 26 June 2021.

15 Admittedly, this is an expansive definition: settlements of between 5,000 and 225,000. See Office of National Statistics, 'Understanding towns in England and Wales: An introduction', available at: www.ons.gov.uk/peoplepopulationand-community/populationandmigration/populationestimates/articles/understanding townsinenglandandwales/anintroduction, last accessed 26 June 2021. Labour's prospects become better at the top end of that population range, not least because those larger towns are likelier to contain universities.

16 Paula Surridge, 'Beyond Brexit: Labour's structural problems', *Political Insight*, 11 (2020), 16–19.

17 Seymour Martin Lipset and Stein Rokkan, 'Cleavage structures, party systems, and voter alignments: an introduction', in Seymour Martin Lipset and Stein Rokkan (eds), *Party Systems and Voter Alignments: Cross-National Perspectives* (Toronto: The Free Press, 1967), pp. 1–64.

18 This is much less true of Scotland, where Remain vs. Leave had to fit around a Yes vs. No divide on independence that not only came first but ran deeper. Even there, however, Brexit left an appreciable mark on voters' political identities. See Ailsa Henderson, Robert Johns, Jac Larner and Christopher Carman, 'Scottish Labour as a case study in party failure: Evidence from the 2019 UK General Election in Scotland', *Scottish Affairs*, 29 (2020), 127–140.

19 Butler and Stokes, *Political Change in Britain*, pp. 276–295.

20 David Deacon, Jackie Goode, Dominic Wring, Cristian Vaccari, John Downey, James Stanyer and David Smith, 'What was all that about, then? The media agenda in the 2019 General Election', in Daniel Jackson, Einar Thorsen, Darren Lillete and Nathalie Weidhase (eds), *UK Election Analysis 2019: Media, Voters and the Campaign* (Poole: Centre for Comparative Politics and Media Research, 2020), pp. 96–97.

21 John Curtice, 'Brave new world: Understanding the 2019 general election', *Political Insight*, 11 (2020), 8–12.

22 Ed Fieldhouse, 'Swings and roundabouts: The potential electoral consequences of Labour's position on Europe', British Election Study, 11 September 2017, available at: www.britishelectionstudy.com/bes-findings/swings-and-roundabouts-the-potential-electoral-consequences-of-labours-position-on-europe/#.XvojEy2ZPOQ, last accessed 26 June 2021.

23 Jonathan Mellon, 'Should Labour have united to remain?', British Election Study, 6 March 2020, available at: www.britishelectionstudy.com/uncategorized/should-labour-have-united-to-remain/#.Xv5Jty2ZPOQ, last accessed 26 June 2021.

24 BES data confirm that Leavers, while less interested in politics in general, were more interested in the 2016 referendum than were Remainers.

25 The advantage of this approach is that the parties and voters are placed on exactly the same scales. The disadvantage is that voters' placements of parties are often ill informed and, given the tendency when guessing to opt for the middle point on the scale, biased towards moderation. An alternative approach is that taken by voting advice applications (e.g. www.whogetsmyvoteuk.com/#!/, last accessed 26 June 2021), which base parties' positions on their policy proposals and then ask voters where they stand on the same proposals. While this does indeed push the parties further out to the extremes, it leads to similar conclusions to those drawn here. See Iulia Cioroianu, Micha Germann and Jonathan Wheatley, 'Who to vote for in the 2019 general election: Why Voting Advice Applications help get out the vote', *iNews*, 25 November 2019, available at: https://inews.co.uk/news/who-to-vote-for-in-the-2019-general-election-why-voting-advice-applications-help-get-out-the-vote-366455, last accessed 26 June 2021.

26 Eric Kaufmann, 'Not all Remainers are liberals', *UnHerd,* 19 December 2019, available at: https://unherd.com/2019/12/not-all-remainers-are-liberals/, last accessed 26 June 2021.

27 Again, this territory is covered more thoroughly by Maria Sobolewska in Chapter 5.

28 Sara B. Hobolt, Thomas J. Leeper and James Tilley, 'Divided by the vote: Affective polarization in the wake of the Brexit referendum', *British Journal of Political Science*, FirstView (2020), 1–18: doi:10.1017/S0007123420000125.

29 Bartle, 'Why the Conservatives lost their majority – but still won'.

30 Mellon *et al.*, 'Brexit or Corbyn?'.

31 See Michael Clemence, 'NHS surges to match Brexit in final Issues Index ahead of the 2019 general election', November 2019, available at: www.ipsos.com/ipsos-mori/en-uk/nhs-surges-match-brexit-final-issues-index-ahead-2019-general-election, last accessed 26 June 2021.

32 See BBC News, 'General election 2019: Labour facing long haul, warns McDonnell', 14 December 2019, available at: www.bbc.co.uk/news/election-2019–50794076, last accessed 26 June 2021.

33 Edward Fieldhouse, Jane Green, Geoffrey Evans, Jonathan Mellon, Christopher Prosser, Hermann Schmitt and Cees Van der Eijk, *Electoral Shocks: The Volatile Voter in a Turbulent World* (Oxford: Oxford University Press, 2019), p. 174.

34 Zachary D. Greene and Matthias Haber, 'The consequences of appearing divided: An analysis of party evaluations and vote choice', *Electoral Studies*, 37 (2015),

15–27; Robert Johns and Ann-Kristin Kölln, 'Moderation and competence: How a party's ideological position shapes its valence reputation', *American Journal of Political Science*, 64 (2020), 649–663.

35 Harold D. Clarke, David Sanders, Marianne Stewart and Paul Whiteley, *Performance Politics and the British Voter* (Cambridge: Cambridge University Press, 2009); Jane Green and Will Jennings, *The Politics of Competence* (Cambridge: Cambridge University Press, 2017).

36 The 'costs of ruling' is the tendency for ruling parties to lose a portion of their support, net of all other factors, between successive elections. See Peter Naanstead and Martin Paldam, 'The costs of ruling', in Han Dorussen and Michael Taylor (eds), *Economic Voting* (London: Routledge, 2002), pp. 17–44.

37 For an analysis of how the mood affected the outcome of the 2017 general election, see Bartle, 'Why the Conservatives lost their majority – but still won', pp. 170–172.

38 Dominic Wring and David Deacon, 'The final verdict: patterns of press partisanship', in Jackson *et al.* (eds), *UK Election Analysis 2019*, pp. 104–107.

39 This might seem odd given his own long-standing Euroscepticism. It probably has less to do with perceived betrayal over Brexit and more to do with other issues on the nationalism–internationalism dimension – such as Corbyn's refusal to sing the national anthem and palpable discomfort with Britain's military traditions and symbols – on which he was poles apart from Leavers.

40 Philip Cowley and Dennis Kavanagh, *The British General Election of 2017* (Basingstoke: Palgrave Macmillan, 2018), p. 412.

41 Bartle, 'Why the Conservatives lost their majority – but still won', p. 179.

42 Jane Green, quoted in Miranda Green, 'Boris Johnson can't afford to squander trust by protecting Dominic Cummings', *Financial Times*, 25 May 2020, available at: www.ft.com/content/e32fa314–9e73–11ea-b65d-489c67b0d85d, last accessed 26 June 2021.

43 See Chris Curtis, 'Conservatives still more trusted on economy, but can they hold their lead?', YouGov 17 June 2020; available at: https://yougov.co.uk/topics/politics/articles-reports/2020/06/17/conservatives-still-more-trusted-economy-can-they-, last accessed 26 June 2021.

44 Ben Walker, 'Labour is closing in on the Conservatives but it still faces an electoral Everest', *New Statesman*, 17 June 2020, available at: www.newstatesman.com/politics/uk/2020/06/labour-keir-starmer-popularity-election-boris-johnson-polls, last accessed 26 June 2021.

45 Maria Sobolewska and Robert Ford, 'Brexit and Britain's culture wars', *Political Insight*, 11 (2020), 4–7.

46 According to an Opinium poll conducted on 18–19 June, 71 per cent of Remainers but only 27 per cent of Leavers said that they supported the Black Lives Matter movement in the UK. See Opinium, *The Polling Report*, 18 June 2020, available at: www.opinium.com/wp-content/uploads/2020/06/Opinium-Political-Report-19th-June-2020.pdf, last accessed 26 June 2021.

47 James Tilley and Geoffrey Evans, 'Ageing and generational effects on vote choice: Combining cross-sectional and panel data to estimate APC effects', *Electoral Studies*, 33 (2014), 19–27.

7

2019: a critical election?

Jane Green

When we ask whether 2019 was a critical election, what are we really trying to establish?[1] This question is about whether an enduring electoral realignment has taken place in Britain, and, if so, *how* the realignment has taken place and whether the decisive point in that process was the 2019 general election. The question demonstrates how we might easily misunderstand the 2019 British general election, a contest that Boris Johnson sought to 'get Brexit done' and which finally secured the Conservative parliamentary majority necessary to pass the EU withdrawal agreement. The question also requires us to think about any realignment in the context of the long-term trend in partisan dealignment in the electorate.[2] Has an electoral alignment provided a new form of stability in electoral behaviour, replacing the once deeper, socialised party attachments that used to characterise British elections?

The question is also important for our national political parties. Interpreting what happened – and did not happen – in the 2019 election will determine how they respond and what happens next. Parties implement the lessons of electoral victories and losses. They adapt their strategies and policies and change leaders. Learning the right lessons, therefore, has important long-term political consequences. The wrong lessons are likely to be learned if attention is focused only on the *outcomes* of elections – for example, the Conservatives' loss of their majority in 2017 (characterised as Theresa May's 'disastrous' campaign) and their success in winning a comfortable majority in 2019 (characterised as Boris Johnson's 'triumphant' campaign). Such a limited comparison risks writing off the underlying changes that were highly significant in the one and exaggerating the degree to which one dramatic change affected the other. It also risks missing the significance of pre-existing trends and systemic dynamics.

We can also ask whether the alignment that now exists in the British electorate is likely to persist. If it does, how do our political parties respond to it? Should they change their appeals or should they simply wait for it to pass, and for 'normal' politics to resume?[3] Whether or not 2019 was a critical election is, then, an important and timely question for our understanding of British politics and British elections.

Because of its importance, and the way the election could be misread, the question makes for an obvious potential exam question. Fittingly, there's even evidence of a potential 'split' among academics, which is always a great place to start an answer to any exam question. For the sake of simplicity, one view is that Brexit was a defining moment – an 'electoral shock' – that was the primary cause of a fundamental restructuring of vote choice.[4] Another view is that the realignment has been gradual and long-term, resulting from the fragmentation of Labour's class-based electoral coalition and the geographic tilting of the political axis that began *prior* to the EU referendum.[5] Neither of these views requires that the 2019 general election was the election in which the electorate realigned (thereby making it *the* 'critical election'), nor do they reject the idea that there has been a realignment. However, it *has* been argued that 2019 was *not* a critical election, because the election result was built on processes underway long beforehand.[6] Academics agree that there has been a fundamental shift in the relationship between both attitudes and demographics and vote choice. Put simply, vote choice used to be strongly structured by a primary traditional left–right axis that was rooted in social class and in turn shaped traditional partisan alignments. That pattern has now changed. Cultural, or second-dimension, issues are now more important than before and rooted in different demographics defined by age and education. Labour has lost a great deal of support in its traditional working-class constituencies and communities as a result.

Why might we think 2019 *was* a critical election, and why is this question being posed? The answer lies in the 2019 general-election campaign and in the result. It was the election to 'get Brexit done', the election that finally delivered the Conservatives a comfortable parliamentary majority, the election where many of Labour's traditional heartland seats fell dramatically to the Conservatives and the election where – in a stunning reversal – more working-class voters supported the Conservatives than Labour.[7] It was also the election that finally made possible Britain's withdrawal from the EU, and in doing so delivered Brexit.

In this chapter I set out a framework for thinking about whether the 2019 general election can be viewed as a critical election. I first consider what we mean by a critical election. I then summarise the evidence for an electoral realignment, and – as a result – argue that 2017 and 2019 were both critical elections that together resulted in a realignment. These elections were two steps in a process through which Brexit reshaped the electorate. The preconditions for this realignment were helped by the long-term shifts in the electorate, but these were not sufficient to make a major realignment inevitable. For there to be an electoral realignment, the mainstream parties had to compete around a 'second dimension' in British politics, which they ended up doing because of the importance of disagreements about Europe. Brexit, the pre-eminent cultural, or second-dimension, issue, realigned and sorted the electorate along party lines. Insofar that 2019 was a critical election, its main consequence was to increase party sorting among those voters who had backed Leave in the referendum – but not among those who had backed Remain – which benefited the Conservatives and contributed to their large parliamentary majority, as Robert Johns describes in Chapter 6. Whether this asymmetric realignment is likely to be a continued feature of British politics remains to be seen. The political parties must navigate this new electoral configuration in which the second dimension of political competition has created new electoral coalitions, accentuated geographic divides and altered Britain's electoral geography. All of this has taken place in the context of a volatile electorate that has the potential to be more volatile in future.[8] These conditions may yet throw up further surprises, depending on how political actors respond and on the longevity of the realignment. I end by reflecting on some of the implications of our new electoral arrangements for ongoing political competition.

Definitions: critical elections and realignments

We first need to separate the meaning of a 'critical election' from the meaning of an 'electoral realignment', although in many cases these two terms can become entwined. A critical election is a turning-point election that causes or first manifests a realignment: that is, an enduring new pattern of voting behaviour around demographics and attitudes. The last example of a critical election in the UK context was the landslide general election of 1997, when Labour transformed its support base by attracting middle-class former Conservative voters under the then Labour leader, Tony Blair.[9] The concept of a 'critical election' was defined much earlier, by V.O. Key, who specified the criteria for critical elections as:

> elections in which voters are, at least from impressionistic evidence, *unusually deeply concerned*, in which the extent of *electoral involvement is relatively quite high*, and in which the *decisive results of the voting reveal a sharp alteration of the pre-existing cleavage* within the electorate. Moreover, and perhaps this is the truly differentiating characteristic of this sort of election, the realignment made manifest in the voting in such elections seems to *persist for several succeeding elections* [emphases added].[10]

If we adhere closely to this definition, we need several succeeding elections to tell if there has been a realignment and if the preceding election was 'critical'. There has been very little attention paid to the first two criteria, salience and participation, but a great deal of attention has been paid to the third. The 'sharp alteration of the pre-existing cleavage within the electorate' is known as an 'electoral realignment', sometimes a 'critical realignment', or an 'ideological realignment'.[11] Each implies that different issues, attitudes and demographics matter to vote choice, such that new coalitions of voters support political parties, changing the association between demographics and vote choice.[12]

Realignments can also happen gradually, without a critical election. Voters can, for example, gradually move away from some parties and towards others. The relative importance of issues and their influence over party support can change over time. These shifts must happen to a very substantial degree to be considered a meaningful electoral – or critical, or ideological – realignment, or they might lay the foundations for a realignment that takes place later. Why, then, might realignments happen particularly due to critical elections, rather than gradually over time?

Here we need a theory of how an electorate realigns. The reason that critical elections take place is that the electorate has the potential to realign *and* that parties adjust their positions and the social groups they appeal to. The conditions for a critical, realigning election are social, ideological and institutional.[13] There may be new, salient polarising issues that cross-cut traditional ideological divisions, accompanying social change and alterations to the way the voting system maintains or facilitates changes within the party system. Thus, critical elections follow longer-term processes, but there is something about the election itself that translates those processes into a substantial change in voting behaviour. For new issues to matter, and therefore for different demographics to support political parties, parties must appeal on those issues and to those groups, providing a way for new concerns to be expressed by vote choice. Elections are the mechanism through which parties do this, raising awareness and providing political opportunities. If parties do this gradually, we might observe a gradual realignment. If they do it relatively suddenly, we might witness a critical election.

The decisions of politicians are a key factor in how and when realignments take place. Political parties can raise the salience or electoral significance of issues in a process of 'issue evolution' and take distinctive positions on those issues in order to increase their competitiveness.[14] Thomas Quinn notes in Chapter 2 that the Conservative Party eventually took a position on Brexit largely in line with their members' hard-Brexit preferences. Similarly, Paul Whiteley, Harold Clarke and Patrick Seyd in Chapter 3 argue that Labour eventually arrived at a Brexit policy that could unite the warring factions in the Labour Party. A minor party can also try to change the issue basis of party competition and upset the 'dominant party alignment'. UKIP, for example, helped raise the importance of Britain's relationship with the EU and immigration. Arguably, this is only possible when voters are concerned about different issues, or have the potential to be, as suggested by the theory of 'electoral shocks'.

Electoral shocks are events or other changes that 'provide political opportunities and create an imperative for parties and political actors to respond'.[15] The effects of such shocks may be absorbed or they may create major and long-lasting changes in the electorate, shaping subsequent elections. They may even lead to critical elections, where the basis of electoral choice alters such that a realignment takes place. In multi-party competition, 'issue entrepreneurs' try to mobilise by emphasising issues that have been relatively ignored by the mainstream, and by adopting distinctive policy positions that fall outside the status quo.[16] This need not cause a realignment. The issues emphasised and positions adopted by political entrepreneurs could simply divert a small number of votes to minor parties. However, a major realignment could take place if mainstream political parties compete on new issues that are highly salient and upset the dominant party alignment. When mainstream parties capture or incorporate new dimensions, those dimensions become far more important to vote choice such that different demographic groups become associated with political parties. While in principle an electoral realignment could take place as a result of gradual processes of social change, they are invariably politicised and made relevant to vote choice by political actors, usually manifested in a decisive election, or elections.

The realignment of the British electorate

The evidence for a realignment in British politics is provided by the changing relationship between both age and education and vote choice. These two demographics historically divided voters on a less salient 'second dimension', associated with cultural issues. This dimension has now risen in prominence. It has not *replaced* the left–right dimension, which remains important, but British elections have become far more two-dimensional. The greater prominence of cultural issues has meant that age and education predict vote choice more decisively than beforehand. These relationships have been widely reported and are also presented below.[17]

In Figure 7.1, we see how age divided Conservative and Labour voters in 2015, with the youngest age groups tending to back Labour and the oldest groups voting Conservative. We also see that the age–vote choice relationship became far more pronounced in 2017 and 2019. The Conservatives increased their lead among older voters in 2017 and then even more so in 2019, while Labour made substantial gains among younger voters in 2017 and did so to a slightly lesser extent in 2019.

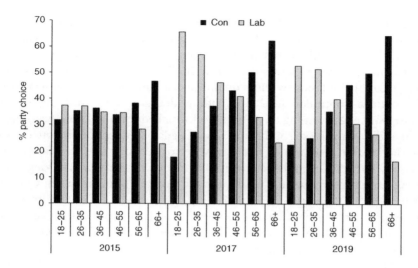

Figure 7.1 Conservative and Labour reported vote by age group, 2015, 2017 and 2019
Source: BES Internet Panel, waves 6, 13 and 19.

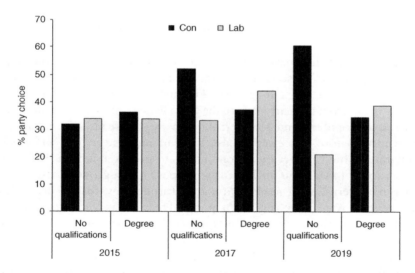

Figure 7.2 Conservative and Labour reported vote by education, 2015, 2017 and 2019
Source: BES Internet Panel, waves 6, 13 and 19.

The association between education and party choice can be seen in Figure 7.2, which compares the reported vote among those with at least an undergraduate degree and those with no formal qualifications. In 2015, the Conservatives did marginally better than Labour among graduates, whereas Labour did marginally better than the Conservatives among voters without qualifications. This pattern switched in 2017, with graduates now tending to vote Labour and those without qualifications tending to vote Conservative. The pattern continued in 2019, with a dramatic and substantial pro-Conservative lead among those with no formal educational qualifications.

In addition to the strengthening role of age and education in vote choice for the two largest parties, there has been a change in the relationship between vote choice and social class (or income).[18] Labour has long been losing support among its working-class voters to other parties or to abstention.[19] At the 2015 general election, for instance, UKIP had its greatest support among working-class voters, but Labour still led the Conservatives among this demographic. The long-term decline in working-class support for Labour subsequently accelerated, and in 2019 the Conservatives enjoyed a clear lead over Labour among working-class voters. As two leading scholars of social class note: 'The historic relationship between being working class and voting Labour, and being middle class and voting Conservative, had reversed in less than five years.'[20]

Long-term evolution *and* short-term disruption

Notwithstanding the question of whether this realignment is enduring, it *has* taken place. It is also clear that the conditions for this sort of realignment have existed for a long time. Labour's working-class voters were moving away from the party before the 2015 general election, and divisions between metropolitan and non-metropolitan areas were already widening.[21] The period before this election also saw an increase in the salience of immigration, the Conservatives committing to a referendum on EU membership to try to stave off UKIP's rising support, and a growing association between concerns about immigration and attitudes towards the EU.[22] That is to say, there were many 'top-down' political reasons, as well as 'bottom-up' social reasons, that explain why the second dimension became more important.

These developments have also led researchers to conclude that the recent electoral realignment is best understood as a long-term process that preceded both the Brexit referendum in 2016 and the 2017 and 2019 general elections. As two prominent political scientists put it:

> This was not a Brexit 'realignment' – in that the vote is better seen as a symptom of a longer-term divide that is emerging between citizens residing in

locations strongly connected to global growth and those who are not ... the relationship far predates the referendum vote and should be expected to continue to reshape British politics in future.[23]

Elsewhere, the same scholars argue that 'While the EU referendum vote put the political divide between Britain's towns and cities into the spotlight, this divide is the product of long-term forces of social and economic changes.'[24] This argument has also been applied specifically to the 2019 general election. Another group of political scientists argue that '2019 is not a critical election but a continuation of longer-term trends of dealignment and realignment in British politics.' They suggest that:

> although Brexit has reconfigured the geographical base of electoral support for the main parties, this process is part of a longer trend that has gathered pace over recent years. Brexit may have paved the way for the Conservatives to make gains deep into Labour's working class heartlands, but these gains have been a long time coming and were only made possible by Labour's weakening relationship with working class Britain.[25]

These different interpretations can be reconciled by referring back to the critical-elections literature and the mechanisms through which electoral realignments take place. Can a persistent and substantial realignment take place without a change in the basis of competition by the dominant political players in the party system? Conversely, can a critical election be expected without some long-term antecedents?

Critical elections follow long-term processes of social, ideological and political change, just as the 1997 general election was a critical election rooted in factors that predated the election itself.[26] However, they also follow substantial changes in the representation of voters by parties. Both 'issue entrepreneurs' and 'issue evolution' can lead to parties 'upsetting the dominant dimensions of political choice'.[27] New issue concerns and political opportunities arise associated with discrete events or electoral shocks. The substantial increase in immigration from Central and Eastern Europe in the 2000s was such a shock, which enabled UKIP to compete successfully for votes.[28] Electoral shocks provide opportunities for political parties and an imperative to respond, by changing both the salience of issues and parties' reputations and images. In short, shocks have the potential to produce critical elections and realignments. Our conclusions about whether we have witnessed a critical election depend on the sharpness of the discontinuity after the 2016 referendum. It also depends on our judgement about whether a realignment would have happened on the same scale had the issue of Brexit been resolved and/or the mainstream political parties *not* 'sorted' the electorate around Leave and Remain.

There has certainly been a sharp discontinuity since 2016. Figures 7.1 and 7.2 showed this using individual-level survey data. The relationship between age and Labour–Conservative vote choice was evident in 2015, but became far stronger in 2017 and 2019. This was coupled with how the historic relationship between social class and vote choice had reversed across these elections. A sharp change is also observable in constituency data and aggregate-level relationships. There was a weak relationship between Brexit support and Labour and Conservative vote share at the constituency level in 2015, but a much stronger relationship in 2017 and an even stronger one in 2019.[29] This pattern was mirrored in a similar discontinuity in the constituency-level relationship between social class and the Labour lead over the Conservatives. This decreased very substantially in 2017 and then especially so in 2019.[30]

In terms of the mechanics behind these discontinuities, the 2017 and 2019 general elections were the elections when the two major parties most clearly competed and were divided over the second dimension, which now included Brexit. This division was nowhere more obvious than at Westminster, where the seemingly intractable issue of Brexit produced deadlock. Following the EU referendum, the mainstream parties fully incorporated this second dimension into their appeals, either because they saw electoral benefit, or because they had to respond to and be judged on this high-salience issue. Their actions squeezed support for the minor parties that had positioned themselves on this second dimension, especially UKIP, and increased the two-major-party share of the vote to levels not seen since the early 1970s. Previously, UKIP had very clearly been an 'issue entrepreneur', mobilising the relatively neglected issues of immigration and European integration, and adopting a distinct policy position of leaving the EU.[31] In 2017, Labour, under Jeremy Corbyn, campaigned for a closer relationship with the EU following Brexit, and the Conservatives, under Theresa May, campaigned to deliver a 'harder' Brexit. While the 2017 election campaign was by no means only about Brexit, voters started to align around these positions.[32] Had the campaign itself not proved very damaging for May and beneficial for Corbyn, the election might have delivered a result closer to the one that eventually materialised in 2019. In the second election, the Conservatives, now under Boris Johnson, took an even harder stance to 'get Brexit done'. Labour's position in 2019 was more ambiguous than in 2017. It advocated a second referendum without committing to campaign for Remain or Leave. In short, the circumstances of the 2017 and 2019 elections and the decisions of the parties increased the relevance of the second dimension and made it a realigning political force.

It was certainly the case that a gradual process of realignment was already in play. However, it is difficult to believe that the scale of the realignment in evidence in 2017 and 2019 would have happened had it not been for the intense political shock of Brexit, and in particular the changes in political competition that followed. Critical elections take place when long-term trends combine with new forms of political representation and competition that realign voters to different political parties. In sum, the electoral realignment in Britain was the result of long-term processes *and* short-term disruption, in the form of Brexit and the 2017 and 2019 elections that followed.

2017 and 2019 as critical elections

It is a moot point which of the two elections was a critical election. They were just two years apart and sharpened the realignment in different ways. Figures 7.1 and 7.2 have shown how processes in play were accelerated in both contests, with Conservative and Labour voters most clearly divided by age in 2017 and by education in 2019. Constituencies became increasingly divided along Leave/Remain lines, and both elections eventually led to a Conservative lead among working-class voters in 2019. The elections were two steps in a process, close together in timing, and they bookended a minority government that tried unsuccessfully to win a parliamentary majority on the biggest question of the day. It is difficult to argue, then, that 2019 was *the* critical election, and problematic to argue that it did not substantially influence the realignment.

What was different in 2019?

If 2017 and 2019 were two steps in a process, two critical elections, why did the 2019 election deliver the Conservatives an eighty-one-seat majority whereas the 2017 election led to a hung parliament?[33] Since Robert Johns provides a comprehensive account in Chapter 6 of why the Conservatives won, this section looks instead at how the votes 'fell out' in terms of Brexit-sorting, the pincer movement on Labour vote shares at the constituency level and the differences in the votes-to-seats relationships between 2017 and 2019, which benefited the Conservatives.

The Leave vote unified

A realignment of the electorate does not need to be symmetrical. Figure 7.3, which draws on data from the BES Internet Panel, enables us to track how the same respondents voted in each election. It shows that they 'sorted' unevenly along Brexit lines.[34] Voters were already divided by Brexit in 2015. Those who would vote Remain one year later split 42 per cent

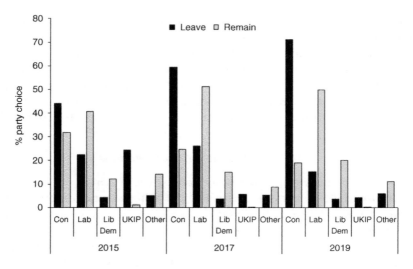

Figure 7.3 Vote choice in 2015, 2017 and 2019 by reported EU referendum vote
Source: BES Internet Panel, waves 6, 9, 13 and 19.

Labour, 32 per cent Conservative and 12 per cent Liberal Democrat. Those who would vote Leave split 44 per cent Conservative, 22 per cent Labour and 24 per cent UKIP. By 2017 almost 60 per cent of those who had voted Leave in 2016 voted Conservative, and by 2019 this had risen to 71 per cent. Some 25 per cent of Remainers voted Conservative in 2017 but only 19 per cent did so in 2019. In short, the Leave vote unified around the Tories. Not only was Boris Johnson more popular among Leave voters, but the Brexit deadlock increased the imperative to move on and, for some, a need to honour the referendum result. The Remain vote did not unify to the same extent. In 2017, 51 per cent of Remainers backed Labour, and 49 per cent did so in 2019. Labour retained the support of 26 per cent of Leavers in 2017 but this fell to just 15 per cent in 2019. The failure to unify Remainers and the haemorrhaging of Leavers cost Labour dearly. The Liberal Democrats increased their share of the vote among Remainers to 15 per cent in 2017 and 20 per cent in 2019.

This individual-level pattern resulted in a far higher proportion of Leave-voting constituencies supporting the Conservatives in 2019. Figure 7.4 uses data on EU referendum constituency-level estimates.[35] It groups UK constituencies into those with the highest Leave vote and those with the highest Remain vote, reporting general-election vote shares in 2017 and 2019.[36] The key difference in 2019, compared with 2017, was the fall in Labour's support in the strongest Leave constituencies, with the

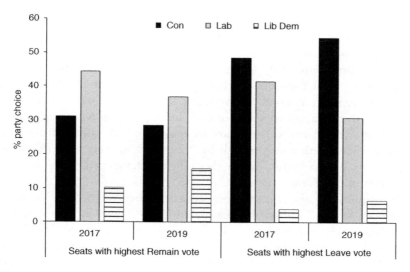

Figure 7.4 Constituency vote shares in 2017 and 2019 by EU referendum vote
Source: BES Internet Panel, waves 6, 9, 13 and 19 (see notes 25 and 36).

Conservatives winning a clear vote-share majority in these seats. In the most Remain constituencies, the Conservatives' vote share largely held up, but Labour lost out to the Liberal Democrats. The Conservatives consolidated the Leave vote, won back voters who had supported Nigel Farage's Brexit Party in the May 2019 European Parliament elections and won a majority of votes among Leave voters and in Leave-supporting constituencies.[37]

Labour was caught in a pincer movement

In 2017 Labour had benefited from the Liberal Democrats' failure to recover from their miserable 2015 performance. The party took just over 7 per cent of the vote and experienced a half-point reduction in its vote share, although it made a net gain of four MPs. Labour had staved off Liberal Democrat inroads by its strong appeal to younger voters (Figure 7.1), and the Liberal Democrats experienced a continuing penalty for the former Conservative–Liberal Democrat coalition (Chapter 4). In 2019, Labour was squeezed on two sides of the second dimension: by the Liberal Democrats on the Remain side, and by the Conservatives on the Leave side.

This squeezing was not just about the flow of the vote, but also where this flow happened. In 2017, Labour made its greatest gains in seats with the highest proportions of university students, where it increased its vote share by 14.2 points on average, and the largest proportions of graduates, where it went up by 10.7 points. But Labour also made vote-share gains of 8.7 points in constituencies with the lowest levels of educational qualifications.[38] Ominously for Labour, the Conservatives also saw vote-share gains of 10.2 points in these constituencies. In 2019, however, Labour was caught in a pincer movement. Its vote share *fell* by 11.9 points in seats with the largest proportions of the population with no qualifications, while the Conservative share increased by 5.5 points in the same constituencies.[39] Labour's vote fell by 7.2 points in seats with the largest proportions of graduates, while the Liberal Democrats' vote went up 9.6 points in these constituencies.

This squeezing also occurred in constituencies defined by economic differences. In 2017, Labour had increased its vote share in seats with both the highest levels of deprivation – by 9.2 points on average – and the lowest levels of deprivation – by 8 points. However, in 2019 Labour's vote share fell by 10 points in the most deprived seats, by 12.8 points in seats with the 'least healthy' populations, by 8.6 points in seats with the highest levels of unemployment and by 9 points in seats with the highest proportions employed in the public sector. Meanwhile, the Liberal Democrats made their greatest gains in the wealthiest constituencies, where their vote went up by 11.4 points, and in those seats with the lowest proportions of deprived households, again ensuring that Labour's vote was squeezed on both sides.

Changes in votes to seats (in)efficiencies

One of the challenges for Remain parties in 2019 was the risk of taking votes from each other and delivering Brexit by handing victory to the Conservatives, whose vote share became relatively more efficient. A 'Remain Alliance' was formed between the Liberal Democrats, the Greens and Plaid Cymru, with the Remain parties agreeing not to run against each other in sixty seats, but in only a few constituencies, if indeed any at all, was this pact decisive. The Greens were unchallenged by the Liberal Democrats or Plaid Cymru in ten constituencies, which might have helped the Greens to hold Brighton Pavilion for MP Caroline Lucas, though she was always likely to have won re-election. The Greens and Plaid in turn stood aside for the Liberal Democrats in forty-three constituencies, but the Liberal Democrats failed to gain any of these seats. Plaid Cymru were given a clear run in seven Welsh constituencies, helping them to hold their four seats from 2017. In seat terms, therefore, the pact resulted in very little change.

The Liberal Democrats succeeded in taking votes away from Labour, even if they did not win a single additional seat from them. Their vote gains helped deliver Brexit, to some degree, by preventing Labour from taking more seats from the Conservatives: Labour gained one, Putney, and lost fifty-nine overall. The Liberal Democrats increased their vote share in 2019 by a mere 1.3 percentage points in those seats they had lost to the Conservatives in 2015, seats that – under normal circumstances – they might have hoped to win back as their overall vote grew. As a result, across all their target seats – those requiring the smallest swing for the Liberal Democrats to win – their vote share increased by just 1.9 points. By contrast, the Liberal Democrats made much larger gains in Remain-voting Conservative-held seats, but many of these were Labour target seats. In thirty-five such constituencies, Labour's vote fell by 8.8 percentage points on average and the Conservatives' fell by 4.2 points, while the Liberal Democrats' vote share increased by 11.9 points.

The Conservatives also increased their vote where it did not matter. Their largest gains were in seats they already held with the strongest Leave votes, where they increased their support by 8.8 points. However, they also dramatically increased their vote where it mattered a great deal: in previously Labour seats with the strongest Leave votes. In such seats the Conservative share increased by 5.4 points, and Labour's vote plummeted by 16.3 points. Many constituencies in Labour's 'red wall' – some once considered its safest seats – had voted very strongly for Leave. The Conservatives repeatedly broke through the wall in those constituencies where the Leave vote had been highest.

These geographic variations provided a bonus to the Conservatives from the electoral system and a penalty for the Liberal Democrats. The geographic efficiencies of the vote and the degree of electoral bias in the system varies between elections.[40] We can see this in Figure 7.5 (a–c), which plots the percentages of votes and seats won for the three largest parties between 1997 and 2019. The gap between the percentages was relatively small for Theresa May in 2017 but widened substantially in 2019. The percentage of Conservative votes increased by just 1.3 points, but the seat share rose by 7.4 points. Labour's vote share, by contrast, fell by 7.9 points but its seat share fell further, by 9.2 points. The variations in the votes-to-seats relationship can be seen clearly for the Liberal Democrats. The electoral system always penalises the party. In 2019, however, the system had a positively perverse impact. Although the Liberal Democrats' vote share increased by 4.1 points, its seat share fell by 0.2 points – that is, one seat.

By unifying the Leave vote, the votes-to-seats translation was more efficient in 2019 for the Conservatives. By splitting the Remain vote, the votes-to-seats translation was particularly inefficient for the Liberal Democrats. Labour lost the bonus it had enjoyed in seats-to-votes translation in previous years.

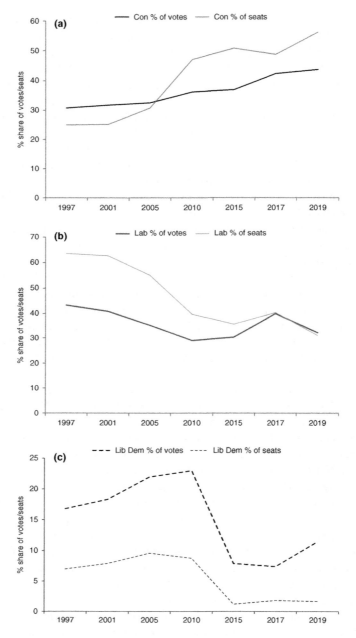

Figure 7.5 Proportions of votes and seats by party, 1997–2019:
(a) Conservatives; (b) Labour; (c) Liberal Democrats
Source: House of Commons Library.

Labour's ongoing decline in Scotland

Any understanding of the 2019 election is not complete without consideration of the plight of Labour in Scotland. While the immediate story of 2019 was the loss of Labour's votes and seats in its English 'red wall', Labour's continued decline in Scotland should not be overlooked.

Scotland was, until recently, a place where Labour dominated and had some of its safest 'heartland' seats. In 2015 Labour lost all but one of its seats in a landslide victory to the SNP, dramatically losing forty MPs and seeing its vote share fall by 17.7 points.[41] The SNP's success was, in large part, due to the issue of Scottish independence, which cut across the left–right dimension. Following the independence referendum in 2014, Labour lost pro-independence voters to the SNP.[42] In 2017 Labour's vote share went up only 2.8 points in Scotland, in contrast to its 9.5-point increase across the UK as a whole. In the same election, the Conservatives' vote share in Scotland went up by 13.7 points, while the SNP vote fell by 13.1 points. Importantly, Labour's long-term decline in Scotland continued in 2019, when the party's vote share fell by a further 8.5 points. That additional loss is not quite on a par with its 2019 losses in northern English regions – Labour's vote fell by 10.1 points in Yorkshire and the Humber and by 12.8 points in the North East – but it is very large in the context of Labour's huge 2015 losses in Scotland and its failure to recover in 2017.

A thorough analysis of the reasons for the SNP's success in 2019 and Labour's ongoing decline in Scotland will have to wait for detailed individual-level survey data. What we can say is that there were few differences in 2019 in the pro-independence or pro-union composition of the seats. The Conservatives' vote share went down in Scotland equally in the most pro-union and pro-independence constituencies (by 4.1 and 4.0 points respectively), Labour did very slightly worse in the most pro-union seats (down 8.2 points versus down 7.0 points) and the SNP were up almost equally in both (8 points in the most pro-union and 7.5 points in the most pro-independence). The Liberal Democrats only increased their share in Scotland in 2019 by 2.8 points. Of course, Scottish independence is not the only dividing line in Scotland, where Brexit, independence and traditional left–right politics intersect. Westminster elections represent judgements on the devolved Scottish government, the government in Westminster and national party leaders. As far as seats are concerned, the SNP had a successful election in 2019, most likely as a result of a combination of negative judgements about Jeremy Corbyn, the Conservatives and Brexit, and positive judgements about Scottish independence. The continued decline of Labour in Scotland is particularly striking, and very challenging for

Labour's future hopes of forming a majority government, since it has traditionally relied on Scottish seats to do so.

Not only Brexit

Just as Scottish politics represents an intersection of Scottish independence,
Brexit and traditional politics, so we should not oversimplify the role of
Brexit and second-dimension politics in England and Wales. As Labour Leave
voters supported the Conservatives in 2019, their reasons could have just as
easily been their liking of Boris Johnson, the reassurance that the Conservatives would spend more money in their constituencies or on the NHS and
other services and their scepticism towards Labour's manifesto commitments
and Jeremy Corbyn's competence as a leader. That they also happened to be
Leave voters does not mean their Brexit preferences decided their vote,
though it was undoubtedly very important for many. Among Conservative
Leave voters who had toyed with UKIP in 2015 and backed the Brexit Party
in the May 2019 European Parliament elections, Boris Johnson's likeability
was an important part of their return to the Conservatives in December.[43]
The Conservative vote among Leave voters was also aided, partly, by the
Brexit Party's decision not to stand in Conservative-held seats.

Similarly, Remain voters who moved from Labour to the Liberal
Democrats might have been alienated by Labour's difficulties in opposition,
convinced that the Liberal Democrats had a better chance of beating the
Conservatives in Remain constituencies; or they might have simply been
erstwhile Liberal Democrats who had forgiven the party for their period in
coalition government with the Conservatives. The sorting of the electorate
along Brexit lines was not only because of Brexit or the so-called 'culture
wars' associated with other second-dimension politics. For this reason, the
apparent polarisation may be somewhat more temporary and changeable
than it first appears, since the sorting is in part due to the normal ebb and
flow of politics. The durability of the electoral realignment in British politics
and elections is considered next.

Lessons and implications

It would be easy to read anything written on the 2019 general election and
assume Brexit is everything. Indeed, this chapter has argued that Brexit has
realigned the British electorate, a highly consequential change. In spite of
this, we should not overstate the degree of polarisation and division on
Brexit and assume that this is an immutable change.

It is certainly possible to exaggerate the degree of polarisation in the electorate. The Brexit realignment is not entirely bipolar, forcing all of the electorate into rigid Leave and Remain positions.[44] While it is true that a majority of voters in around 60 per cent of constituencies are estimated to have supported Leave in 2016, this includes constituencies whose estimates fell close to 50:50. There were 211 constituencies (32 per cent) where the estimated Leave/Remain vote was within a 45–55 percentage point margin (+/- 3 per cent of the result).[45] Meanwhile, in a 2019 BES post-election survey, 35 per cent of respondents reported attitudes about EU integration that were neither extremely pro- nor anti-EU.[46] Taken together, roughly a third of voters and a third of constituencies cannot be easily classed as very strongly Leave or very strongly Remain. This is not to deny that there may be a degree of Brexit-related 'affective' polarisation among parts of the electorate. Some people's views on Brexit are clearly associated with stereotyping, prejudice and evaluative biases.[47] Yet there are also grounds for suggesting that variations in competence, leader likeability or some other non-Brexit factor could overcome Brexit-based resistance.

It is far from clear whether the electoral realignment is enduring. We can make a reasoned guess by factoring in our knowledge about *how* these realignments come to take place. Since they arise due to parties aligning with positions, their continuation is, in part, dependent on the positions that political parties come to take. If the Conservatives softened their Brexit position or Labour hardened theirs, we could expect to see some weakening or strengthening respectively of the realignment. Since realignments are a consequence of the increasing salience of issues (or issue-dimensions), their continuation depends, in part, on the ongoing salience of those issues to voters and in party competition. The salience of Brexit could diminish now the UK has left and secured a new trade deal with the EU, especially if Brexit is no longer discussed in the media or contested politically. Alternatively, British politics may have become frozen around the Brexit dividing line, expressed in new Brexit identities and the force of those identities on ongoing evaluations of political crises and events.[48] If Brexit identities come to shape partisan identities, if new Conservative voters develop a strong partisan identity for the Conservatives on the basis of Brexit, then this part of the realignment may continue. At present, the evidence suggests that a Leave–Conservative alignment is likely to be stronger than one for any of the Remain parties.

This, in turn, highlights the difficulties in determining what might be a Brexit-based alignment and what might be a traditional party-based alignment. We have seen how issue entrepreneurs can try to change the dimensionality of political competition for electoral advantage, leading to issue evolution. Electoral alignments are contingent: they are – at least in part – the outcome of political strategies. The theory of electoral shocks suggests that future issue competition is the product of unpredictable and largely exogenous political 'events'.[49] Among all this uncertainty, there is, then, a possibility that British politics becomes more polarised, reducing volatility due to stable attachments and issue-alignments. If polarisation increases, the effects of future shocks are likely to be dampened.

In order to understand how parties compete in this new environment, we need to consider the fluctuation in recent elections. As John Bartle describes in Chapter 4, the gradual decline in the two major parties' share of the vote culminated in minor and 'other' parties winning 35.1 per cent in 2015. This was followed by a substantial resurgence for the two major parties: the Conservatives and Labour combined won 82 per cent of the vote in 2017 and 76 per cent in 2019. In two- or three-dimensional political space, smaller parties can splinter votes on cross-cutting dimensions and/or squeeze the mainstream parties on the traditional centre ground. When the second dimension becomes incorporated into the principal dimension by the mainstream parties, as happened at least for the Conservatives on Brexit and to a lesser extent for Labour, smaller parties, such as the Brexit Party, find it difficult to gain a foothold. The difficulties facing challenger parties are increased by the powerful mechanical and psychological effects of Britain's first-past-the-post electoral system.[50]

The major battle lines, at least in England and Wales, are between Labour and the Conservatives. Labour needs to appeal to its former voters who defected to the Conservatives in its traditional heartland seats, while retaining and building on its new electoral coalition in metropolitan constituencies. The Conservatives need to deliver on their key campaign promises: to 'get Brexit done' and 'level up'. If the major parties succeed, they will continue to structure party politics. But it is possible, too, that we will return to a more fragmented party system. If there is one lesson from Labour's experience in Scotland, it is that even loyal voters are not immune to switching parties when faced with major realigning events, or shocks, such as the 2014 referendum on Scottish independence. The defection of Labour voters to the Conservatives in its former heartlands in northern England has created a new group that could switch back relatively easily in the future. The Conservatives will also need to retain former UKIP and Brexit Party voters: those who have switched to smaller 'other' parties in the past have a greater propensity to switch parties in the future. This implies that the two largest parties have an incentive to contest the success of Brexit.

Contesting Brexit will also matter for electoral competition in Scotland. If Brexit brings economic benefits, support for Scottish independence may also diminish, and with it, some of the SNP's electoral strength. If Brexit is not successful, and Scotland is particularly badly affected, support for independence may grow and produce greater constitutional conflict.

These discussions naturally raise the question of whether the second dimension in British electoral competition will continue to be as important. My answer – as will be clear by now – depends on how it became more prominent. Did the salience of 'identity politics' occur because of a long-term and perhaps indeterminate process of cultural change, or did it happen through a series of political decisions that temporarily diminished the ideological left–right differences between the two major parties, led to a rapid rise in immigration and/or paved the way for a referendum on Brexit? A sharp global financial crisis may temporarily change voters' priorities and increase the salience of economic issues. Priorities have also shifted as a result of the global coronavirus pandemic, but this is not guaranteed to send British politics back to left–right politics. Since electoral shocks fundamentally shape voter priorities, party images and parties' reputations, and can lead to realignments under the right conditions, I expect the outcomes of British politics to be determined by future shocks, and therefore for the dimensionality of British politics to be unpredictable. The party or parties that will prosper in this environment are those that can learn, adapt and respond to electoral shocks most effectively.

Conclusion

In this chapter I explored whether the 2019 general election was a critical election. To answer this question, I looked to the literature on how critical elections and electoral realignments happen, and in my account emphasised the importance of political competition in driving these phenomena. Political competition was certainly driving changes before the 2016 Brexit referendum, and the geographic divides beginning to emerge were very perceptible and, importantly, identified and acted upon.[51] We could see the clear electoral signs of this in the rise of UKIP in the general election in 2015, as well as in the increasing metropolitan basis of Labour's vote. However, the Brexit referendum, which started the process of Britain's departure from the EU, only increased the salience and political significance of Brexit, and both Labour and the Conservatives used that issue to mobilise voters. Would the degree of the electoral realignment that took place in 2017 – and then in 2019 – happened had it not been for these 'Brexit elections'? And would we have called such a smaller and more gradual change in the significance of the second dimension a full electoral realignment? We cannot know the answer to this counterfactual. However, I have argued that these elections – and the political competition that surrounded them – have the characteristics of critical elections.

To focus on 2019 as *the* critical election would be misleading. To understand this we need to first appreciate the degree to which 2017 also had the hallmarks of a critical election. Some of the decisive changes took place in 2017. Subtly different patterns were exhibited in 2019, and some changes in 2019 simply amplified the patterns that took place in 2017. Also, while the Conservatives won a dramatic majority in 2019 and took many of Labour's 'red wall' seats in the process, this was largely a result of the more asymmetric sorting of the electorate that took place in 2019 compared with 2017: the Leave vote was unified behind the Conservatives, but Labour lost a sizeable proportion of Remain voters to the Liberal Democrats. This sorting followed the pincer movement on Labour by the Conservatives in constituencies with low levels of education and high levels of deprivation, and by the Liberal Democrats in constituencies with high levels of education and wealth. It also followed Labour's continued electoral decline in Scotland. The result was a particularly efficient distribution of votes to seats for the Conservatives and a particularly inefficient distribution for the Liberal Democrats, with Labour losing any advantage.

There is no disagreement about *what* has happened in British politics. There is, rather, a potential difference in emphasis on the relative importance of short-term political processes and longer-term sociological ones. Amid the long-term changes, there has been a weakening of Labour's working-class vote, which has been taking place over many elections, and a widening centre–periphery geographic divide. There has also been a process of partisan dealignment, making elections more volatile and susceptible to shocks. Whether we think this realignment is now a stable feature of British politics – and so faithfully fulfils one of the criteria of V. O. Key's definition of a critical election – comes down to whether you conclude that realignments are essentially a feature of political competition and the changing salience of issues and dimensions, or a longer-term sociological and cultural process.

Notes

1 Thanks to Alma Rottem for excellent research assistance and also to ITN and Professor Colin Rallings for ITN constituency categorisations used on ITV News's election-night results programmes.
2 Edward Fieldhouse, Jane Green, Geoffrey Evans, Jon Mellon, Christopher Prosser, Hermann Schmitt and Cees van der Eijk, *Electoral Shocks: Understanding the Volatile Voter in a Turbulent World* (Oxford: Oxford University Press, 2019).

3 Note that 'normal' was not static. The 2017 election saw the highest levels of volatility on record and the 2015 general election a substantial rise in votes for minor parties. The party system was in considerable flux, and even the stable period between 1945 and 1970 was relatively brief in long-term perspective, as John Bartle argues in Chapter 4.

4 Jonathan Mellon, Geoffrey Evans, Edward Fieldhouse, Jane Green and Christopher Prosser, 'Brexit or Corbyn? Campaign and inter-election vote switching in the 2017 UK general election', *Parliamentary Affairs*, 71 (2018), 719–737; Fieldhouse *et al., Electoral Shocks*; Edward Fieldhouse, Jane Green, Geoffrey Evans, Jon Mellon and Christopher Prosser, 'Volatility, realignment and electoral shocks: Brexit and the UK general election of 2019', *PS: Political Science & Politics* (forthcoming).

5 Will Jennings and Gerry Stoker, 'Tilting towards the cosmopolitan axis? Political change in England and the 2017 general election', *Political Quarterly*, 88 (2017), 359–369; Paula Surridge, 'The fragmentation of the electoral left since 2010', *Renewal*, 26 (2018), 69–78; David Cutts, Matthew Goodwin, Oliver Heath and Paula Surridge, 'Brexit, the 2019 General Election and the realignment of British politics', *Political Quarterly*, 91 (2020), 7–23; Paula Surridge, 'Beyond Brexit: Labour's structural problems', *Political Insight*, 11 (2020), 16–19; Paula Surridge, 'A mountain to climb: The Labour together 2019 election review', *Political Quarterly*, 91 (2020), 659–663.

6 Cutts *et al.*, 'Brexit, the 2019 General Election and the realignment of British politics'.

7 Geoffrey Evans and Jonathan Mellon, 'The reshaping of class voting', British Election Study, 6 March 2020, available at: www.britishelectionstudy.com/bes-findings/the-re-shaping-of-class-voting-in-the-2019-election-by-geoffrey-evans-and-jonathan-mellon/#.Xz_EBUBFx9A, last accessed 26 June 2021.

8 Will Jennings and Gerry Stoker, 'The divergent dynamics of cities and towns: Geographical polarisation after Brexit', *Political Quarterly*, 90 (2019), 155–166.

9 Geoffrey Evans and Pippa Norris (eds), *Critical Elections: British Parties and Voters in Long-term Perspective* (London: Sage, 1999).

10 V. O. Key, 'A theory of critical elections', *Journal of Politics*, 17 (1955), 3–18.

11 David R. Mayhew, 'Electoral realignments', *Annual Review of Political Science*, 3 (2000), 449–474; Peter F. Nardulli, 'The concept of a critical realignment, electoral behavior, and political change', *American Political Science Review*, 89 (1995), 10–22; Alan I. Abramowitz and Kyle L. Saunders, 'Ideological realignment in the US electorate', *Journal of Politics*, 60 (1988), 634–652.

12 Note that we are not talking about a realignment to the party system that might have seen the Conservative coalition fragment in parliament, Labour split between moderates and more left-wing Corbynites and a new centrist-Remain party emerge at the centre. For a time in 2019, that didn't seem a ridiculous idea. Notwithstanding the intense disillusionment that existed among MPs, the first-past-the-post electoral system is a strong force, drastically reducing the incentives of MPs to switch sides with a reduced chance of re-election, as eventually proved to be the case.

13 Evans and Norris, *Critical Elections*.

14 Edward G. Carmines and James A. Stimson, 'On the structure and sequence of issue evolution', *American Political Science Review*, 80 (1986), 901–920; Edward G. Carmines and James A. Stimson, *Issue Evolution: Race and the Transformation of American Politics* (Princeton: Princeton University Press, 1989); Edward G. Carmines and James A. Stimson, 'On the evolution of political issues', in William H. Riker (ed.), *Agenda Formation* (Ann Arbor: University of Michigan Press, 1993), pp. 151–168.

15 Fieldhouse *et al.*, *Electoral Shocks*, p. 48.

16 Sara B. Hobolt and Catherine De Vries, 'Issue entrepreneurship and multiparty competition', *Comparative Political Studies*, 48 (2015), 1159–1185.

17 John Curtice, 'General election 2017: A new two-party politics?', *Political Insight*, 8 (2017), 4–8; Christopher Prosser, 'The end of the EU affair: the UK general election of 2019', *West European Politics*, 23 (2020), 1–12; Cutts *et al.*, 'Brexit, the 2019 General Election and the realignment of British politics'; Fieldhouse *et al.*, *Electoral Shocks*; Fieldhouse *et al.*, 'Volatility, realignment and electoral shocks'.

18 See Fieldhouse *et al.*, *Electoral Shocks*, p. 183.

19 Geoffrey Evans and James Tilley, *The New Politics of Class: The Political Exclusion of the British Working Class* (Oxford University Press, 2017); Surridge, 'Beyond Brexit: Labour's structural problems'; Surridge, 'A mountain to climb'.

20 Evans and Mellon, 'The reshaping of class voting'.

21 Cutts *et al.*, 'Brexit, the 2019 General Election and the realignment of British politics'; Jennings and Stoker, 'Tilting towards the cosmopolitan axis?'.

22 Fieldhouse *et al.*, *Electoral Shocks*.

23 Jennings and Stoker, 'Tilting towards the cosmopolitan axis?', p. 35.

24 Jennings and Stoker, 'The divergent dynamics of cities and towns', p. 155.

25 Cutts *et al.*, 'Brexit, the 2019 General Election and the realignment of British politics', 8.

26 Evans and Norris, *Critical Elections*.

27 Hobolt and De Vries, 'Issue entrepreneurship and multiparty competition'; Carmines and Stimson, 'On the structure and sequence of issue evolution'; Carmines and Stimson, *Issue Evolution*; Carmines and Stimson, 'On the evolution of political issues'.

28 Fieldhouse *et al.*, *Electoral Shocks*.

29 Cutts *et al.*, 'Brexit, the 2019 General Election and the realignment of British politics', 8.

30 Cutts *et al.*, 'Brexit, the 2019 General Election and the realignment of British politics', 17.

31 Hobolt and De Vries, 'Issue entrepreneurship and multiparty competition'.

32 Mellon *et al.*, 'Brexit or Corbyn?'.

33 Calculating the government's majority is less straightforward than it appears. A simple majority is merely the governing party's (or parties') number of MPs minus the total number of other MPs. In 2019 the Conservatives won 365 seats out of 650, giving them a simple majority of eighty. The situation is complicated by the position of the speaker and three deputy speakers, none of whom usually

vote. It is further complicated by the decision of Sinn Féin MPs not to take their seats. This chapter follows the convention adopted by the House of Commons Library of excluding only the speaker when calculating the government's majority, resulting in the figure of eighty-one.

34 For a similar breakdown, see Prosser, 'The end of the EU affair'.
35 Chris Hanretty, 'Areal interpolation and the UK's referendum on EU membership', *Journal of Elections, Public Opinion and Parties*, 27 (2017), 466–483.
36 ITN election-night programme analysis, compiled by Professor Colin Rallings.
37 Evans *et al.*, 'The Conservatives and the radical right'.
38 These classifications are based on ITV News's constituency classifications, with the top and bottom groups defined as proportions across the distribution of demographics provided by the UK 2011 census.
39 This was one of the Conservatives' highest gains in any of the types of constituency we analysed on ITV on election night. Credit also to Ian White for his graphical display of key groups on ITN's election-night programmes.
40 Ron Johnston, Galina Borisyuk, Michael Thrasher and Colin Rallings, 'Unequal and unequally distributed votes: The sources of electoral bias at recent British general elections', *Political Studies*, 60 (2012), 877–898.
41 Jane Green and Chris Prosser, 'Party system fragmentation and single-party government: The British general election of 2015', *West European Politics*, 39 (2016), 1299–1310.
42 Fieldhouse *et al.*, *Electoral Shocks*.
43 Evans *et al.*, 'The Conservatives and the radical right'.
44 Sara B. Hobolt, Thomas J. Leeper and James Tilley, 'Divided by the vote: Affective polarization in the wake of the Brexit referendum', *British Journal of Political Science*, FirstView (2020), 1–18: doi:10.1017/S0007123420000125.
45 Hanretty, 'Areal interpolation and the UK's referendum on EU membership'.
46 Using the post-2019 general election BES Internet Panel data and self-placements on the 0–10 EU integration scale (where 0 = unite fully with the EU and 10 = protect our independence), 35 per cent occupy positions between 3 and 7 (rather than the 'extreme' ends, 0–2 and 8–10).
47 For a helpful review of polarisation as it impacts the UK, see Bobby Duffy, Kirstie Hewlett, Julian McCrae and John Hall, *Divided Britain? Polarisation and Fragmentation Trends in the UK* (The Policy Institute at King's College London, 2019), available at: www.kcl.ac.uk/policy-institute/assets/divided-britain.pdf, last accessed 26 June 2021.
48 Hobolt *et al.*, 'Divided by the vote'.
49 Fieldhouse *et al.*, *Electoral Shocks*.
50 Evans *et al.*, 'The Conservatives and the radical right'.
51 Jennings and Stoker, 'Tilting towards the cosmopolitan axis?'; Jennings and Stoker, 'The divergent dynamics of cities and towns'.

8

Comparative perspectives

Sarah Birch

The chaos caused by the coronavirus pandemic in 2020 made the previous year seem like a fairly 'normal' period in British politics. It did not seem so at the time. The 2019 general election took place in highly unusual circumstances, as documented in other chapters, and was in many respects very different from previous polls. While the election can best be understood in relation to factors specific to UK politics, certain aspects of it have important parallels with phenomena experienced in other established Western democracies, specifically technological change, the decline of social democracy and the rise of populism. At a time when the world is rapidly evolving, comparative analysis is useful in helping to understand underlying drivers of change such as these. Placing recent British political developments in a comparative context also highlights the ways in which the UK differs from other developed democracies with similar economic, social and political profiles.

This chapter assesses the extent to which recent changes in UK politics have parallels with those witnessed elsewhere. It focuses on the general political, policy and demographic challenges that have caused havoc in the political systems of developed democracies in the first two decades of the twenty-first century, as well as their distinct manifestations in the UK. The chapter also compares the 2019 election outcome with the results of recent elections in other established democracies. Its main argument is that the UK has been affected by a series of political developments that have many of the same roots as, and bear similarities to, developments observed in other democracies, but that their impact has been shaped greatly by the UK's unique institutional and political set-up. It is this set-up that continues to make contemporary British electoral politics so distinctive.

Socio-economic and political change in contemporary democracies

The digital and technological revolution that began in the second half of the last century has profoundly affected most aspects of economic, social and political life across the globe. It has engendered an unprecedented rate of social and economic change that has brought both opportunities and dislocations, ranging from the automation of many jobs and the advent of new forms of electoral manipulation to a rapid rise in social connectedness and novel ways of holding leaders to account. It has also accelerated the processes of globalisation that have had substantial impacts on economic and social structures across the globe. Other technological advances have led to increases in life expectancy and have produced lifestyles radically different from those of previous generations. The immediacy of social media has made letter-writing seem quaint, internet search engines have consigned telephone directories to service as doorstops, and weekend breaks take people to Marrakesh instead of Margate. The sheer volume of change and its rapid pace have been both exhilarating and disorienting for many citizens. In this context, it makes sense to review the underlying demographic, economic and structural developments that have affected twenty-first-century developed democracies, to discuss the impacts these changes have had on people's attitudes and behaviours, and to trace through in comparative perspective the impact of attitudinal shifts on party support and electoral results.

Demographic and structural changes

Recent decades have reshaped the lives of those living in developed democracies. There are many changes that could be identified from a comparative perspective, but five have arguably played the largest role in conditioning political attitudes and behaviours: de-industrialisation, the rising cost of housing, ageing populations, underemployment among certain groups of young people and climate change. Let us consider each of these in turn.

De-industrialisation: The historical decline of traditional manufacturing industries in developed countries, documented in Figure 8.1, has been accompanied by an increase in service-sector, high-tech and 'knowledge economy' employment. Unfortunately, the groups and geographical areas that have seen increases in service- and knowledge-based jobs are in many cases not the same as those that have seen declines in industry. The result is that there are in many countries 'rustbelt' regions with high levels of unemployment, underemployment, emigration and deprivation. Well-known examples include the Pas de Calais in France, the Ruhr region in Germany and the former car-manufacturing cities of the US Midwest. In contrast with areas of post-industrial decline, many cities are vibrant, increasingly expensive and offer ample employment in well-paid jobs for those with the specialised skills to fill them. The result is a widening social and geographic chasm between 'winners' and 'losers' from globalisation that has led to increased economic inequality in many established democracies.[1]

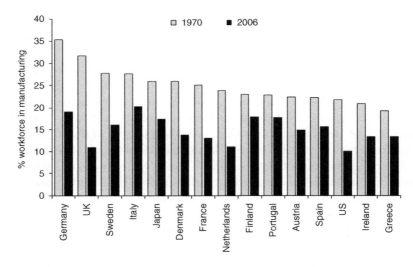

Figure 8.1 Workforce employed in manufacturing, 1970–2006
Source: David Hope and Angelo Martelli, 'Replication data for: The transition to the
knowledge economy, labor market institutions, and income inequality in advanced
democracies', available at: https://dataverse.harvard.edu/dataset.xhtml?persistentId=
doi:10.7910/DVN/EUC80S, last accessed 26 June 2021.

Rising cost of housing: As a result of both increasing life expectancy and
the migration of people to cities in search of employment, many urban areas
in developed societies have experienced housing shortages, which has made
it especially difficult for young people to get on to the property ladder.
Recent economic trends have further affected the fortunes of those who
have been able to purchase property: those in affluent cities have watched
the value of their most important asset skyrocket, while those in more
deprived areas have seen house prices stagnate or fall. Geographic variations in the property market have thus exacerbated differentials in people's
resources and their prospects for the future.[2]

Ageing population: Population ageing in developed countries, shown in
Figure 8.2, is a product of declining birth rates, increased life expectancy
and hesitancy to welcome young migrants who could supply much needed
demographic balance. The result in many established democracies is a crisis
in pension funds, battles around proposals to push up retirement ages and
increases in healthcare costs as a proportion of gross national income. Population ageing has also contributed to housing shortages, and resulting price
increases, especially in societies where it is conventional for older people to
live independently rather than moving in with their children.

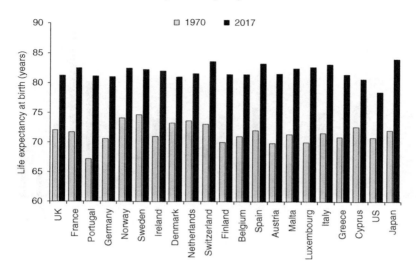

Figure 8.2 Changes in life expectancy, 1970–2017
Source: World Bank Open Data, available at: https://data.worldbank.org/, last accessed 26 June 2021.

Underemployment of young people: In post-industrial societies where many jobs are based on knowledge and knowledge-processing skills, those who have missed out on formal education often find themselves with limited employment opportunities. Their only option is often to work in low-paid, low-security service-sector jobs, sometimes holding down multiple part-time jobs to make ends meet (Figure 8.3). To make matters worse, automation is now threatening many such roles. The resulting income inequality can be effectively mitigated, however, by systems of coordinated wage bargaining; economic inequality has risen fastest in Anglo-Saxon economies that lack such practices.[3]

Climate change: In addition to problems experienced on a daily basis, climate change is beginning to produce periodic extreme weather events that can have catastrophic consequences for communities in the areas affected. The European heatwave of 2003 led to an estimated 70,000 excess deaths.[4] Floods in Central and Eastern Europe in 2013 left 33,000 temporarily homeless.[5] The Australian wildfires of 2020 burned more than 24.7 million acres of land.[6] The knowledge that global heating brings greater risk can cause anxiety to those in vulnerable areas. Moreover, the fact that current extreme weather episodes are a harbinger of problems to come adds to the concern caused by floods, coastal erosion, wildfires and crop failures.

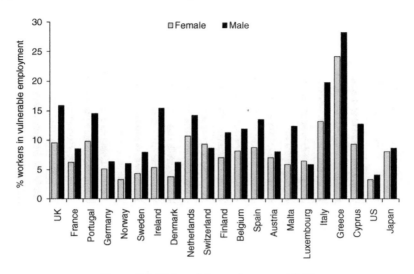

Figure 8.3 Vulnerable employment, 2019
Source: World Bank Open Data, available at: https://data.worldbank.org/, last accessed 26 June 2021.

Taken together, these five developments have generated inequalities within advanced democratic societies, which, in turn, have led to widespread unease and a sense of relative deprivation. Those in previous generations had a reasonable expectation of being better off than their parents, whereas many now do not view their prospects so favourably. Moreover, many citizens today are aware that others in society are far better off than they are. To add to their plight, advanced democratic societies have experienced declining relative affluence, as people in other parts of the world have started to compete successfully in the globalised world. The West is no longer the indisputable economic 'top dog'. The relative success of countries such as China, South Korea and Taiwan in combating the covid-19 pandemic has served to underline this shift. For some, the recent socio-economic changes reflect opportunities; for others, they represent a closing off of hope. How people react and the political consequences of those reactions is the topic of the next section.

Attitudinal and behavioural change

Comparative studies of political behaviour have since the 1950s recognised an attitudinal divide between socially liberal, cosmopolitan values on the one hand, and authoritarian, place-based values on the other.[7] Individuals who espouse more socially liberal or libertarian views tend to be more tolerant of alternative lifestyles and people who are culturally different from themselves, and they are more open to new experiences. Individuals who have more authoritarian mindsets, by contrast, are less tolerant of people unlike themselves, less open to new experiences and more sympathetic to hierarchical and traditional modes of social organisation.[8] Although political scientists have long been aware of the libertarian–authoritarian dimension of political competition, the left–right economic dimension – which reflects different ideas about the size of the state and levels of public spending – has largely defined party-political competition in Western democracies during most of the post-war period. In recent years, however, the libertarian–authoritarian dimension has become far more prominent in electoral competition and in society more generally, as Maria Sobolewska describes in Chapter 5. This change has generated a series of 'culture wars' between those who espouse more traditional values among the majority ethnic populations, on the one hand, and those among the majority group whose views are more cosmopolitan and more socially liberal, as well as ethnic minorities whose values are often socially conservative, on the other.

In as much as most political elites on both the left and the right of the political spectrum are relatively liberal in their orientations towards social issues, the more authoritarian traditionalists in the wider population have often felt alienated by politicians in general. This anti-elite backlash, often described as populism, commonly goes hand in hand with anti-immigrant sentiment and proposals that could limit the enjoyment of equal rights by all groups. In countries such as Greece, Spain and Italy, populism has a prominent left-wing manifestation, but in most places, the majority of populists have aligned with cultural conservatives on the political right whose views conform more closely to authoritarian values. Populism also has two other characteristic features of relevance to democratic politics: a tendency to value social and economic outcomes over democratic processes, and a preferrence for polices that deliver immediate benefits, regardless of their long-term social, economic and environmental consequences. Just as many democracies have seen an increase in the political salience of the libertarian–authoritarian dimension of public opinion, they have also witnessed a rise in the prominence of populist attitudes and parties that espouse them.

Party-system change

The changes in popular attitudes documented in the previous section have been associated with shifts in the electoral fate of political parties across the ideological spectrum. In many countries new challenger parties have emerged to represent the views of authoritarians as well as populists. Some established large parties have seen their support fall as voters have switched to the political newcomers.[9]

On the right of the political spectrum, challenger parties include those that have appealed to the anti-outsider attitudes and xenophobia found among those on the authoritarian end of the political spectrum. Like UKIP and the Brexit Party in the UK, far-right parties such as Golden Dawn in Greece, the National Front (since 2018 the National Rally) in France, the Freedom Party of Austria and the True Finn Party have employed nativist rhetoric to win votes. Left-wing challengers, including Syriza in Greece, Podemos in Spain and the Five Star Movement in Italy, have tended to shy away from explicit nativism. But like their counterparts on the right, left-wing challenger parties have framed their appeals around antipathy towards elites and 'experts' and valorised the opinions of 'ordinary' people.

Long-established parties with experience of governing have been the main casualty of challenger parties' rising popularity. The worst-affected have in many cases been social democratic parties that rose to prominence in the early part of the twentieth century as champions of workers' rights. The net result of these changes has been to make party systems both more fragmented and more volatile, with larger numbers of small parties exhibiting dramatic shifts in vote share from one election to the next. In the UK context this volatility is evidenced by the spectacular rise of UKIP in the 2015 general election, its crash in 2017 and the Brexit Party's dramatic change of fortunes in 2019, when it came first in May's European Parliament elections but won just 2 per cent of the vote in December's general election.

Given that substantial portions of voters in established Western democracies hold views that can broadly be described as populist and/or authoritarian, many older parties have also been tempted to jump on the populist bandwagon and channel illiberal views.[10] This has led to the phenomenon dubbed 'contagion of the right'.[11] Established political parties, notably in France, Switzerland and the Netherlands, have mimicked the tactics of challenger parties in the hope of retaining the votes of citizens who might otherwise be tempted to defect.

Socio-economic and political change in the UK

The processes described above can all be traced in the UK, but the ways in which they have affected political values and vote choices have been conditioned by factors specific to the British case. The UK is culturally and geographically located between continental Europe and North America, and has unusually centralised and majoritarian national-level political institutions. Some of the trends noted above have been muted, while others have taken forms different from those that have occurred in established European democracies.

The most significant differences can be summarised under three broad headings. First, xenophobic sentiment has been focused largely on the UK's relationship with the EU, especially in the wake of rising immigration from the post-2004 Eastern European member states and the post-2009 Eurozone crisis. Not only was membership of the EU seen to be an increasing threat, but the benefits of membership were seen as dwindling.[12] Sentiment that might otherwise have been channelled towards longer-standing immigrant groups was therefore concentrated on the policy response seen as best suited to addressing the UK's perceived immigration 'crisis': leaving the EU. And when the decision to leave the EU was made, public anxiety over immigration appears to have waned.[13]

Second, the UK's labile constitution means that regional inequalities are often channelled into demands for greater decentralisation. Problems in Scotland, Wales and Northern Ireland tend to be filtered through proposals for greater devolution – or in Scotland's case, independence – while problems in London and England's large northern industrial and post-industrial cities have led to the creation of new regional authorities. The ease with which constitutional precedent can be set also means that unscrupulous politicians have an incentive to engage in political manoeuvres that undermine democratic accountability if they think they can achieve popular policy outcomes. As the nineteenth-century Liberal prime minister William Gladstone famously remarked, '[The British constitution] presumes more boldly than any other the good sense and the good faith of those who work it'. It appears that this good sense and faith are ebbing away as politicians feel less inclined to adhere to traditional standards of 'good' behaviour.[14] When this happens, democracy is imperilled.

Third, Britain's first-past-the-post electoral system means that the bar for entry for new political parties is very high, as John Bartle describes in Chapter 4, even if they or their leaders are able to gain considerable media exposure. Parties that win substantial numbers of votes can still fail to gain seats in Parliament. In 2015, for example, UKIP won nearly 13 per cent of the popular vote but only one of its candidates was elected to the House of Commons. The consequence is that challenger parties are a more limited threat to the dominant parties in the UK system. This, in turn, incentivises Britain's two major parties to chase the votes of the disaffected and those who might in other countries turn to parties that seek to position themselves as outsiders. The Conservatives' efforts to appeal to UKIP supporters has led to a British version of 'contagion of the right', as Tory policies have become more aligned with the xenophobic orientation of the far right. There has also been a limited 'contagion of the left' in Britain, with

Labour seeking – albeit with somewhat less success – to accommodate the concerns of potential Green and SNP supporters.

Demographic and structural changes in the UK

As previously outlined, five major social and demographic changes have affected many developed democracies in the early twenty-first century. These changes are also apparent in the UK, where they have been refracted through the country's geography and economic structure. They manifest themselves in distinct ways.

De-industrialisation: The North and the South of England have long had different economies and different cultures, yet de-industrialisation has turned these differences into stark inequalities. Successive Conservative-led governments since 2010 have talked of reviving the North and turning it into a 'Northern Powerhouse' through infrastructure investment and industrial strategy, but this had failed to materialise to any great extent at the time of the 2019 general election. On the contrary, 'austerity' and widescale cuts to public spending meant that local authorities and other public-sector bodies had limited resources to ease the pain for these areas, further exacerbating the stark divide between the relatively affluent South East of England and the hard-hit North. In addition to regional tensions, the UK is also beset by a skills shortage in fast-growing service-sector industries such as high tech and hospitality.

Rising cost of housing: The concentration of economic opportunities in the South East of England has increased demand for housing in this region and put intense pressure on costs. Many younger people perceive themselves as falling into 'generation rent': they have no realistic chance of ever purchasing their own property, as most of their parents had done. The problem is exacerbated by the fact that the UK is one of the only developed countries in the world not to levy direct property taxes in the form of annual taxes on the value of real estate. People instead pay stamp duty, a tax on property values when they move house. Moreover, while local taxation is tied to property values through the Council Tax, in England these values reflect what the property was worth, or would have been worth, in 1991. They do not reflect how property values have changed as result of differential regional changes in demand for housing. One of the consequences of the UK tax system has been a rise in under-occupation, as elderly people remain living in large family homes long after they cease to need the space. All of this puts further pressure on the availability of homes for younger, growing families.

Ageing population: As the UK population ages, so the distinct views and interests of young and old have diverged. Moreover, the turnout gap between these groups has grown, with older voters more likely to make it to the polls and younger voters less likely to.[15] This means that the interests of older citizens are better represented than those of their younger counterparts, leading to policies that benefit pensioners, such as the 'triple lock' that protects state pensions and generous tax relief for private-pension contributions. Perhaps not surprisingly, there was little policy movement in the run-up to the 2019 general elections on issues of more concern to younger voters, such as the cost of housing and university tuition fees. The logical antidote to such representational imbalances is to make voting mandatory and thereby compel politicians to pay attention to the needs of all sectors of society, young and old, rich and poor, majority ethnic and minority ethnic. Yet, despite the fact that compulsory voting is favoured by a significant portion of the UK citizenry, few members of the political elite endorse it, and it is unlikely to be adopted at any time soon.[16]

Under-employment of young people: The UK's flexible labour market has led to an historically unusual situation of near-full employment, combined with employment insecurity as many young people struggle to find full-time jobs that guarantee them a secure income. The rise of zero-hours contracts and the 'gig economy' has created a swathe of society disproportionately populated by young people and their families who are 'just about managing' but not thriving. Many are in precarious employment and are often unable to afford more than the bare necessities without racking up dangerous levels of household debt. Theresa May had made it a personal priority help these so-called JAMs at the start of her premiership, as described in Chapter 1, but her government, sidetracked by Brexit, did little to help in practice.

Climate change: A spate of strong storms and floods in the run-up to the 2019 general election brought climate change into focus, an issue that has steadily risen up the political agenda in recent years. Theresa May had made a surprise commitment to a net-zero carbon Britain as one of her last deeds as prime minister, and the flooding that hit large parts of the UK in the summer and autumn of 2019 reinforced popular anxiety about the likely future impact of global heating and increased storm intensity. Indeed, the environment appears to be a far larger concern to voters in 2019 than it had been in previous elections (Table 1.2).[17]

Attitudes and behavioural change in the UK

The specific structural changes just outlined are associated with attitudinal developments that resemble those elsewhere. In recent years, as described in more detail by Maria Sobolewska in Chapter 5, there has been much talk in UK political circles of a new political alignment around the cultural cleavage between cosmopolitan social liberals and more traditionally minded citizens with stronger ties to place and more authoritarian values.[18] Though the latter group has long made up a substantial part of the UK electorate, a decade of economic austerity – which hit this section of the electorate especially hard – combined with the debate around Brexit and the eventual referendum outcome, gave them increased visibility and arguably greater political confidence. Theresa May's view of 'citizens of the world' being 'citizens of nowhere' – a targeted critique of irresponsible bosses, especially heads of tax-avoiding corporations – grounded an attempt to build a Conservative alliance around this group, an effort which continued when Boris Johnson assumed the premiership. The Conservative Party was remarkably successful in convincing voters 'left behind' by the double blows of globalisation and austerity that their woes were caused instead by immigration and the EU, despite abundant evidence to the contrary.[19]

The rise to prominence of traditional-authoritarian values has three components that are of particular relevance to the 2019 general election campaign: anti-elite sentiment characteristic of populism, xenophobia and support for anti-democratic proposals.[20] It is worth pausing to consider, in turn, how each of these manifested itself at the time of the 2019 election.

Anti-elite sentiment: Britons have for decades been sceptical of political elites.[21] However, several factors have in recent years converged to enhance this scepticism. Some scholars have pointed to the gradual professionalisation of UK political parties as a factor in populist sentiment. Regardless of partisan affiliation, politicians now resemble each other more in terms of background and lifestyle than they resemble those they purport to represent.[22] The 2009 parliamentary-expenses scandal, when numerous MPs were found to have been living high on the hog at public expense, also served to compound the sense that politicians are 'in it for themselves' and not aligned with the popular interest. Nor is it just politicians who are targets of the anti-elite mood. Inspired perhaps by the success of populist rhetoric in the US, Brexit campaign leader and Conservative cabinet minister Michael Gove famously claimed in the run-up to the 2016 referendum that people had 'had enough of experts', even though virtually all public- and private-sector institutions in the UK, as elsewhere, are run by experts of some description.[23] Experts rose to favour again in the struggle to combat covid-19 several months later, but the 2019 general election was fought in a context in which large sectors of the public had a jaundiced view of elite expertise.

Anti-immigrant sentiment and appeals to nativism: Popular support for the UK to leave the EU had strong xenophobic undertones.[24] In the months leading up to the Brexit referendum, concern about immigration focused on migrants from other European countries. To be sure, the focus of debate was more about 'control' rather than stopping immigration completely: there was widespread recognition that the UK needed migrants to address skills shortages, and that immigrants made a net positive contribution to the economy. This emphasis on control also characterised the two major parties' positions on immigration ahead of the 2019 general election campaign. The Conservatives pledged an 'Australian-style points-based immigration system' in their manifesto, while Labour promised an approach 'built on human rights and aimed at meeting the skills and labour shortages that exist in our economy and public services'. Nevertheless, there remains a darker, anti-immigrant side to political discourse. During the referendum campaign, this was most clearly reflected in UKIP's controversial campaign poster showing large numbers of non-white migrants under the slogan 'Breaking Point'. Ahead of the 2019 election, the Tories were dogged by claims of Islamophobia, Labour by claims of anti-Semitism.

Anti-democratic and illiberal policy proposals: British governments have always occasionally pursued policies that run counter to liberal-democratic norms and the rule of law. The Labour government under Tony Blair, for instance, challenged the right of habeas corpus by introducing detention without trial for suspected terrorists in the Terrorism Act 2000.[25] But in recent years, there has been a noteworthy spate of illiberal conduct in UK politics. Boris Johnson's illegal prorogation of parliament in the autumn of 2019, accompanied by inflammatory language around Brexit, aroused suspicions of his government's willingness to run roughshod over civil liberties and political rights. These suspicions were further fuelled by thinly veiled threats to the BBC, Britain's public-service broadcaster, and hints that the Conservatives might politicise the judiciary and the civil service. Although the covid-19 pandemic returned a degree of political consensus and moderation to political tone, suspicions remained about the Johnson government's commitment to liberal norms. They reappeared in late 2020, when proposed legislation, intended to protect the integrity of the UK's internal market, overrode parts of the withdrawal agreement recently negotiated with the EU. Brandon Lewis, the Northern Ireland secretary, admitted that parts of the Internal Market Bill would 'break international law in a specific and limited way'.[26] In the event, the government removed the offending parts ahead of securing a new trade deal with the EU.

Party-system change in the UK

The party-political consequences of the new cultural and political alignment are dealt with by John Bartle in detail in Chapter 4. It suffices here to summarise briefly how the developments just described affected the outcome of the 2019 general election and to compare it with electoral results in other established democracies.

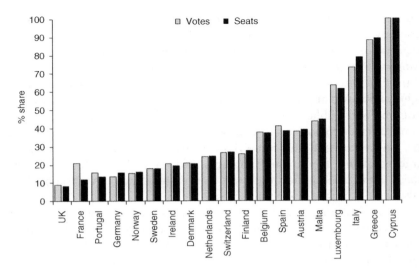

Figure 8.4 Support for populist and/or authoritarian parties in recent Western
European elections
Source: Compiled by author from various national electoral management bodies and
IFES Election Guide, available at: www.electionguide.org/, last accessed 26 June 2021.
The figures reported here are from the lower-chamber parliamentary elections that were
most recent at the time of the 2019 UK general election. For two-round elections
(France), data include second-round (definitive) vote share. For mixed systems, the
proportional-representation component of the vote share is shown.

The UK's first-past-the-post electoral system sets a very high hurdle for
entry into Parliament. This goes a long way towards explaining why the
Brexit Party won 31.6 per cent of the vote in the May 2019 European
Parliament elections but secured not a single seat in the general election held
six months later. The two-party dominance of British politics means that
smaller rivals are very unlikely to win seats, unless they enjoy concentrated
regional support. Voters know this, so tend to be unwilling to 'waste' their
votes by casting their ballots for another party. The end result in comparative terms is a relatively strong degree of 'containment' of populist and
authoritarian pressures within the UK's two-party system. Figure 8.4 shows
the share of populist and/or authoritarian party vote and seat shares in
recent parliamentary elections in a number of Western European democracies.[27] As can be seen, the UK's voting system has been an effective bulwark
against left- and right-wing versions of populism, such that it has the lowest
proportion of populist and/or authoritarian parties in any national
parliament in Western Europe.

But this is not to say that populist and authoritarian parties do not exert influence in the UK. They can in some cases drain sufficient support from one of the two main parties to shift the balance of power in a constituency and alter outcomes. Thus the main effect of smaller parties in the UK system is to influence the stances taken by the two large parties. In the case of the 2019 general election, this 'contagion effect' came from both Labour and the Conservatives being pressed to take new policy positions in the hopes of retaining their traditional supporters. The Conservatives were pushed to the right on social issues to avoid losing votes to the Brexit Party, whereas Labour was pressed on the left by the Liberal Democrats, Greens, Scottish Nationalists and Plaid Cymru, all of which were on many issues more socially liberal than Labour. Both large parties were, however, faced with the incontrovertible fact that their traditional electorates hailed from both socially conservative and socially liberal groups. They thus faced a dilemma, which the Conservatives resolved more decisively than Labour by taking a clear step towards social conservatism and embracing authoritarian values.

Understanding British politics in 2020

Drawing together the information presented, it is evident that recent UK politics and the 2019 general election have features in common with developments in other established democracies, but that the UK remains distinctive in important respects. Commonalities in popular attitudes are refracted through the prism of British politics in specific ways that yield outcomes – and potential future trajectories – that set the UK apart from other countries.

Commonalities

Two features of the 2019 general election invite comparison with other established Western democracies: the apparent decline of social democracy and the potential for authoritarian backsliding. In each case there are parallels between the UK experience and experience elsewhere, but also differences that can be traced to the UK's social and institutional context.

Labour's poor performance in the 2019 general election was undoubtedly in part due to local factors: the party's failure to take a clear stance on Brexit, ongoing doubts about Jeremy Corbyn's leadership and the party's perceived obsession with identity politics and issues that were far removed from the concerns of much of its traditional support base. However, Labour's failure in the past four general elections must also be viewed in the broader context of the pan-European decline of social democracy, a phenomenon that has been in evidence since the 1980s. This decline can be in part attributed to economic change, including a reduction in the proportion of workers in secure manufacturing jobs and attendant economic restructuring, and in part to ideological shifts and the rise of cultural issues that preoccupy socially liberal elites on the left.[28] European electorates may also have become less favourably disposed towards universal welfare policies in the wake of the 2008 economic downturn: in hard times, many voters come to resent resources being devoted to collective goods.[29] Western democracy may thus have entered an era of more oppositional politics where people view benefits for others as being losses for themselves and consequently look askance at the universalist aspirations of social democracy. The most significant threat to social democracy may thus not be far-right populist authoritarianism, but rather traditional conservatism that favours looking after one's own. This threat is abundantly apparent in the British context, where the two-party duopoly offers the electorate clear choices between more extensive and more restrictive versions of the post-war welfare state, and between open or closed approaches to cultural diversity. Electoral results since the 2008 economic downturn have suggested that the UK public is edging closer and closer towards restricting economic and social rights to a smaller circle of beneficiaries.

The evidence also suggests an increased appetite for restricting political rights and traditional civil liberties in the name of enacting policies favoured by the majority, a trend that was magnified during the covid-19 crisis by the introduction of widely accepted public-health surveillance systems. This appetite could be seen as a characteristic feature of so-called authoritarian backsliding, which has manifested itself in a variety of twenty-first-century democracies. Indeed, scholars of democratic politics are increasingly looking to the literature on authoritarianism to help make sense of the rise of right-wing populism and xenophobia.[30] Two scholars define the phenomenon of authoritarian backsliding as 'a decrease in competitiveness (or the potential for competitiveness) of the electoral playing field due to increasing concentration of power in the hands of the incumbent executive, relative to other actors'.[31] Worryingly, several recent studies have revealed declining support for democracy and increasingly favourable attitudes towards authoritarian rule in established Western democracies.[32]

Is authoritarian backsliding taking place in the UK? If it is, it is not through the vehicle of new authoritarian parties, as Figure 8.4 attests. But there is some evidence that politicians across the political spectrum have in recent years been prepared to contemplate infringements of long-accepted legal and democratic rights. Moreover, the attitudes of a significant proportion of the UK population reflect values that are difficult to square with the basic democratic principle of equality. Nostalgia for the political institutions of a bygone era carries with it a favourable disposition towards the politics of opacity and political centralisation. The new-found love of some in the UK for referendums betokens a worrying lurch towards majoritarianism that potentially threatens the rights of minorities.

The British have experienced a very large number of changes over the past several decades to their communities and the lives they lead. From the buildings they live in, the jobs they undertake, the food they eat, and the stores they shop in to the television programmes they watch, the mobile technology they use and the language they use, life in Britain in the twenty-first century is vastly different from that of a generation ago. Yet there is one change that has preoccupied some voters far more than any other development: the presence of larger numbers of foreign-born and ethnic minorities in the population. The change is relatively modest in comparison to the more dramatic ways in which people's living spaces, jobs and leisure activities have been transformed over the same period. Nevertheless, the rate of net immigration did increase by 83 per cent between 1991 and 2019, from 329,000 to 612,000 per year, and a significant portion of the electorate has focused on immigration as having a negative impact on local communities.[33] This focus could well be in part due to the right-wing press, which misattributed the effects of austerity to immigration. Shortages of hospital beds, school places and public housing can be directly traced to the massive public-sector cuts that were implemented following the economic downturn of 2008, yet these shortages are blamed by some on the impact of immigrants who put pressure on local services.

The language used by politicians also reveals signs of movement in the direction of authoritarianism. A typical authoritarian discursive ploy is to discredit the legitimacy of a speaker if you disagree with their ideas, rather than engaging with the substance of their argument.[34] This is the essence of Donald Trump's frequent sneering at 'fake news', which is effectively anything he does not want to hear. There is evidence that this approach is creeping into British political discourse, such as when Conservative MP Jacob Rees-Mogg claimed the UK treasury was 'fiddling' data on the impact of Brexit on the UK economy, or when Boris Johnson dismissed other MPs' concerns about his inflammatory language around Brexit as 'humbug'.[35]

Differences

Although recent UK experience has features in common with politics in other established democracies, there are also some noteworthy differences. The 'culture wars' apparent in other democracies were in the UK context channelled through the Brexit referendum, which brought them into starker relief and, as described in Chapter 5, may have accentuated them. But this process also imbued in Britain's 'culture war' a constitutional component lacking elsewhere.

For a start, the Brexit referendum may well have skewed public understandings of democracy in some quarters through its emphasis on majority opinion and underplaying of minority rights and institutional checks on majority rule. Referendums have long been a favoured tool of political manipulation by authoritarian leaders, from Adolf Hitler in Nazi Germany to Vladimir Putin in Russia and Recep Tayyip Erdoğan in Turkey. It was their utility as an instrument of manipulation – enabling leaders to invoke majority support as a justification for bypassing opposition – that led Clement Attlee, the former Labour prime minister, to reject them as being 'so alien' to British democracy.[36] For some Leave campaigners, such as Conservative MP Sir Bernard Jenkin, the success of the referendum in promoting Britain's withdrawal from the EU has encouraged them to think about using the device more widely in future. For many others, especially Remainers, Brexit has provided a clear lesson in the dangers of reducing democracy to the expressed view of the voting public on a given question on a given day, rather than seeing it as a vibrant and densely woven fabric of ideas and practices that place accountability and political equality at their heart. It is for this reason that, despite their appeal to some, referendums have been criticised by voices from across the political spectrum.[37]

The intellectual muddle around ideas about sovereignty is also striking in the wake of the Brexit referendum.[38] Many of those wishing to 'take back control' by leaving the EU apparently pined for some nostalgic pre-accession constitutional settlement in which Parliament alone was sovereign. At the same time, many Brexit supporters also favoured the conceptually incompatible embodiment of popular sovereignty as expressed through the referendum device. Though originally a Remainer, Theresa May accepted the mandate imposed by the referendum and took the view that, on this issue at least, her government was directly accountable to the people rather than to Parliament.[39] These alternative visions were a far cry from earlier debates over the merits of 'pooling' national sovereignty at the EU level, where the interests of UK citizens were defended by directly elected members of the European Parliament. The institutions of a liberal world order may be needed now more than ever, but a substantial portion of the UK public appears to have turned away from them.

At this juncture one might pause to wonder whether Britons were ever all that liberal in the past. Illiberal and 'little Englander' attitudes have long been part and parcel of many voters' mindset.[40] In-group favouritism and out-group antipathy may even be hardwired into our brains: psychological research suggests that people are naturally 'hivish' and oriented towards people like them.[41] Lord Hailsham's warnings in 1976 of 'elective dictatorship' and the tendency of the UK political system to be dominated by a small and potentially illiberal inner circle has been voiced by others.[42] Perhaps the 'democratic hubris' of the post-war period blinded commentators to the fact that there have always been strong strains of socially illiberal views and authoritarian attitudes in all democracies. Or perhaps it led them to ignore those views in the expectation that they were relics of a former time that would gradually wither away as the world moved towards an ever more perfect democratic state of affairs. At any rate, the sentiments underlying the drive to amputate the UK from the EU are not new. They have been with us for a long time. It is only recently that they have been harnessed politically.

However, some things were truly different in 2019. The use of a majoritarian tool such as the referendum to make a hugely significant policy decision, without the checks that normally counterbalance majoritarian decision-making, was something that had not been attempted at national level for nearly four decades between 1975 and 2011. Britain's first national referendum, the 1975 vote on continued membership of the Common Market, as the EU was then known, was arguably an opportunity for voters to ratify a decision taken in the conventional way: MPs had only recently voted for Britain to join the European Community. The 2011 AV referendum on introducing the 'alternative vote' in Westminster elections and the 2016 Brexit vote were fundamentally different, in that they both asked voters to decide on policies that were opposed by a large majority of MP. The use of referendums in such circumstances raises serious questions about the coherence of the democratic process that can probably only be resolved by means of a codified constitution.

The extreme concentration of the most important political powers in the hands of any government with a strong majority in Parliament means that authoritarian tendencies are more worrisome in the UK than elsewhere. In political systems characterised by federalism, the separation of powers, strong bicameral parliaments and/or multi-party politics, it is much harder for any single political party or individual to gain full control over the state apparatus. The UK has relatively few formal checks and balances. A government with a solid parliamentary majority has considerable freedom to legislate, even if some powers have been devolved to administrations in Edinburgh, Cardiff and Belfast. And a prime minister who has the support of their party can dominate the government. The main accountability mechanisms in the British system are the independent judiciary, independent civil service and an independent media. When the independence of these institutions is threatened, as has been the case in the wake of the 2019 general election, British democracy is truly under threat. Although the political attitudes and voting behaviours of the British public may not be all that different from those of other Western democracies, the unique concentration of political power in a compact party system and dominant executive is highly unusual, and vulnerable to manipulation by unscrupulous leaders.

Notes

1 Thomas Piketty, *Capital in the Twenty-First Century* (Cambridge, MA: Harvard University Press, 2014).
2 David Adler and Ben Ansell, 'Housing and populism', *West European Politics*, 43 (2019), 344–365.
3 David Hope and Angelo Martelli, 'The transition to the knowledge economy, labor market institutions, and income inequality in advanced democracies', *World Politics*, 71 (2019), 236–288.
4 Jean-Marie Siu Lan K.Cheung, Sophie Le Roy, Herman Van Oyen, Clare Griffiths, Jean-Pierre Michel and François Richard Herrmann, 'Death toll exceeded 70,000 in Europe during the summer of 2003', *Comptes Rendus Biologies*, 331 (2008), 171–178.
5 *The Economist*, 'Central European floods: A hard lesson learned', 6 June 2013, available at: www.economist.com/eastern-approaches/2013/06/06/a-hard-lesson-learned, last accessed 24 June 2021.
6 BBC News, 'Australia fires: A visual guide to the bushfire crisis', 31 January 2020, available at: www.bbc.co.uk/news/world-australia-50951043, last accessed 24 June 2021.
7 See Robert Merton, *Social Theory and Social Structure* (Glencoe: Free Press, 1957); and Seymour Martin Lipset, 'Democracy and working-class authoritarianism', *American Sociological Review*, 24 (1959), 482–501.
8 Pippa Norris and Ronald Inglehart, *Cultural Backlash: Trump, Brexit, and the Rise of Authoritarian Populism* (New York: Cambridge University Press, 2019).
9 Catherine E. De Vries and Sara B. Hobolt, *Political Entrepreneurs: The Rise of Challenger Parties in Europe* (Princeton: Princeton University Press, 2020).
10 John Bartle, David Sanders and Joe Twyman, 'Authoritarian populist opinion in Europe', in Ivor Crewe and David Sanders (eds), *Authoritarian Populism and Liberal Democracy* (Basingstoke: Palgrave Macmillan, 2020), pp. 49–71.
11 Norris and Inglehart, *Cultural Backlash*.
12 Harold D. Clarke, Matthew Goodwin and Paul Whiteley, *Brexit: Why Britain Voted to Leave the European Union* (Cambridge: Cambridge University Press, 2017).
13 Rob Ford, 'Immigration: Is public opinion changing?', in Anand Menon (ed.), *Brexit and Public Opinion 2019* (London: UK in a Changing Europe, 2019), pp. 13–15.
14 Andrew Blick and Peter Hennessey, *Good Chaps No More: Safeguarding the Constitution in Stressful Times* (London: Constitution Society, 2019), available at: https://consoc.org.uk/wp-content/uploads/2019/11/FINAL-Blick-Hennessy-Good-Chaps-No-More.pdf, last accessed 26 June 2021.
15 Sarah Birch, Glenn Gottfried and Guy Lodge, *Divided Democracy: Political Inequality in the UK and Why It Matters* (London: Institute for Public Policy

Research, 2013), available at: https://www.ippr.org/files/images/media/files/publication/2013/11/divided-democracy_Nov2013_11420.pdf, last accessed 26 June 2021.

16 Sarah Birch, *Full Participation: A Comparative Study of Compulsory Voting* (Manchester: Manchester University Press, 2009).

17 Fiona Harvey, 'Climate crisis topping UK election agenda is "unprecedented" change', *Guardian*, 21 November 2019, available at: www.theguardian.com/environment/2019/nov/21/climate-crisis-topping-uk-election-agenda-is-unprecedented-change, last accessed 26 June 2021.

18 David Goodhart, *The Road to Somewhere: The New Tribes Shaping British Politics* (London: Hurst, 2017).

19 Nicola Gilpin, Matthew Henty, Sara Lemos, Jonathan Portes and Chris Bullen, *The Impact of Free Movement of Workers from Central and Eastern Europe on the UK Labour Market*, Department for Work and Pensions, Working Paper No 29, 2006, available at: https://cream-migration.org/files/Working_paper_291.pdf, last accessed 26 June 2021.

20 Norris and Inglehart, *Cultural Backlash*.

21 Nicholas Allen and Sarah Birch, *Ethics and Integrity in British Politics: How Citizens Judge Their Politicians' Conduct and Why It Matters* (Cambridge: Cambridge University Press 2015).

22 Peter Allen, *The Political Class: Why It Matters Who Our Politicians Are* (Oxford: Oxford University Press, 2018).

23 Geoffrey Evans and Anand Menon, *Brexit and British Politics* (Cambridge: Polity Press, 2017), p. 62.

24 Clarke *et al.*, *Brexit*, pp. 146–174.

25 Lord Hoffman's judgment in A and Others v Secretary of State for the Home Department (2004) criticised detention without trial in no uncertain terms: 'The real threat to the life of the nation, in the sense of a people living in accordance with its traditional laws and political values, comes not from terrorism but from laws such as these. That is the true measure of what terrorism may achieve. It is for Parliament to decide whether to give the terrorists such a victory.' The opinion is available at: https://publications.parliament.uk/pa/ld200405/ldjudgmt/jd041216/a&oth-1.htm, last accessed 26 June 2021.

26 BBC News, 'Northern Ireland Secretary admits new bill will "break international law"', 8 September 2020, available at: www.bbc.co.uk/news/uk-politics-54073836, last accessed 26 June 2021.

27 The classification of populist parties follows that in Norris and Inglehart, *Cultural Backlash*.

28 See, among others: Jonas Pontusson, 'Explaining the decline of European social democracy: The role of structural economic change', *World Politics*, 47 (1995), 495–533; David Rueda, 'Insider–outsider politics in industrialized democracies: The challenge to social democratic parties', *American Political Science Review*, 99 (2005), 61–74; Michael Keating and David McCrone (eds), *The Crisis of Social Democracy* (Edinburgh: Edinburgh University Press, 2015); and Adam Przeworski, *Crises of Democracy* (Cambridge: Cambridge University Press, 2019).

29 Christopher J. Anderson and Jason D. Hecht, 'Crisis of confidence? The dynamics of economic opinions during the great recession', in Nancy Bermeo and Larry M. Bartels (eds), *Mass Politics in Tough Times: Opinions, Votes, and Protests in the Great Recession* (Oxford: Oxford University Press, 2014), pp. 40–71.

30 See, for example, Steven Levitsky and Daniel Ziblatt, *How Democracies Die: What History Reveals about Our Future* (London: Penguin, 2018); Robert R. Kaufman and Stephan Haggard, 'Democratic decline in the United States: What can we learn from middle-income backsliding?', *Perspectives on Politics*, 17 (2019), 417–432; Robert Mickey, Steven Levitsky and Lucan Ahmad Way, 'Is America still safe for democracy? Why the United States is in danger of backsliding', *Foreign Affairs*, 96 (2017), 20–29; Norris and Inglehart, *Cultural Backlash*; Przeworski, *Crises of Democracy*; and Cass R. Sunstein, *Can It Happen Here? Authoritarianism in America* (New York: Harper Collins, 2018).

31 Jennifer Raymond Dresden and Marc Morjé Howard, 'Authoritarian backsliding and the concentration of political power', *Democratization*, 23 (2016), 1122–1143: p. 1123.

32 Norris and Inglehart, *Cultural Backlash*; Przeworski, *Crises of Democracy*.

33 Georgina Sturge, *Migration Statistics*, House of Commons Library, Briefing Paper CB06077 (London: House of Commons, 2020), available at: https://research-briefings.files.parliament.uk/documents/SN06077/SN06077.pdf, last accessed 26 June 2021.

34 Levitsky and Daniel Ziblatt, *How Democracies Die*; Emre Toros and Sarah Birch, 'Framing electoral impropriety: The strategic use of allegations of wrong-doing in election campaigns', *British Journal of Middle Eastern Studies*, 47 (2019), 794–810.

35 Damien Gayle, 'Rees-Mogg claims Treasury is "fiddling" Brexit figures', *Guardian*, 3 February 2018, available at: www.theguardian.com/politics/2018/feb/03/jacob-rees-mogg-treasury-fiddling-figures-brexit-report, last accessed 26 June 2021; Rowena Mason and Frances Perraudin, 'Boris Johnson refuses to apologise for language about Jo Cox', *Guardian*, 26 September 2019, available at: www.theguardian.com/politics/2019/sep/26/boris-johnson-refuses-to-apologise-for-language-about-jo-cox, last accessed 26 June 2021.

36 See Anthony King, *The British Constitution* (Oxford: Oxford University Press, 2007), pp. 46–47.

37 Andrew Blick, *Stretching the Constitution: The Brexit Shock in Historic Perspective* (London: Hurst, 2019), p. 41.

38 Albert Weale, *The Will of the People: A Modern Myth* (Cambridge: Polity, 2018).

39 Blick, *Stretching the Constitution*, pp. 55–56.

40 Ivor Crewe, 'Authoritarian populism and Brexit in the UK in historical perspective', in Crewe and Sanders (eds), *Authoritarian Populism and Liberal Democracy*, pp. 15–31.

41 Jonathan Haidt, *The Righteous Mind: Why Good People Are Divided by Politics and Religion* (London: Penguin, 2012).

42 Blick, *Stretching the Constitution*, pp. 249–254.

Appendix

Results of British general elections, 1945–2019

Election year	Percentage of popular vote							Seats in the House of Commons					
	Turnout	Con	Lab	Lib Dem	Nats	Other	Swing	Con	Lab	Lib Dem	Nats	Other	Government majority
1945	72.8	39.7	47.7	9.0	0.2	3.4	-12.2	210	393	12	0	25	147
1950	83.9	43.3	46.1	9.1	0.1	1.4	+2.6	298	315	9	0	3	6
1951	82.6	48.0	48.8	2.6	0.1	0.6	+1.0	321	295	6	0	3	16
1955	76.8	49.6	46.4	2.7	0.2	1.1	+2.0	345	277	6	0	2	59
1959	78.7	49.4	43.8	5.9	0.4	0.6	+1.2	365	258	6	0	1	99
1964	77.1	43.3	44.1	11.2	0.5	0.9	-3.2	304	317	9	0	0	5
1966	75.8	41.9	47.9	8.5	0.7	1.0	-2.6	253	364	12	0	1	97
1970	72.0	46.4	43.0	7.5	1.7	1.5	+4.7	330	288	6	1	5	31
1974 Feb	78.8	37.8	37.2	19.3	2.6	3.2	-1.4	297	301	14	9	14	none
1974 Oct	72.8	35.7	39.3	18.3	3.4	3.3	-2.1	277	319	13	14	12	4
1979	76.0	43.9	36.9	13.8	2.0	3.4	+5.3	339	269	11	4	12	44
1983	72.7	42.4	27.6	25.4	1.5	3.1	+3.9	397	209	23	4	17	144
1987	75.3	42.2	30.8	22.6	1.7	2.7	-1.7	376	229	22	6	17	101
1992	77.7	41.9	34.4	17.8	2.3	3.5	-2.0	336	271	20	7	17	21
1997	71.4	30.7	43.2	16.8	2.5	6.8	-10.0	165	418	46	10	20	178
2001	59.4	31.6	40.7	18.3	1.8	7.7	+1.8	166	412	52	9	20	166
2005	61.4	32.4	35.2	22.0	2.2	8.2	+3.1	198	355	62	9	22	65
2010	65.1	36.1	29.0	23.0	2.2	9.7	+5.0	306	258	57	9	20	77
2015	66.2	36.8	30.4	7.9	5.3	19.6	-0.4	330	232	8	59	21	11
2017	68.8	42.3	40.0	7.4	3.6	6.6	-2.1	317	262	12	39	20	none
2019	67.3	43.6	32.1	11.6	4.4	8.4	+4.6	365	202	11	52	20	81

Note: Figures are taken from House of Commons Library Briefing Paper CBP7529, *UK Election Statistics: 1918–2019: A Century of Elections*. 'Lib Dem' refers to the Liberal party (1945–1979), the Liberal–SDP Alliance (1983–1987) and the Liberal Democrats (1992–2019). 'Nats' refers to the SNP and Plaid Cymru. 'Swing' refers to the Butler swing and compares the results of each election with the results of the previous election. A positive sign denotes a swing to the Conservatives; a negative sign denotes a swing to Labour. Labour formed a minority government after the February 1974 election, just as the Conservatives did in 2017. The Conservatives and the Liberal Democrats formed a coalition government after the 2010 election. The speaker is excluded when calculating the size of the government majority.

Index